THE DELAWARE RIVER STORY

THE DELAWARE RIVER STORY

Water Wars, Trout Tales, and a River Reborn

LEE HARTMAN

STACKPOLE BOOKS

Essex, Connecticut
Blue Ridge Summit, Pennsylvania

"*The Delaware River Story* chronicles the natural and unnatural history of the Delaware, one of America's most popular designated 'Wild and Scenic Rivers,' that many believe is the best wild trout fishery east of the Mississippi. Having been a disciple of its fisheries for nearly half a century, Lee Hartman is well-qualified to author a book about this river. He has witnessed how the river's ecology, fish life, and recreational assets have been abused by mismanaged water releases from New York City reservoirs. Lee has been among the leaders in devoting his time and energy to any and all organizations working to protect and preserve the Delaware River and its fisheries."

—Ed Van Put, author of *Trout Fishing in the Catskills*, and
The Beaverkill: The History of a River and Its People

"Lee Hartman has fished all over the world—Russia, Greenland, Cuba—but he's made his name on the Delaware River as a guide and conservationist. In *The Delaware River Story*, Hartman offers the full sweep of the Delaware's story and makes the case for its protection as a historically and ecologically important river that just happens to host a wild trout fishery that's unparalleled east of the Mississippi."

—David Kinney, author of *The Big One: An Island, an Obsession,*
and the Furious Pursuit of a Great Fish

"A gripping story of the rescue of one of America's great rivers—from a choked and contaminated commercial waterway in the nineteenth century to today's thriving wild trout fishery."

—Garth Hallberg, author of *Boon Juster* and *The Piketty Problem*

"From childhood fishing experiences in heavily polluted headwaters of the Pennsylvania anthracite coal region to eyewitness accounts of devastation, reparation, and astonishing creation, Lee Hartman documents the history of and ongoing struggle to sustain what is commonly known as the Upper Delaware tailwater trout fishery.

You may ask is this a book about fishing, conservation, economics, politics, or history. My answer, 'all of the above, and more.'"

From Supreme Court justices, far-thinking government officials, and conservationists to people simply trying to make a living, Lee recounts the battles for water rights of the Lenni Lenape Indians, early day colonists, and industrialists and current demands and allocation of water in the Delaware River watershed. Ever hear of chemical factories and the causes of the demise of Pennsylvania's state tree, the hemlock? Read the book. Want to know more about the bewildering number of laws, rules, decrees, agreements, compacts, and advocates for the allocation of water captured and stored in the New York City reservoirs in the Catskill Mountains? Read the book. Want to know about the creation and management of cold-water ecosystems? Read the book.

One could claim that the central focus of the book is trout. But trout serve merely as the framework of the relevance of fish such as the sorry decline of the river's shad fishery and the importance of such resources. One learns about the success and failure of introducing West Coast rainbow trout and the European immigrant the brown trout. And perhaps, above all, one can see what happens both good and bad as people unendingly change a natural resource as magnificent as the Delaware River."

—Robert Bachman, PhD

STACKPOLE BOOKS

An imprint of Globe Pequot, the trade division of
The Rowman & Littlefield Publishing Group, Inc.
4501 Forbes Blvd., Ste. 200
Lanham, MD 20706
www.rowman.com

Distributed by NATIONAL BOOK NETWORK

British Library Cataloguing in Publication Information available
Library of Congress Control Number: 2019953812

ISBN 978-0-8117-3938-2 (hardcover)
ISBN 978-0-8117-6933-4 (e-book)
ISBN 978-0-8117-7225-9 (paperback)

♾™ The paper used in this publication meets the minimum requirements of American National Standard for Information Sciences—Permanence of Paper for Printed Library Materials, ANSI/ NISO Z39.48-1992.

To the memory of Phil Chase and Dr. Peter Bousum for their sacrifices to protect and preserve the Delaware River cold–water fishery

Phil Chase
CATSKILL FLY FISHING MUSEUM

Dr. Peter Bousum
LEE HARTMAN

CONTENTS

Acknowledgments x

Foreword xiv

Introduction xviii

CHAPTER 1: Rivers of Coal 1

CHAPTER 2: A Place Called Stockport 23

CHAPTER 3: The Admiral of the Delaware 42

CHAPTER 4: The Vanishing Brook Trout 65

CHAPTER 5: The Legacy of Tocks Island 90

CHAPTER 6: The Fish That Saved America 108

CHAPTER 7: Birth of a Trout River 129

CHAPTER 8: The Ghost of Lordville 149

CHAPTER 9: Fishing When the Sun Don't Shine 171

CHAPTER 10: Unnatural Flows 191

CHAPTER 11: Water, Water, Everywhere 213

CHAPTER 12: Rainbows Under a Pot of Gold 237

Index 257

About the Author 268

ACKNOWLEDGMENTS

While writing this book my bedroom was turned into an office cluttered with old, yellowed newspaper clippings from every major newspaper, history books from local historical societies, outdated Trout Unlimited chapter newsletters, Delaware River Foundation newsletters, Upper Delaware Council publications, Gordon's Quill newsletters, old magazines, and saved emails as far back to before laptops were in vogue. My computer and many visits to local historical societies were the greatest assets to find the history of the legendary people who once lived along the waters of the Delaware. Without these modern-day conveniences, *The Delaware River Story* could never have been completed.

After the completion of Cannonsville Reservoir on the West Branch of the Delaware in 1968, the cold-water bottom releases began to change the aquatic life of the river. Wild trout soon became the dominant fish in the Upper Delaware. The number of fly fishermen who fished for trout during the early years could not fill up a school bus. Those that did told no one about the fishing except for a few choice friends. As the years passed, fly-fishing articles began appearing in popular fishing magazines, which upset the Delaware's fly-fishing fraternity.

John Randolf, publishing editor of *Fly Fisherman* magazine, permitted a glowing article about fishing the Upper Delaware soon after a warm-water crisis that led to a fish kill. In response to the written article, I wrote to Mr. Randolph that any Delaware River piece should be about protecting the river's cold-water habitat rather than exploiting its fishing. He kindly wrote back in so many words: "A river must have friends; without them the river cannot be safeguarded." His response hit home. It was a valid argument of how important it is to have allies in order to protect this unique trout fishery for future generations.

Today the Delaware River has many new friends and organizations that are currently active in protecting this unique wild trout river. Writing this book about the Delaware watershed and its history was made possible by the encouragement and assistance of friends, family, and many visits to regional historical societies. There are many individuals to thank who have supported and shared their experience and knowledge of the river:

Chris Wood—President of Trout Unlimited, for recognizing the importance of protecting the cold-water value of the Upper Delaware River.

Trout Unlimited committee members of Pennsylvania, New York, and New Jersey—Garth Pettinger, Jeff Plackis, Rich Thomas, Greg Malaska, and Ron Urban—who continue to work together to gain the proper flows and temperature regimes for the wild trout fishery in the Upper Delaware system.

Dan Plummer—A great friend of the river and a frequent fishing companion who joined Friends of the Upper Delaware River (FUDR) in 2006. "Troutboy," as we call him, became the backbone of FUDR for many years and is a major factor in the success of the organization.

Dr. Robert Bachman—A special friend whose longtime advocacy for the river comes with a wealth of knowledge about trout behavior that few men possess.

Al Caucci—Al, a co-founder of FUDR, has spent much of his life on the Delaware, both fishing and collecting insect samples. There is no one more knowledgeable about the river and its aquatic life.

Jeff Skelding—Jeff's skills and hard work as executive director has steered FUDR into the halls of Washington, DC.

Ed Van Put—The legendary Catskill angler was one of the first to fish the river and deserves a special thanks for his efforts and the knowledge that he shared with me, which was the inspiration to put this book together.

Joe Humphreys—A longtime friend and early river companion whose encouragement and advice made me a better angler.

Carol McMaster—Curator of the Equinunk Historical Society, the former Cannonsville resident is a true historian of the region. Her information and photos were invaluable.

Mike Romanowski—Under Mike's leadership the Stanley Cooper Chapter of Trout Unlimited was the foremost chapter to address the release issues to maintain the cold-water fishery.

Dr. Peter Kolesar—Who helped develop the Flexible Flow Management Plan and continues to work with state and local agencies for better flows.

Michael Gondell—For sharing his early fishing experiences on the West Branch.

Sherri Resti Thomas—Executive coordinator for FUDR, who was there for me in a time of need.

Garth Hallberg—An author of three books who gave me encouragement and advice when needed.

Elizabeth (Liz) Davidson—An architect and true friend of the river who provided information and support.

Sara Becker—Sara was a major asset who gave me early assistance in the development of Indian Springs Fly Fishing Camp.

The Indian Springs Fly Fishing Club members who continue to support Friends of the Upper Delaware River—Mike Cartechine, Terry DiSabatino, Ron Dudginski, Peter Grimbilas, Ed Jacoby, Steve Mongiardo, Ken O'Connor, Paul Robino, Bob Rodeheaver, and Chuck Rudershausen.

Joe Whalen—A lifetime friend and former high school classmate who for many years sacrificed his time to maintain Indian Springs Fly Fishing Camp.

Joe Demarkis—A great friend I couldn't be without. He became my first guide for Indian Springs. Today he continues to guide on the Lehigh River.

Don Baylor—Don is a certified aquatic biologist, a talented artist, and a true friend of the Delaware River. It is always a learning experience when fishing with Don.

Steve Ribustello—A longtime area resident and fly fisherman on the Delaware River who supplied me with books on local history.

And a big thank you goes to my editor Barbara Gogan. Her experience and professionalism as a Time-Life editor were invaluable.

A special thank you to Donita Pinto, who gave me the time and support I needed while writing this book.

And to my family—my son, Scott, and daughter, Nicole Merges, who have put up with my fishing addiction during much of their young lives. And to my ice skating granddaughter, Allison Merges, whom I love and adore.

FOREWORD

Few people know, and love, the Upper Delaware wild trout fishery as well as Lee Hartman.

Lee discovered the Upper Delaware in 1973, a few years after the Cannonsville Reservoir was built, with its bottom release of cold, clean water. Lee's habit was to take a few days every year and mark a space on the map to camp and fish for trout. His wall map of Pennsylvania and New York was filled with pushpins. Until then, the Upper Delaware remained blank.

He stopped at Pete and Lovey's Tavern (now MicBree's) on the Pennsylvania side of the Upper Delaware. He had a beer and asked where he might camp for the evening. The bartender pointed him toward a farmhouse on the hill.

"The stocky, overalls-clad dairy farmer didn't miss a beat when I asked him if we could camp by the river for the night. 'Sure can,' he said politely. 'Just give me two bucks and you can drive through the pasture and park next to the maple trees below the river junction. . . . If you are here to fish you ain't goin' to catch nothin' but trout. Ever since they put in those damn reservoirs the bass and bullheads have all but disappeared.'

"Our jaws dropped as we gaped at each other like two kids in a candy store," Lee said. "Without another word we gave the man two bucks."

On his second cast, Lee caught a football-sized trout. His two-day vacation turned into a week. And then a lifetime.

The Upper Delaware—one of America's great wild trout fisheries—was discovered.

The great conservationist Aldo Leopold once described the "oldest task in human history is to live on a piece of land without spoiling it."

No landscape better describes Leopold's challenge than the Upper Delaware River. As Lee Hartman so well describes, this is a river system whose lower tributaries, the Lehigh and the Schuylkill Rivers, were essentially killed and recovered by the discovery, production, and distribution of coal.

To be certain, Pennsylvania's coal fired the productive capacity of the United States during the Industrial Revolution and helped us win two world wars. The exploitation of rich timber reserves, initially pine for the masts of sailing ships and later any wood that could be burned to fire the insatiable demands of the acid factories, also nearly killed the Upper Delaware.

Hunting and fishing, once a mainstay for American Indian tribes and pioneers—whose intersected history Lee so well tells—nearly vanished. American ingenuity, however, always strikes back. Seth Green and other "fish culturists" figured out how to artificially breed the progeny of rainbow trout that grew up in the McCloud River in California, and through a combination of sweat, ingenuity, and luck transported them back East.

Meanwhile, brook trout, the native resident of eastern streams, began to blink out.

The passage of federal environmental laws such as the Clean Water Act, the vision of several elected leaders, and the work of countless Trout Unlimited volunteers, chapters, and staff helped to set the Upper Delaware on the path to recovery. Republican governor James Henderson Duff deserves a lot of the credit for starting the recovery of rivers such as the Schuylkill and other water bodies.

Rivers are remarkably resilient. If given a respite and half a chance, they will bounce back. Given the fact that Lee is a phenomenal angler—and one of the people who "discovered" the Upper Delaware's trout fishery—it is surprising how little *The Delaware River Story: Water Wars, Trout Tales, and a River Reborn* is about fishing. To be certain, Lee covers the commonwealth's luminaries, describing, for example, George Harvey's nymphing technique, later perfected by Joe Humphreys. He also uses personal recollections and memories to ground us in the area as a jumping-off point to describe its history.

Lee takes us on a journey of the people and places that define the lands and waters that he calls home. This is important. Conservation is a lot less about policy than it is about people and place.

Inside this book, you'll read about Zane Grey, the famous writer of Western novels, and how his fishing experience on the Delaware led to a back pocket full of rod-line records in previously undiscovered fisheries such as Australia.

Famous anglers, such as Ed Van Put and his decades of meticulous research on water temperatures and catch records, cut their teeth on the nascent Upper Delaware. Later, luminaries such as Joe Humphreys came with Lee to camp at and fish the rivers.

Learn about the pioneer who witnessed his father's murder by the Mohawks, and claimed vengeance on ninety-nine Mohawk souls before he perished. If you are like me, you will get the chills when you see what some claim is his ghost looking out at you from a three-story building in Lordville.

The Upper Delaware is a completely contrived wild trout fishery, previously known and well written about in this book for its native shad, eel, and sturgeon fisheries. Lee, one of the first and perhaps the best guide in the area, could be forgiven for being a homer for the introduced wild rainbow and brown trout.

That never happens. Lee's description of how the lumber boom and later the acid factories took their toll on native brook trout is poignant. When New York City was authorized to build dams to supply their drinking water, inundating a nine-generation town such as Cannonsville, it is clear Lee's sympathies lie with the lost farms, traditions, and families.

The book, however, is a story of hope, not loss. Witness the activism of a forty-one-year-old mom, Nancy Shukaitis, and her efforts over several years to mobilize her community and stop the ill-conceived Rocks Island Dam project, which would have displaced fifteen thousand people and created a thirty-seven-mile lake of their farms and home places. More recently, people such as Dan Plummer, the former chair of the Friends of the Upper Delaware River, are drawing connections between the health of the river and the economic vitality of the local communities.

Trout Unlimited is replete with people such as Dan and Nancy who work daily to stop, for example, the equally stupid Pebble Mine project from being developed in Bristol Bay, Alaska. Bristol Bay is home to the world's most prolific and important commercial, recreational, and subsistence salmon fishery. We have spent eighteen billion dollars to try to recover wild salmon and steelhead from the Columbia and Snake Rivers in the Pacific Northwest. All we need to do to keep Bristol Bay—a fishery that provides half, half, of all of the wild sockeye in the world—intact, is to have the wisdom to leave it alone.

The Delaware River Story: Water Wars, Trout Tales, and a River Reborn is a story of one man's love affair with a river. Lee built Indian Springs Fly Fishing lodge, the first overnight lodge on the river, which he owned and operated for decades. Later he helped form the Friends of the Upper Delaware River (FUDR). Along with Trout Unlimited, with whom Lee has worked for decades, FUDR works to ensure that New York City's insatiable and, quite often, unreasonable demand for drinking water allows for stable summer flows and rational management of reservoir releases.

Too often today in the hottest months, the Upper Delaware flows are cut off, impairing the bugs and riverside vegetation the trout depend on. Other times the reservoir engineers will impair the fishery with so-called yo-yo flows, where they open and close the flow of the reservoir suddenly.

The Upper Delaware is composed of formerly resource-dependent communities—towns dependent on coal, then timber, then acid factories. Boom and bust, and largely bust for the past few decades.

Flowing through their centers lies the source of their potential wealth and future prosperity.

If New York City and the four states that control the flow of the rivers on the Upper Delaware could agree to reasonable and incremental changes that allow for a little more water to be left in the river in the summer, and to desist the practice of running the reservoirs like a faucet, the communities of the Upper Delaware would see a direct and material benefit from having America's finest wild trout fishery flowing through their backyards.

—Chris Wood

INTRODUCTION

The Delaware, which extends some 330 miles from its headwaters near Hancock, New York, to the mouth of the Delaware Bay, is one of this country's most important rivers. It remains the longest free-flowing river east of the Mississippi. Its historical, cultural, and economic significance is unparalleled, and in many ways the Delaware River has been directly involved in events that have shaped the course of our national lives.

When Europeans set foot on the bank of the Delaware River in the early seventeenth century, they discovered that they were not alone. The indigenous people called the river Lenape Wihittuck, which means "the rapid stream of the Lenape." For over ten thousand years the Lenni Lenape lived peacefully along the clean river and its tributaries, surviving on its wealth. In less than one hundred years, the colonial population grew from roughly 2,000 to over 2.5 million, and soon displaced the Native Americans.

In America's infancy the rapid growth along the Delaware threatened the nature of the waterway, spewing out sewage and industrial waste that soured the river, causing sickness and a decline of its fish. It became apparent that the way to ruin a river is to build a city along its banks.

After the discovery of anthracite in southeastern Pennsylvania in 1792, the Delaware's two lower tributaries, the Lehigh and the Schuylkill, turned black from unregulated coal mining operations. European settlers began expanding northward into the Appalachian and Catskill regions, where timber cutting, acid factories, and tanning operations denuded the forestland, which led to the corruption of nearly every unspoiled mountain stream. Without the mighty hemlock and pine, silt poured into the pristine waterways, suffocating stream life and warming the water—and fish like the native brook trout found it difficult to survive.

Slowly, over the course of the nineteenth century, the Delaware River tributaries began to heal the wounds of mankind. Transplanted fish were introduced to replenish native species. New forest growth began to appear, and soon a new class of fish, the brown and the rainbow trout, replaced the once-abundant brook trout.

In the mid-twentieth century, four states, a city, and the federal government—known as the "Compact"—proposed to build a major dam in the middle of the river, just above the Delaware Water Gap. This dam would have obliterated the historic Minisink Valley and cut the free-flowing river in half, seriously impairing the migration of American shad. After a fifteen-year battle led by a lady and a freshman congressman, the Tocks Island Dam project was de-authorized.

The most far-reaching change to the Delaware was the construction of two enormous reservoirs, located on the river's East and West Branches, to supply drinking water to everyone within a 150-mile radius, including the millions of people in New York City. The Delaware was never considered a wild trout river until the reservoir dams disrupted the natural flows and turned nature upside down. The dams gave the once-warm waterway cooler flows, which created a self-sustaining wild trout population and established a modern-day fishing and boating industry to fuel the economy of the Upper Delaware River communities. However, questionable reservoir release management practices during the next forty years have continued to play havoc with the self-sustaining trout of the Upper Delaware River.

Protecting the Delaware that has served as the backbone of our nation is a daunting task. There are many heroes, both living and dead, who have labored to keep its flows clean, healthy, and prosperous over the past four centuries. This book is about the individuals and organizations who have—and are still today—sacrificing their time and effort to keep the Delaware River flowing free and clear without detriment to its flora and fauna. Without a doubt their sacrifices are for the love of the river.

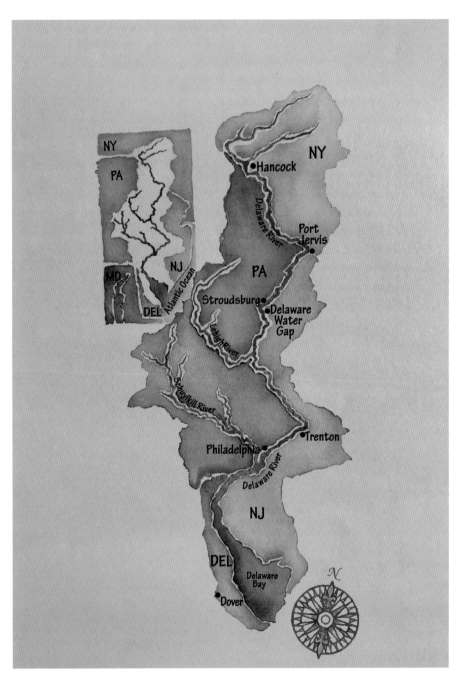

DELAWARE RIVER BASIN COMMISSION

Rivers of Coal

A cold rain began to fall on the mountaintop where Philip Ginter sat in search of deer with his Pennsylvania Long Rifle. It was 1791 when the German-born immigrant moved to the hills of southeastern Pennsylvania

Honey Brook coal breaker. Coal deposits are scattered around the world; however, the coal from a five-hundred-square-mile region of eastern Pennsylvania is special. During the Paleozoic era, three hundred million years ago, what is now rugged mountainous terrain was a steamy plain filled with swamps. Tropical plants grew and died here, and the decaying matter sank to the bottom of these swamps to form a dense organic substance known as peat. Over millions of years, shifts in the earth's plates and other landscape changes compressed prehistoric peat deposits into mineral layers known as coal. Artist Theodore R. Davis traveled into the anthracite coalfields of Pennsylvania in 1869 to sketch scenes for *Harper's Weekly*. THEODORE R. DAVIS

known as Panther Valley. Ginter (sometimes spelled Ginder), being literally a hunter of the backwoods, built a small log cabin for his wife and children and settled in the mountains of eastern Pennsylvania to support his family by hunting in the Appalachians.

His hunting day had been extensive and yet not a shot had been fired. Legend has it the distraught and wet hunter set his course for home before the daylight faded. Stepping down the side of the 1,440-foot Sharpe Mountain was a serious chore, and he stumbled against a hard object, dislodging a shiny black stone by the force of his foot. There was just enough light remaining to distinguish what it might be. He had often listened to the country legends about the possible existence of coal in the region. It occurred to him that the curious-looking black rock could be a deposit of that "stone coal" he had heard about.

Philip Ginder Memorial, Summit Hill, Pennsylvania. Philip Ginter's discovery of coal would eventually fuel an industrial revolution by the mid-nineteenth century in the Appalachian region of Pennsylvania, but there would be no rewards for the German immigrant. Deprived of his claim and cheated out of his land, Philip Ginter later died in obscurity. MARK KRAJNAK

Ginter took the mysterious rock to his cabin. He then waited until the following spring before traveling in his canoe down the Little Schuylkill River to Fort Allen (now Weissport, Pennsylvania), located on the Schuylkill River. There he met with Colonel Jacob Weiss of the Continental Army. The colonel, who was aware of anthracite stone, brought the rock specimen to Philadelphia where three inspectors confirmed it was indeed anthracite coal. They authorized the colonel to satisfy Ginter's find on the condition that he point out the precise spot where he had found the coal. Ginter agreed.

The Ark of 1814

As the sun was setting on Bethlehem, Pennsylvania, on August 14, 1814, a crudely built ship, called an "ark," was floating by on the Lehigh River. Its cargo would bring Bethlehem into a new industrial age. The ark contained twenty-four tons of "black diamonds," or anthracite coal, from the Room Run Mine. The ark was sixty-five feet long, fourteen feet wide, and built with hemlock wood. It began its journey at the landings at Lausanne with a crew of six men. Within a quarter mile the ark collided with a slate ledge, causing a large gash in its side. The crew ripped off their clothing and successfully plugged the hole. The ark stayed afloat all the way to its Philadelphia destination, five days later.

The War of 1812 had raised the cost of coal and limited its availability through the British blockade of Chesapeake and Delaware Bays. This inspired a new attempt at transporting coal from the Lehigh Coal Mining Company down the river to the Philadelphia market. The Lehigh Coal Mining Company began leasing their mines to other enterprising men, hoping to increase the value of its mines. Some of the original investors had passed away. The next generation of investors (Jacob Weiss, Isaac Chapman, Jacob Crist, Charles Miner, and John Robinson) took their chances with the mining and selling of anthracite. Arks were produced at the Jacob Weiss sawmill at Lausanne Landing, Pennsylvania. Each ark could carry from twenty to thirty tons of coal.

Josiah White and Erskine Hazard purchased a carload of the coal that was piled on the ark that passed through Bethlehem in 1814. They wanted to investigate its usefulness for heating the furnace at their mill,

3

Historic Lausanne, also often called Lausanne Landing in the 1790s to 1820s, was a small settlement at the mouth of Nesquehoning Creek on the Lehigh River in marshy delta-like floodplain. KARL BODNER PAINTING, 1862

the Fairmount Nail and Wire Works, at the Falls of the Schuylkill. They experimented with lighting the coal for several hours but soon gave up. Disgusted, they shut the furnace door and left the mill.

One of the workers realized he left his jacket in the mill. He returned thirty minutes later to find the furnace red-hot. The closed furnace door had increased the flow of oxygen and facilitated the combustion. White and Hazard discovered the great potential of anthracite coal. Their involvement in the anthracite mining industry solved many of the Lehigh Coal Mining Company's problems. Karen M. Samuels, Lehigh Valley History.

American industry was in its infancy at the time anthracite coal was discovered, and relied primarily on wood and charcoal for fuel. As industrialization progressed, alternative sources of energy were needed; there were simply not enough forests to power the hungry factories of

A breaker boy was a coal-mining worker in the United States whose job was to separate impurities from coal by hand in a coal breaker.
LIBRARY OF CONGRESS

the burgeoning nation. With its high carbon content, anthracite appeared to offer a solution, but digging it up, getting it to market, and making it suitable for commercial and household use would prove costly to life in the Schuylkill River watershed, the largest tributary to the Delaware River.

By the Civil War era, coal was king in the United States. The great anthracite mining industry boomed in southeastern Pennsylvania and was soon making company bosses very rich and providing a good living for many coal managers and businessmen. With no mining regulations, they spread their collieries, coal mines, and coal breakers across the landscape. Coal companies hired men and their children to work the mines, then built small patches of homes in town, each with a well-stocked company store. Mining was unregulated, but the money was not. The coal barons gouged family paychecks for house privileges, work tools, and food costs—making the miners and their families practically slaves to the company.

About twenty-two thousand coal miners worked in Schuylkill County, Pennsylvania. Fifty-five hundred of these were children between

There were forty-one working collieries in the Mahanoy Valley (1858-1953) during the peak years of deep mining. Seventeen other collieries in the Schuylkill County region, including more than seventeen thousand miners, fueled the steel and industrial revolution, provided a critical energy source for WWI and WWII operations, and led our entire nation in setting the foundation for organized labor. COLLIERIES AND COAL BREAKERS OF SCHUYLKILL COUNTY

the ages of seven and sixteen years, who earned between one and three dollars a week separating slate from the coal. Injured miners, or those too old to work at the face, were assigned to picking slate at the "breakers," where the coal was a manageable size. Thus, many of the elderly miners finished their mining days as they had begun them in their youth. The miners lived a life of bitter and terrible struggle.

Wages were low, working conditions were dreadful, and deaths and serious injuries numbered in the hundreds each year. On September 6, 1869, a fire in the Avondale Mine took the lives of 110 coal miners. The families blamed the coal company for failing to finance a secondary exit for the mine.

Day of the Rope

The disaster also caused thousands of miners to join the Workingmen's Benevolent Association, one of the first unions to represent coal miners in the United States. Continuing labor and social strife in the Pennsylvania anthracite coalfields resulted in an increase of activities by the "Molly Maguires," a controversial organization that conducted violent attacks against anthracite coal mine operators. These conflicts eventually resulted in the trial and execution of twenty members of the Molly Maguires in Pottsville and Mauch Chunk (now Jim Thorpe).

Thirteen years after the Day of the Rope, the unions prevailed and the United Mine Workers was created. Unable to cope with the prospect of treating workers well, Franklin Gowen, president of the Reading Railroad, who had served as chief prosecutor at the trial, committed suicide. Several years later, evidence surfaced that suggested Gowen had been behind many acts of sabotage attributed to the Molly Maguires. In 1979 a posthumous pardon was granted for the Mollies, with Governor Milton Shapp denouncing Gowen's fervent desire to wipe out any signs of resistance in the coalfields. "All Pennsylvanians," Shapp said, "should pay tribute to these martyred men of labor."

Life in the Coal Region

It is often said that trout don't live in ugly places. This revelation became apparent to me at an early age.

7

Throughout my youth the anthracite coal mining industry continued its onslaught in the region. By 1950 many company coal mines had closed, as electrically powered cranes replaced deep mining by digging mammoth open pits (stripping holes) sometimes a mile long and one hundred feet deep, scraping away layers of earth, exposing the tops of vertical black veins of anthracite. The coal breakers, often described as "enormous preying monsters," crushed and separated the hard, black coal into different sizes, processing it for market. Huge culm piles (coal waste) littered the landscape.

During the early nineteenth century, nearly 175,000 anthracite workers had supported a million people. The aboveground strip-mining operations cut the workforce to fewer than 2,000 workers. Their mining operations pumped out acid-laced water that polluted most rivers and streams. Any beer-colored stream, commonly known as a "sulphur creek," was a telltale sign that the stream would be without fish and other aquatic life forms.

Acid mine drainage, like that of Shamokin Creek in Pennsylvania, is one of mining's most serious threats to water. A mine draining acid can devastate rivers, streams, and aquatic life for hundreds of years under the "right" conditions.

Delano is a former mining village and railroad center in northern Schuylkill County, Pennsylvania. The Lehigh Valley Railroad company operated the center until its closing in 1963. JAMES SHAUP

Trout Unlimited—or any other local conservation organizations—did not exist back then to challenge the decimation of land and waterways. Did people care? Not really. Those who had been born in the coal regions knew no better and accepted this as a way of life. Abandoned strip mines became swimming holes; towns had a bar and church on every street; high school football was the number one sport enjoyed by all on Friday nights; the first day of deer season was treated like a national holiday; and church and firehouse block parties were popular events that featured ethnic food, beer, and live polka bands. Life was good!

Coal mining wasn't the only source of pollution in the area. In my preteen years, waste treatment facilities in the anthracite region were nonexistent in most rural communities. My hometown of Delano, Pennsylvania, located in northern Schuylkill County, was no exception. The toilet water from the small patch of homes where I lived drained into a tiny mountain brook that everyone called "Shit Creek."

My father was not the fishing type. In fact, my only recollection of fishing (of sorts) with him was when I was four or five years old. He drove

9

my older brother, Eugene, and I to a small lake to go fishing for snapping turtles. When we reached the lake, Dad hoisted me onto an old wooden rowboat anchored at the lake's edge. Gene was at the helm and I sat in the front, presumably so my dad could keep an eye on me.

We spent the day paddling around the large pond while my father sat in the back smoking a cigarette and dragging a small piece of red flannel cloth along the bottom. Suddenly my father hollered, "I got something on!" His fishing rod got bent in half in a fierce struggle to get the beastly looking reptile into the boat. I don't have a recollection of how long it took, but the excitement of my father catching that huge snapping turtle left an everlasting impression that inspired in me a desire to fish.

A few years later brother Gene joined the 82nd Airborne. This was at the height of the Korean War, and I had no indication of when he would be back. Before leaving he gave me an old metal telescopic fly rod equipped with an automatic reel. During Gene's enlistment, Dad became very ill with tuberculosis, leaving me without a fishing tutor. I was heartbroken.

One spring afternoon my fourteen-year-old neighbor, Bobby Kahley, walked home with a stringer full of brook trout. "Wow," I said. "Where did you catch those fish, Bobby?" "In Shit Creek," he said with a smile. This was the same creek that if my mother caught me playing in or near it, she'd spank me. Nevertheless, it was my playground. But I never saw anything in the stream, which was so tiny you could jump across it, except strings of toilet paper and an occasional crayfish.

The following week Bobby was outside preparing to go fishing again. "Can I go with you?" I asked politely. "No, you are too young. Besides, it's too far of a walk," he retorted. "I'll never get to go fishing with anyone," I said to myself. Dejected but not discouraged, I plotted to follow him, and in preparation went to the garden and dug up some worms. The following day I waited patiently for him to leave his house.

He finally snuck out the back door and scurried up the backyard hill across from where our sewer pipe drained into the back-alley creek. A bit confused by the direction he was taking, I followed behind with my metal fishing rod and can of worms. Bobby was well ahead of me on the country roadway, but he never left my sight.

The walk was longer than I'd expected and in the midst of my struggle to keep up, Bobby disappeared over a hillcrest. When I reached the top, there he stood waiting. Obviously, he'd known I was behind him. "Okay, smarty pants, I'll take you fishing. But you better listen to me." And he shook his finger in my face. I was elated.

Together we trudged another mile along the hillcrest, nearing the valley at a sharp bend in the road everyone knew as "horseshoe curve." Bobby stopped and led me to the edge of a steep ridge at the corner of the mountainside. He looked concerned about taking me down an unbeaten trail to the creek below. Spilling my can of worms was my only worry. We took each step carefully, holding on to small trees and bushes, until we reached the bottom.

The stream, called Pine Creek, was no wider than five feet and no deeper than the thighs above my knees. From its back-alley origin in Delano, the water picked up speed and tumbled over rocks and deadfall three or so miles through steep, mountainous terrain, naturally cleansing itself to produce bright, clear water that exposed every submerged rock and bit of vegetation.

Little Pine Creek

After a brief critique of my hand-me-down equipment and some basic instruction about where to fish, Bobby quickly vanished through the mountain laurel, leaving me alone at a small pool. My futile attempts to fish resulted in tangles, snags, and frustration, often losing my worms in rapid succession and reducing my supply. I did not catch or even see a fish the entire morning. I gave up and sat helplessly on the bank, gawking at the water and wishing for Bobby to come back.

After a while a fish suddenly swam out from beneath an overhanging bush and grabbed one of my lost worms before dashing back to its cover. That little fish had my heart pumping a mile a minute. Quickly, I put another worm on the hook, plopped it into the water, and quietly waited.

Frozen in place, I was staring intently at the shallow pool when not one but two trout suddenly made a mad dash to the helpless worm on my hook. Spellbound, I watched the spooky fish dart back to cover, leaving half the worm dangling on the hook. Despite that setback I dropped the

Little Pine Creek is the upper most tributary of the Schuylkill River and begins in the town of Delano, Pennsylvania. LEE HARTMAN

bait back into the same spot and waited again, eyeing one of the fish hovering just outside its cover. After a few minutes the trout slowly moved toward the worm and ate it. With one swift jerk of the rod, I plopped the fish onto the bank and pounced on it.

My eyes magnified the trout's size. The colorful brook trout measured just five and a half inches, half an inch short of legal size. Suddenly I found myself in a dilemma. Bobby heard the commotion and appeared out of nowhere. "Whatcha got?" he said. "A trout," I said with a smirk on my face. "But it's only five and a half inches. Can I keep it?" He silently pulled out his knife, cleaned it, and stretched out the brook trout on his tape measure. "There, now it's six inches."

My day was complete. Bobby had four or five trout no bigger than eight or nine inches on a stringer. I tied my brookie through its gill with a leader and a stick, hooked it to my belt, and proudly followed Bobby home with a big smile on my face. The memory of catching that little brook trout in that bright, clear stream taught me the importance of clean water.

The water you touch in a river is the last of that which has passed, and the first of that which is coming; thus, it is with time.
—*LEONARDO DAVINCI*

A few years went by before my brother returned home from his stint in the 82nd Airborne. Bait fishing with worms and corn were still my only means to fish. Gene took me under his wing and taught me how to cast a fly with his new white fiberglass Shakespeare Wonder Rod. Another golden memory occurred when I caught a twelve-inch brook trout on a homespun wet fly. It was another milestone that remains with me today.

The Schuylkill River

The Schuylkill River is a source of drinking water for approximately 1.5 million people. Before the founding of Philadelphia, the Schuylkill—then known by its Indian name Manayunk ("where we go to drink")—was an important part of the landscape for the Lenni Lenape tribes. William Penn originally intended for his "green country town" to spread evenly between the Delaware and Schuylkill Rivers, situating the city at the

Common fish on the Schuylkill River include trout, catfish, perch, sunfish, carp, and bass. Depending on the season and river conditions, you may also catch shad and eel. LEE HARTMAN PHOTO

narrowest point between the two. However, residents had other ideas, developing bustling neighborhoods along the Delaware River and leaving the Schuylkill River largely as a country retreat with pastoral estates, institutional uses, and larger farm tracts through the late 1700s.

The Schuylkill River (the Dutch name for "Hidden River") is the largest watershed to the Delaware River. The Schuylkill watershed is over 130 miles long, includes over 180 tributaries, and drains an area of 2,000 square miles. The watershed is located in southeastern Pennsylvania, encompassing eleven counties and over three million residents. The headwaters of the Schuylkill River drain approximately 270 square miles of Schuylkill County, flowing in a southeasterly direction into the tidal waters at the river's confluence with the Delaware Estuary. The basin includes large parts of Schuylkill, Berks, Montgomery, Chester, and Philadelphia Counties and smaller parts of Carbon, Lehigh, Lebanon, Lancaster, Bucks, and Delaware Counties. The major towns and cities along the river are Pottsville, Reading, Pottstown, Phoenixville, Norristown, Conshohocken, and Philadelphia.

In 1825 the Schuylkill Navigation Company opened a canal on the Schuylkill to provide transportation and water power. The "canal" was actually a system of interconnected dams and slack-water pools in and along the river, called a routing.

The river was the least expensive and most efficient method of transporting bulk cargo at a time when the eastern seaboard cities of the United States were experiencing an energy crisis due to deforestation. It fostered the mining of anthracite as the major source of industry between Pottsville and eastern markets. Along the towpaths, mules pulled barges of coal from Port Carbon through the water gaps to Pottsville, some locally to the port and markets of Philadelphia, and some by ship to neighboring ports in New Jersey.

The Industrial Revolution, which continued into the twentieth century, was hardly conservation friendly. Coal interests ruled the land and turned the Schuylkill River into an inky black mess from the upriver coal banks continually feeding into the river. As villages and hamlets grew into cities and towns along the Schuylkill, industry leaders turned their backs on the river's quality. River dams were built to harness the water for

A coalfield is an area of certain uniform characteristics where coal is mined. The criteria for determining the approximate boundary of a coalfield are geographical and cultural, in addition to geological. A coalfield often groups the seams of coal, railroad companies, cultural groups, watersheds, and other geographical considerations. LEE HARTMAN

power; forests were cut; and tons of wastewater and culm deposits poured into the river, killing fish and other aquatic life and eventually threatening Philadelphia's drinking water.

State and local officials sounded the alarm. After numerous studies of the Schuylkill River in 1936, it was estimated that twenty-two million cubic yards of coal waste had accumulated in the river's channel. Traces of culm deposits were also found in the Delaware River ten miles above and thirty miles below its confluence with the Schuylkill. If the practice continued it would eventually stop navigation on the Delaware River.

Only the extreme headwaters above the coal operations survived the onslaught. Efforts by public officials encouraged the federal government to play a role in cleaning up the Schuylkill River, which continued until 1941, when it took a backseat to the war effort.

For there are many who still haven't found out that pure streams are necessary in Pennsylvania, not only in order that we may live but also that the people of Pennsylvania may properly make a living—that water is important in the daily life of us all.

—GOVERNOR JAMES H. DUFF

After World War II, Philadelphia and all of southeastern Pennsylvania remained among the most densely populated parts of America. The Schuylkill River, a major source of drinking water for millions of people, was more polluted than ever—considered the most polluted river in the country. Mine acid drainage, raw sewage, and coal waste deposits continued unabated until the river became an environmental disaster, leaving it in a lifeless state.

To rejuvenate the coal-laced river and reclaim it as a viable source of water, the State of Pennsylvania in 1942—led by Pennsylvania's Attorney General James H. Duff, who had served on the Pennsylvania Game Commission from 1905 until 1924, under Governor Edward Martin—declared war on river pollution, not just for the Schuylkill River but for all waterways in Pennsylvania.

James "Jim" Henderson Duff was an American lawyer and politician. A member of the Republican Party, he served as US senator from Pennsylvania from 1951 to 1957. Previously he had served as the thirty-fourth governor of Pennsylvania from 1947 to 1951. HTTP://BIOGUIDE.CONGRESS.GOV/ SCRIPTS/BIODISPLAY.PL?INDEX=D000516 (PUBLIC DOMAIN)

As attorney general, he did something no other politician had done to date. He pushed for enforcement of the 1937 Clean Stream Law to prevent the discharge of pollutants and waste into all Pennsylvania streams.

Duff believed the government should do for people what they could not do for themselves.

After Governor Martin's term ended, James H. Duff was handpicked by Martin as the Republican candidate for governor, and he was elected in 1946 by an overwhelming margin. The newly elected governor began heated discussions with state and federal government officials to clean up the Schuylkill River.

Although skeptical of Pennsylvania breaking from its past coal mining practices, the federal government joined in and imposed certain conditions on any proposed Schuylkill cleanup initiative. When the governor accepted the US government recommendations, the cleanup plan, called the Schuylkill River Project, was adopted.

Pennsylvania's first state-federal joint cleanup project officially got underway in 1947, helmed by Governor Duff. The 1945 Desilting Act was the cornerstone of the project. The Commonwealth made use of previously built dams and land holdings of the Schuylkill Navigation Company, which had gone out of business in 1931. The lower basin dams that had been acquired in the 1930s served as desilting pools once dredging operations began.

Three more desilting basins were completed on the upper reaches located between Tamaqua (Schuylkill County) and Hamburg (Berks County), some thirty miles apart. Once the desilting basins filled with water, the pools could stand until all the silt deposits settled to the bottom. The dredges excavated the siltation and trucked it to impoundments along the river. The problem that had to be faced was what to do with the silt? It was an environmental hazard.

After analyzing the sediment for content and combustibility, it was determined that 70 percent could be sold for profit as fuel. Power plants and other compatible industries bought the reclaimed coal deposit for as little as thirty-one cents a ton.

Reclamation projects persisted for many years after the official Schuylkill River Project was completed in 1951. The coal sludge continues to be collected, stored in containment sites, and sold by the ton to this day.

The Schuylkill River Project was the first major environmental cleanup effort undertaken by a government agency in the United States. At the time it was also the largest operation of its kind in the world. The historic Schuylkill River, once considered the dirtiest river in the country, rebounded from the past and came back to life in a dramatic way. The river improved significantly as fish and fauna returned throughout much of its length, and in 1978 it was designated a National Wild and Scenic River under the 1968 Wild and Scenic Rivers Act.

I did not know of Governor Duff's efforts until he died in 1969, when I read of the love he held for the great outdoors. He was unlike most politicians of his time. Serving as attorney general, governor, and later a senator on behalf of the state of Pennsylvania and its citizens, his conservation efforts are still felt today. He is a true environmental hero of his time.

The Lehigh River

The Lehigh River, the longest river in the Delaware watershed, rises in the Pocono Mountains in southern Wayne County and zigzags its way for 109 miles until it reaches the Delaware River. The Lehigh has been flowing through eastern Pennsylvania for thousands of years. It is one of nine rivers in the Commonwealth of Pennsylvania that is navigable. Until the nineteenth century it was called the West Branch of the Delaware River. Only after the river acquired its own individuality as a transportation base for coal in the early 1800s did we begin to use the English version, Lehigh, of the name the Native American Lenni Lenape Indians gave the river, Lechewuekink. This tongue-twisting word means "where there are forks," hence the name Forks of the Delaware.

———

I walked away, finally a free man. No more saluting generals, no more spit-shining boots or parading in marching bands. My three years of life in the military ended August 17, 1964. Hooray! The Vietnam War was heating up when my discharge papers were handed to me. Now don't get me wrong; I loved the military service. Why not? They obliged me with an electronics school that lasted a year, then put me in a windowless

The Lehigh River below the river gorge. LEHIGH COLDWATER CONSERVANCY ALLIANCE

cinderblock building with five army mates for the next two years to maintain and repair a complicated control system for the Nike Hercules missile that circled Philadelphia.

The first thing I had to do was buy a car and find a job. Without either I couldn't go fishing. After mustering out at Fort Dix, I bummed a ride to a used car dealer in Philly, bought the first vehicle available, and headed home to Delano in a used black-and-white 1959 Chevy Impala.

Hidden in a four-foot-high cubbyhole in the third-floor attic of my parents' house was the remainder of my fishing gear—an old telescopic metal fly rod, a box of moth-eaten wet flies, and a Perrine automatic reel spooled with an old HDH floating line. Salvaging what was usable, I replaced the rust-stained pole with a new eight-foot, six-weight Fenwick fiberglass fly rod, a double-tapered six-weight Cortland line, and a model 1498 Pflueger hand-cranked fly reel—just enough gear to get back to fly fishing.

Most streams and rivers in coal mine country were not yet suitable to fish. However, the coal culprits who spewed out their waste products were losing money, and the volume of coal production soon declined. Sewage treatment plants and strict regulations became the law of the land—a double whammy for coal operators—which initiated a recovery process for many neglected streams and rivers of the coal region.

The Lehigh River above White Haven had always been an exception—an area where coal deposits had never been discovered. The upper reaches of the river, where I routinely fished during my high school days, had a special place in my heart. This uninhabited section, with trout-friendly water, had no public access points until the town of White Haven. After three years in the military, I yearned to float and fish the mighty Lehigh again.

Deliverance Down the Lehigh

"That fiberglass canoe won't work on the Lehigh River," I said to the rental agent. "Where I'm going is rough-and-tumble water." "Of course it will. This canoe will handle any whitewater situation," the rental agent answered confidently. I paused for a moment, reflecting on my own experience navigating the Lehigh in a two-person rubber raft during my teen years. That twelve-foot inflatable was like a giant Ping-Pong ball, and it had safely bounced us down the river over rock and rubble as easy as having breakfast.

Oh well, he was the expert. I paid the man the two-day rental fee, strapped the fiberglass-constructed fourteen-foot Old Town to the rooftop, and drove away to pick up my paddling partner, Mike Rachuck, a high school friend and fishing companion.

The Lehigh River, a tributary of the Delaware River, is 103 miles long and located in eastern Pennsylvania. Parts of the Lehigh River, along with some of its smaller tributaries, are designated as Pennsylvania Scenic Rivers. LEE HARTMAN

The weather was pleasantly cool despite the bright sunlight poking through the car window in our two-hour drive. It was mid-May, and the float trip down the rugged Lehigh, planned weeks in advance, attracted four more of our fishing pals, in aluminum Grumman canoes, to join us.

Men cannot have too many shotguns and fishing poles.
—*General Norman Schwarzkopf*

The Route 115 highway bridge stretching over the Lehigh was our only access point. Below the bridge the river water tumbled violently, spilling its wetness over a picturesque ten-foot falls. One by one the six of us carried our gear and canoes around the steep waterfall through an unbeaten path of heavy laurels. Long rapids skimmed the riverbanks as we began our eleven-mile journey through a heavily forested gorge before reaching the newly built Francis E. Walter Dam.

The clear, rocky bottom of the thirty-foot-wide river was ripe with aquatic morsels for trout to feed on, perfectly suited for my style of fly fishing, dropping nymphs or wet flies below the surface. Fly fishing for trout was unthinkable for my coal region colleagues. Casting spinning rods, using lure or bait, was a popular choice for coal country anglers. I was a purist, fly fishing or bust—nothing else mattered.

Somebody behind you while you are fishing is as bad as someone look-ing over your shoulder while you write a letter to your girl.
—*Ernest Hemingway*

Trailing our friends, Mike and I coasted with the waves, entranced by the seclusion of the wild forest until we were interrupted by a wading angler who warned us the land was private property. "No problem, sir," Mike blurted. "We're just passing through." Suddenly, like a scene from the movie *Deliverance*, another man emerged from the woods with a shot-gun, screaming at us to get out of the water. When you have a double bar-rel pointing at you, stopping is not an option. We immediately paddled like Olympic rowers, praying he wouldn't shoot. He didn't.

The river held numerous stocked trout, a clue to why the armed vigilante had a shotgun. "Most probably he was a disgruntled fishing club member," I reasoned. It didn't matter. We were out of reach of their sacred grounds and were soon landing trout, lots of them. Catch and release wasn't in vogue those days. We caught them, kept them, and threw them on the evening campfire at our camp near the junction with Tobyhanna Creek.

The early morning sun peeked over the mountain ridge to wake us. That one angry guy who decided not to shoot had nearly spoiled the previous eventful day. The six of us brushed off the encounter, broke camp, and prepared to float and fish until reaching the take-out at the dam. The entrance of Tobyhanna water made the Lehigh noticeably deeper and wider, forcing us to lash our gear more securely. The aluminum-built Grummans preceded our canoe.

A few hundred yards downriver, large waves of fast-gushing water exploded against rocks and deadfall. Protruding boulders punished our front-running friends in their aluminum canoes, but fortunately they made their way unscathed through the swift channel. We followed in our plastic-looking Old Town through the heavy turbulence, banging our way over rocks that worked like a chain saw against the fiberglass sides until the vessel came apart and slowly sank like the Titanic in a yard of water.

With only our egos bruised, we dragged the broken craft to shore. The battered canoe was maybe salvageable but definitely not river worthy. Now what? The take-out was six more miles away—and we were stuck with six people, two serviceable canoes, and one that was barely floatable. Forced to put three to a boat, and with the equipment stowed in the damaged canoe, we limped down the river, paddling carefully until crossing the newly constructed Francis E. Walter Dam. The two-day river odyssey was finally over.

My personal ordeal wasn't quite complete until I'd returned the Old Town. "What, if any, would be my financial responsibility?" I wondered. Apprehensive, I pulled into an empty parking lot in the late evening only to find the rental agency closed. Still two hours away from home, I unloaded the canoe and taped a note onto the bow with my name, address, and phone number. I'm still waiting for a reply.

- 2 -

A Place Called Stockport

The white man came to plant a home on this spot, and it was then that great change began; the axe and the saw, the forge and the wheel were busy from dawn to dusk, cows and swine fed in the thickets whence the wild beasts had fled, while the ox and the horse drew in chains the fallen trunks of the forest. The tenants of the wilderness shrunk deeper within its bounds with every changing moon. . . . The open valley, half-shorn hills, the paths, the flocks, the buildings, the woods in their second growth, even the waters in the different images they reflect on their bosom, the very race of men who come and go, all are different from what they were.

—Susan Fenimore Cooper

My anxiety grew with each passing minute as I waited in my truck camper for new friend Joe Humphreys. The unmarked, grassy road from the two-lane highway was the only entrance to the sixteen-acre, partially wooded field. Joe's only point of reference to the well-hidden turnoff was a small sign one-half mile away that stated "Stockport Cemetery est. 1804." No town or road map bore the name Stockport in Wayne County. The cemetery, far from any town, was a mystery. The numerous tombstones, well hidden within a dense forest, revealed the names of many early settlers in the area.

The absentee owner of the river property allowed anglers access to the quiet, unnamed site along the cool flows of the Delaware River. The early spring morning was picture-perfect when Joe pulled his car under a bank of sugar maples not yet in their full glory.

The Appalachian Mountains, often called the Appalachians, are a system of mountains in eastern North America. Early Pennsylvania settlers began arriving in the covered forest during the late eighteenth century. GARTH LENZ

I had met Joe in the fall of 1977 during the National Trout Unlimited conclave held at the Pocono Environmental Education Center in Dingmans Ferry, Pennsylvania. Joe Humphreys was no ordinary fisherman. He was in his fifth year of teaching the angling course at Penn State University after taking over from the legendary George Harvey. Harvey was a fishing icon who spent twenty-five years teaching fly fishing before retiring from that position in 1972.

The great charm of fly fishing is that we are always learning.
—THEODORE GORDON

During the previous winter Joe had been the guest speaker for the Cumberland Valley Chapter of Trout Unlimited. Humphreys's program, advertised as "Tactics for Catching Big Trout," piqued my interest. His presentation topic excited me enough to make the three-hour drive to Carlisle, Pennsylvania.

The first large trout I ever caught happened during my teen years when my brother drove me to Fisherman's Paradise on Spring Creek, a regulated fly-fishing stretch located in Bellefonte, Pennsylvania. The Pennsylvania Fish Commission at the time stocked pellet-fed trout the size of your arm. Whether it's stream-bred or stocked, catching a fish that size is every angler's dream.

Joe Humphreys's program was more of a lecture. Using a piece of chalk on a blackboard, the Penn State professor scribbled a rough outline of a stream, a rock structure, and a large fish lying next to an overhanging bank. He marked an X to the front, side, and back of the fish, then asked the audience, "Where would you first cast your fly?" "In front," the group confidently responded. "NO!" he replied emphatically. "The first cast is behind the trout. The fish senses movement and often will turn on it. And should the trout not react to the fly, you then cast to the side of the fish. Now if that doesn't work, throw a cast above it and let the fly drift down to him." It was a stunning declaration, contrary to the gospel of many of his fly-fishing peers.

I drove 150 miles back home to Pennsburg, Pennsylvania, disappointed by the program. One of my duties that year as co-chairman of the Delaware River Committee for the Pennsylvania Council of Trout Unlimited was to recruit guest speakers for the Trout Unlimited National Conclave scheduled in the fall at the Pocono Environmental Education Center in Dingmans Falls, Pennsylvania. I crossed Joe Humphreys's name off the list.

One Sunday morning in August 1977, I picked up the Allentown *Morning Call* newspaper to read Tom Fegley's outdoor column. My eyes bulged with disbelief as I stared at a picture of a fifteen-pound, three-ounce brown trout held by Joe Humphreys, which he'd caught on a fly—a Pennsylvania fly-fishing record that stands today. That catch made me a believer. The Penn State professor of fly fishing practiced what he preached, and I immediately called him to do a casting presentation at the national conclave.

At the end of the day's festivities, a crowd of anglers surrounded Joe at the bar. They were curious about his record trout, caught in the dead of night on Big Fishing Creek. "What fly did you use, Joe?" I heard someone ask? "A wet fly!" he answered sarcastically. Despite five more minutes of coaxing by the audience, Joe remained evasive.

When the conversation began to subside, I took the opportunity to formally introduce myself. After some light banter I confessed that I knew his secret fly pattern. His lips tightened and with eyes of a cat glaring at a mouse, he declared, "You don't know! In fact, you can't find this pattern in any fly shop!" Humphreys's demeanor briefly stunned me. To ease the tense moment, I offered to buy a round of drinks if I was wrong. Joe gave a nod. "It was a pusher fly." His brows rose and his eyes opened wide. He turned to the bartender. "I'll buy! Give us two drinks."

Joe was unaware of a dinner engagement I'd had with Jim Bashline a few weeks prior to the conclave. The Philadelphia outdoor writer had revealed Joe's mystery fly to me that evening, a nighttime pattern designed by George Harvey called the "pusher fly." Jim became aware of the fly pattern through his wife, Sylvia, who'd photographed Humphreys's record trout for the outdoor news column. Joe Humphreys is a man of his word. Out of respect for his devoted friend and mentor George Harvey, he did not want to divulge the fly to anyone.

My own personal secret was "wild" trout fishing on the Upper Delaware River. At the time, few anglers knew trout even existed in the Delaware. Those who did know rarely shared it with anyone except a few choice friends. I broke the rule and invited Humphreys up to fish the river the following spring.

Joe Humphreys's three-day visit to Stockport included a day of fishing on a few Delaware nursery waters in search of stream-born trout. Joe's prowess isn't just catching big fish. He loves to fish small, tight quarter streams for brook trout the size of your hand. Brook trout were all but gone in most Delaware feeder streams, replaced with juvenile brown and rainbow trout.

One of the tributaries I'd fished during earlier visits to the Delaware was Hollister Creek, a personal favorite. The stream is no wider than my kitchen. It dumped its water through a steep, rocky trough six miles out of the foothills of Wayne County into the Delaware, with pocket water reaching no higher than your knees.

We arrived at Hollister mid-morning under a bright sun. Humph took the lead, poking his thermometer into the cool current. "Sixty degrees. Perfect!" he summed up in three words. The Penn State professor paused for a moment surveying the surroundings before taking a stealth approach upstream in the shallow pocket water. He paused below a five-foot shallow pool crowded with hemlocks along the bank. On one knee Joe cast his fly perfectly under the shady limbs. The float of his green humpy lasted but a foot when a fish exploded to the surface grabbing the fly. He was rewarded with a small crimson jewel—a junior-sized rainbow streaked with gray parr markings down its side.

That morning Joe Humphreys hit every pocket, pool, and riff and managed to land a half dozen stream-bred rainbow trout and one nice foot-long brown. Unfortunately, posted signs curtailed our upstream walk on Hollister Creek. After a streamside lunch we headed a dozen miles north to Big Equinunk Creek.

Equinunk Creek is heavily stocked in early spring with brown and brook trout, generally a one-time stocking during mid-April just before opening day. Trout anglers often crowd both banks of the small tributary

An early camping spot located near the Stockport Cemetery. LEE HARTMAN

during opening week and bombard it with night crawlers, mealworms, and salmon eggs until they fill their stringers with fish.

Now it was mid-May, and there wasn't another angler in sight. But the fishing was suspect. Both of us went our separate ways, Joe going north and me heading south, casting to each pocket and riff with a bushy attractor fly but coming away without a sniff or tug. The hatchery fish had either been caught or were gone, nor were there any signs of wild fish. "Let's try Shehawken Creek," I coaxed Joe. "It's about three miles past the Stockport campsite."

Greeting us was a plume of heavy smoke that blackened the sky next to the river, less than a football field away from where I parked. "The river is burning," I teased. "Let's try there first." A jeep-sized trail to the river was partially hidden with trees and underbrush; it led us to the billowing smoke near the mouth on the West Branch. We waited briefly on the bank of the river, staring at the clean, rippling water, looking for any surface-feeding fish. Not a head bobbed to the top, but the moderate flows looked perfect to dredge the bottom with nymphs.

Joe stayed below the Shehawken outlet, and I walked forty or so yards toward the burning brush pile, where the owner of the river property routinely burns community rubbish. We tagged the pool "Burning Dump." The popular fishing spot is referred to by that name today.

Smoke filled the air as I made an upstream approach with a pair of golden stoneflies, covering the tailout of the pool. It wasn't long before I landed a plump rainbow trout. My luck didn't change as two more fish fell into my net. To share the joy of my catch, I turned around to look for Joe. He wasn't fishing—just sitting on the bank relaxing and watching me fish. "Where did you learn how to tuck cast?" He said. "What's a tuck cast?" I answered, a bit confused. "You know doggone well what it is. I've been watching you. You're getting the flies below the surface before the line hits the water. That's a tuck cast!"

I really didn't know the cast had a name. My fly fishing began when I was twelve years old, but seldom with dry flies. As a ten-year-old, I drifted worms or salmon eggs with a tight line and a sixth sense of when to strike. In my teen years, wet flies and nymphs occupied my fly-fishing time. There were no strike indicators such as most fly anglers use today. In the years that followed, I discovered that stopping the forward upstream cast before the line hit the water got the nymph to the bottom more quickly, resulting in a longer and more natural drift.

Joe explained that he'd learned the tuck cast from George Harvey. Joe Humphreys is a master at it, far better than anyone I know. His offhand compliment pleased me. I was doing something that Harvey had mastered and Humphreys had perfected. He not only was a master angler but a great teacher. Most of all he is a great friend.

Joe and I completed the weekend in the quiet woods by a roaring campfire, reminiscing about the day's fishing. Over the years, we spent many more nights at the Stockport campsite, fishing the river and familiarizing ourselves with the area. Stone boundary walls submerged into the undergrowth graced much of the landscape. Collapsed wooden structures and often barely visible stone foundations showed that an early settlement had been here, only to vanish and leave but a cemetery. Where did all the people go?

The Founding of Stockport

About one hundred years earlier, the Munsee tribe migrated northward along the Delaware and soon held jurisdiction on the Pennsylvania side of the river. Their pathways were used as ancient highways that led them to fishing stations we use today. One of those places, three miles below the river junction, included a large flat of land known by the Indian name Tock Pollock (Tockpollock).

During the American Revolution, the Munsee- and Unami-speaking Lenni Lenape (also called Delaware) bands were deeply divided over which side, if any, to take in the conflict. The Munsee were generally northern bands originally from around the Hudson River and Upper Delaware River region. The Unami were from the south reaches of the Delaware. The Lenape began migrating westward from their territory on the mid-Atlantic coast to try to escape colonial encroachment, first to the Susquehanna Valley and later to Ohio.

On March 8, 1782, the Lenape were surprised by a raiding party of 160 Pennsylvania State Militia led by Captain David Williamson, who accused the Christian Lenape of attacking Pennsylvania settlements finally rounded them up in Ohio. Although the Lenape denied the charges, the militia held council and voted to kill them. After the Lenape were told of the vote, they requested time to prepare for death and spent the night praying and singing hymns.

Militia soldiers placed the men and women in separate buildings. The militiamen were ordered to execute their captives the following morning. In all, Williamson's men murdered twenty-eight men, twenty-nine women, and thirty-nine children. Two boys survived to tell of the massacre.

The bounty of fish and wild game along the Delaware attracted Lenni Lenape, Munsee, Minisink, and other tribes from the Hudson Valley and elsewhere. They made seasonal forays into the mountains and left trails that were later used by early European pioneers, who carved their homesteads from the Catskill forest. Other settlers followed, lured by wealthy landowners anxious to develop the land patents they held on vast tracts across eastern New York and later northeast Pennsylvania.

Prior to the Revolutionary War, only a few squatters had come to the Upper Delaware Valley region. The earliest Pennsylvania arrivals were Quakers from the Philadelphia region. In 1787 Samuel Preston, a Bucks County resident, and John Lukens, surveyor general, were sent by the government of Pennsylvania, which was seated at Philadelphia, to Northumberland County to survey unmarked lands.

Sam Preston was not only an agent but a good friend of Philadelphia merchant Henry Drinker, a wealthy Quaker and large landholder in Pennsylvania. Drinker, old enough to be Preston's father, gave Preston complete authority to acquire and develop the unsettled wilderness in the Upper Delaware region, what was then called Northampton but would shortly become Wayne County.

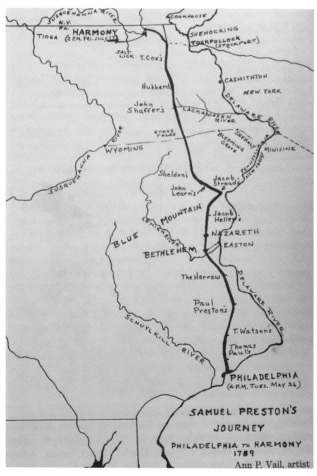

Mapping route of Sam Preston, courtesy of Equinunk Historical Society.

During the same season Sam Preston and Edward Doyle, another Bucks County resident and a member of his crew, surveyed three miles of riverfront sites starting at the junction of the East and West Branches down to Tockpollock Creek (now Stockport Creek). The virgin woodland and picturesque river valley were abundant in natural resources. Magnificent century-old hemlocks and sugar maple trees mixed with white pine, chestnut, cherry, ash, and oak covered the mountainside.

Preston recognized the easily available timber as a valuable resource. He was intrigued by the wide alluvial flats on both sides of the Delaware River, created by high water deposits. The rich and fertile land was ripe for planting seasonal crops, a perfect place to establish a colony of his own.

The Bucks County pioneer admired the Tockpollock Creek area where the clean-flowing mountain stream entered the Delaware River. Preston wasted no time purchasing the 150-acre plot from an early Connecticut settler named Josiah Parks for an unknown amount. He named his new land purchase Stockport, after a town in England where his ancestors once resided.

During the nineteenth century, sawmills were placed on many small Delaware River tributaries. The only water-powered mill, built by William Holbert & John Branning in 1873, remains in northeastern Pennsylvania. LEE HARTMAN

Two years later, Sam Preston, who had little money, formed a partnership with Henry Drinker. Drinker had the wealth but not the physical strength to develop the land for profit. Both men were fully aware of land values, and after much discussion between the two about land rights, obligations, and finance, they amicably agreed to a business arrangement to begin developing the area.

Henry Drinker's dream place to settle was on a bank of the Susquehanna River in an area known as Harmony, where he owned eight thousand acres of land. Preston held a commission from Drinker to sell the Susquehanna acreage at Harmony. Preston favored the forested land of Pennsylvania along the Delaware River, and he hired six men to cut a road from Stockport to Harmony to both lure and ease passage for other settlers.

On June 9, 1789, Sam Preston and his crew, equipped with ox power, hoes, and adzes, began carving their way through trees, rock, and heavy brush. One can hardly imagine the difficulty of hacking out an eighty-mile roadway with simple tools and a few oxen. During the summer trek Preston met a soon-to-become legendary backwoods figure, William Cooper, the founder of Cooperstown (and the father of James Fenimore Cooper). The Portage Highway, as they called it, was completed October 29, 1789. Today it is called Stockport Road.

On November 2, just as he was packing up to head to his winter quarters in Bucks County, a message arrived: "A team of oxen would be needed to bring critical supplies at Shaffer's farm located on the last lap northward through the woods to Harmony." Preston collected his team of men and set out the following day. About seven miles from Harmony, a snowstorm descended on them, forcing Preston and his crew to take shelter in a bark cabin that had been built when cutting the road.

He would later write to Drinker: "There came a hard gale of wind & blew down a large dead hemlock tree on the cabin (of which I have little or no remembrance)." Scarcely realizing what was occurring as the tree started to break apart above them, the men in the cabin stumbled blindly in the dark. "It was my particular misfortune," he wrote, "to run directly under the main segment of the falling tree. I was knocked unconscious and very much hurt by this."

Sam Preston suffered fractures to the shoulder and ribs. The accident not only delayed his trip home but also impaired him for the rest of his life. John Hilborn managed affairs at Stockport for the winter while Preston recuperated from his injuries in Philadelphia. Though he recovered, his strong frame was weakened by the accident. Drinker often chided in subsequent years that Preston was "chicken-hearted under affliction and sickness." The arthritic twinges and feeble hand Preston had to contend with were genuine reminders of that terrifying night.

The following spring the thirty-four-year-old pioneer came back to Stockport flats in a Durham boat—an early means of river transportation—filled with food, tools, supplies, and a half dozen hired hands. During the summer months his men cleared and planted the fertile flatlands along the river, built a small sturdy cabin, and constructed outbuildings for food storage and animal housing.

Among the tall hemlocks and white pine trees that adorned the valley were the sturdy sugar maples. Preston, operating out of a simple log cabin built a year earlier, began a large-scale production of maple sugar with the help of his friend John Hilborn. The evaporation process was done in a seven-hundred-pound cast-iron kettle seven feet across the top and three feet deep.

The kettles were brought upriver in Durham boats from Trenton, New Jersey. The shallow-draft flat-bottom boat, capable of carrying fifteen tons, was propelled upstream by manual labor using twelve- to eighteen-foot iron-shod setting poles. "Walking boards," a foot wide, ran the length of the boat on either side. The crew members set their poles on the bottom of the river and walked from the forward end of the boat to the stern, driving the boat forward. The captain, who steered, held the boat from going back with the current with a pole while the crew returned to the bow to repeat the process.

Traversing more difficult rapids called for ingenuity and strength in overcoming rough, rushing water. Iron rings were drilled and bolted into large shoreline rocks. A rope attached to the boat was threaded through the rings and pulled hand-over-hand by the crew, propelling the boat with greater ease than by poling.

Preston, as a manager-developer-expediter, had to contend with a lack of supplies, unreliable workers, foul weather, and the challenges of bringing the product to market. When the first batch of maple sugar was made, he mailed a package of maple sugar to Henry Drinker in Philadelphia who, in turn, sent it to newly elected President George Washington, who responded as follows:

New York

June 18, 1790

Sir: Mr. Morris has presented me, in your name, with a box of maple sugar, which I am much pleased to find so good a quality. I request you to accept my thanks for this mark of attention; and being persuaded that considerable benefit may be derived to our country, from a due prosecution of this promising object of industry. I wish success to its cultivation, which the person concerned in it can themselves desire. I am, Sir, your obedient servant.

George Washington

In 1791 Sam Preston was not satisfied to do just seasonal work. Consequently, he needed a reservoir of water for the grist- and sawmill to increase his operations to the entire year. After eyeing a large beaver dam one mile upstream of Tockpollock Creek, Sam went to work fortifying it and created a one-hundred-acre body of water. Though his judgment was well founded, the following two years were a disaster. By September a prolonged dry spell sapped the water out of the creek bed, putting his mill out of business. The dry spell lasted most of two years. The numerous eel weirs placed in the river made navigation to Philadelphia impossible until the weirs were battered down by spring freshets.

During the next few years, the weather turned favorable, and timber was cut in abundance and floated down in makeshift timber rafts to the Philadelphia market. Preston, with the help of a family friend, John Knight, an eleven-year-old boy whose father had been a guardsman for George Washington during the Revolutionary War and died a year earlier, added to the Stockport settlement a blacksmith shop, an axe factory,

In 1903, many years after his death, Sam Preston's beloved mansion burnt to the ground, leaving but a stone chimney. EQUINUNK HISTORICAL SOCIETY

a store, a school, a post office, and a beautiful family home on the river modeled after George Washington's mansion at Mount Vernon, Virginia. When the rafting season was in full swing, the Preston home was a favorite resting stop for weary raftsmen.

After the formation of Wayne County in 1798, Governor Mifflin (first governor of Pennsylvania) appointed Samuel Preston as the first associate judge for Wayne County. In the ensuing years the town blossomed into an important business center along the Delaware River. The continued expansion of his enterprise kept Preston busy, and he retired his judgeship in 1813.

According to writings, the judge had many peculiarities, but they were often harmless. Once he asked a man to dine with him who said he was not hungry. But shortly the man said, "I guess I will take some dinner," and drew up to the table. Preston reached over and took away the man's plate, knife, and fork. Supposing it to be a joke, the man asked Mrs. Preston for a new set. "Thee do not let him have any," said Sam. Then, addressing the man, he said, "Thee cannot now eat at my table. Thee said thee was not hungry. If thee is not hungry, thee ought not to eat; and if thee is hungry, then thee has told a lie, and I do not wish to eat with a liar." The man left.

Three years after the death of his partner, Henry Drinker, in 1809, Preston became the sole owner of 2,222 acres of land at a tax sale at Safe Harbor (renamed Equinunk Manor). The purchase included a gristmill operated by Josiah Parks. Preston identified it as the "county seat." After his bid was accepted, Preston wrote to the previous owners advising of his purchase and for how long it was redeemable. On March 10, 1812, Sam Preston received the deed for Equinunk Manor from John and William Penn, grandson and great-grandson of William Penn.

In January 1831, for an unknown reason, Preston gave the Equinunk Manor acreage to his sons Paul, Samuel, and Warner. A short time later Preston's three sons put the acreage up for sale. Samuel J. Preston died in December 1834, just months after the New York and Erie Railroad had been chartered by the governor of New York to connect north of New York City and west along the Delaware River to Lake Erie. Construction began by laying the rail bed along the river corridor to Binghamton, New York.

Around this time, Alexander Calder, an ordained minister who hailed from Deposit, New York, reportedly had decided to go to Africa as a missionary. He fashioned a crude raft, assembled with leftover wood, that would float, and on this he built a crude cabin to move his family. His goal was Philadelphia and from there, a ship to Africa. After floating for one day, he stopped for repairs at Safe Harbor near the mouth of Equinunk Creek (Equinunk is a Lenape word for "a place where clothes are distributed"). The area was so enticing Calder decided to stay; he removed the cabin from the raft, placing it on a convenient site, and began establishing himself in the community, which was where he befriended Israel Chapman.

On July 9, 1832, Alexander Calder and Israel Chapman bought the 2,222 acres from Sam Preston's three sons. By 1851, the railroad system was complete. The Erie was an innovator, being the longest railroad in the United States, over four hundred miles, linking the Atlantic seaboard with the Great Lakes, and the first to construct a telegraph line along its right-of-way.

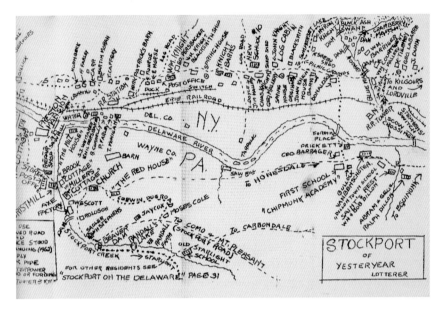

Historical map of Stockport settlement. EQUINUNK HISTORICAL SOCIETY

Following the creation of the Erie Railroad on the New York side of the river, four newly constructed railway stations were placed on a twenty-mile stretch of river—Chehocton, Stockport, Lordville, and Cochecton. The settlement of Chehocton, to avoid confusion with the Cochecton station, changed their name to Hancock in 1849 in honor of the Declaration of Independence's first signer, John Hancock.

River Eels

Freshwater eels are the only catadromous fish in North America. "Catadromous" means that they spawn in salt water and live as adults in fresh water. Anadromous fish, like salmon and American shad, spawn in fresh water but live as adults in the ocean. On this continent, eels are represented by a single species, the American eel (*Anguilla rostrata*). Although the eel looks snakelike, it is a fish.

Many settlers in the region relied on food provided by nature. Hunting wild game and fishing was a common practice. Brook trout, North American eels, maple syrup, and venison were prime food

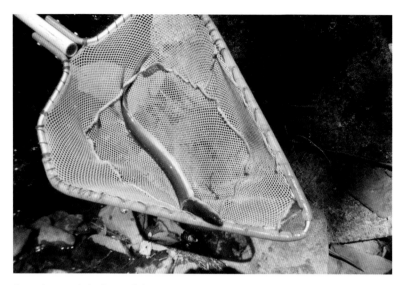

An eel netted during a fish survey study of Factory Creek in Equinunk, Pennsylvania. LEE HARTMAN

sources in the home economy. Fishing laws were nonexistent. It was common practice to harvest large quantities of fish, game, and eel to store for winter use.

Nothing went to waste with eels. Those soaked in brine and smoked were considered a delicacy. The skins were saved and dried, and the dry skin worked by hand until it became pliable. It was used in many ways, such as bands for injured arms or wrists and as tie-down straps.

As the population of Stockport grew, food supplies began to dwindle. Settlers learned to recognize the seasonal habits of the snakelike creatures that came from the ocean and began thinking of other means to catch more of them besides with a hook, line, and sinker. The villagers built two stone wings (weirs) across the shallowest point in the river, angled to each shore. After the V-shaped stonewalls were completed, a wooden rack designed to trap eels was placed at the center, or neck, between the two weirs. Like a magnet, river life came to the opening. Present-day anglers who fish the Stockport area can easily recognize the rock wing once used by local villagers stretched across the river. The remains of old eel weirs can also be seen in other Delaware and Susquehanna River watershed streams.

Until the early 1900s, eels supported an intense commercial fishery in the Susquehanna and Delaware River systems. Harvesting eels was a fall tradition. When eels reach maturity and the river is at its highest level, at the dark time of a new moon, they begin to swim on their ocean-bound journey to the Saragossa Sea. The low, V-shaped barricades made of rocks, called wing dams, trapped adult eels on their downstream migration toward the sea. The eels entered a wooden rack from the wide upstream side and swam through the small funnel opening downstream into holding baskets. Even in a poor harvest year, the eel take was staggering. In 1912, called an "off year," fifty thousand eels weighing more than forty-four thousand pounds were caught in Pennsylvania.

The Life of a Modern-Day Pioneer

Catching and trapping eels is a centuries-old tradition on the Delaware River. Charlie Howard operated an eel weir on the East Branch in the early 1900s, and when he died in 1948, the front-page headline in the *Walton Register* read, "Hancock Recluse Lived in Lonely River Cabin." The obituary described Howard as being "as close to the popular idea of a hermit as was Thoreau." The article said, "He conducted an eel rack near his home, gaining part of his sustenance from the eels."

Howard was an eccentric whose personal belongings included a box of women's discarded shoes and a jar of silver dollars. He lived upstream in a tarpaper shack by the river on Pea's Eddy Road near the village of Hancock, New York.

Ray Turner now lives across the river from Charlie Howard's old residence and calls it Eel Weir Hollow. Turner is a modern-day pioneer who currently has the last remaining eel weir in the Upper Delaware River system. No one knows who was the first to build a weir, but historians tell us that Native Americans collected eels from "traps" during pre-settlement years.

Ray's weir and smoke shop, established in 1988, after a twenty-year stint in the US Army, sits deep in the hemlocks on the bank of the East Branch of the Delaware a few miles north of Hancock, New York. Turner can harvest up to 2,500 eels during a fall season. Ray Turner hot-smokes his eels and sells them to tourists, as well as to restaurants and retailers. Prior to Turner's operation another eel weir was operated by Francis Bennett at Stockport; it closed in the early 1960s. Remnants of the weir still remain in the river today.

The life history of the North American eel was revealed only in this century. Even today they are not completely understood. The principal puzzle for many years was where do eels spawn? Their spawning grounds have been identified as the Saragossa Sea, in the northern Caribbean-Bermuda region of the Atlantic Ocean. The eels arrive there to spawn from two directions: the American eel from the west and the European eel from the east. But how young eels of each species know which continent to go to has yet to be explained.

After the adult eels spawn, they die. The larval eels, called leptocephali, are ribbon-like and transparent. These "glass eels" drift with other tiny organisms in the northward-flowing ocean currents. The transforming young eels, called "elvers," enter river estuaries when they reach the continent. The females don't stop, but continue swimming many miles upstream, mainly at night, even to the river system's headwaters. The trip from the spawning grounds in the ocean to the eel's freshwater home takes about a year.

The male eels, unlike the females, stay in the lower reaches of the coastal river and in the brackish tidewater estuaries just off the river's mouth. After remaining in fresh water for ten to twenty years, the adult females, now called "silver eels" because of their silvery appearance, migrate downstream in the fall on their long way back to the Sargasso Sea. A sexually mature female eel may contain two million or more eggs.

Eels are predators. They eat a wide variety of aquatic insects, crayfish, and other crustaceans, frogs, fish, and worms, feeding mostly at night.

The Admiral of the Delaware

Daniel Skinner, founder of timber rafting, was the lynchpin of the area's economy during the eighteenth and early nineteenth centuries. Thousands of timber rafts rode the spring freshets to markets along the Delaware River, where the vessels were disassembled and the pine and hemlock logs fashioned into spars and masts for the lordly ships of the British Main. Almost two hundred years would pass before his honorary title would be given to a new generation of people and boats drawn to the river.

⚬ ⚬

I could not believe what I was seeing. "What is that thing floating out there?" I said to myself. There was a large fish carcass floating on its side; it looked to be about three feet long as it slowly glided in the eddy by the New York bank. The curious sighting interrupted my trout fishing, just below the outlet of Abe Lord Creek.

Anxious to investigate what appeared to be a lifeless fish bobbing on the surface in a backwater, my curiosity got the best of me and I quickly waded to the shoreline to identify it. The sun-exposed fish was too decayed to recognize. Carefully I turned the dead creature over to the unexposed side for another view. My eyes widened in disbelief. With its skin unspoiled there was no question: It was a brown trout that taped out at thirty-three-and-a-half inches—one-half inch less than the size of Joe Humphreys's record brown caught five years earlier in Fishing Creek, Centre County, Pennsylvania.

I laid the dead beast on the riverbank and went to get my camera and tape measure at the Equinunk Campground. As I was wading back to the fish, a large boat the size of an "ark" drifted toward me. It was a sixteen-foot high-sided McKenzie drift boat—the biggest watercraft I

A steersman checks on his young crew members as they sail their timber to a southern port. EQUINUNK HISTORICAL SOCIETY

had witnessed on the Delaware since my introduction to the river thirteen years ago.

"How ya doin'?" greeted the lone boatman as he anchored above me. "Not bad. Just a few rainbows this morning." I responded in a friendly tone. "What was that you were draggin' by the shore? That didn't look like no rainbow," he muttered. I muzzled up momentarily, not wanting to reveal the trout, but seconds later relented. "Come on, I'll show you," I confessed weakly. He peered intensely at the decayed specimen, marveling at the size of the fish.

His name was Brian Wilson and he lived in Hankins, New York. Brian was on a scouting mission with his new fishing boat, planning to start a guide service business on the Delaware. He requested I send him a picture of the fish for advertising purposes. "No way," I reasoned self-ishly to myself. Fishing articles were already circulating across the country revealing the Upper Delaware's worth of "wild trout," and with every new season anglers were coming in increasing numbers. My head filled with

43

negative replies to his plan, but I held my cool and gave him a slight nod of assent. I never did send him the picture.

It was 1984, and since the construction of the branch reservoirs, the Delaware River had been rapidly growing in recognition as a great trout river. Many Delaware fishing pioneers did not want to exploit the river fishing any further, including myself. But as an active conservationist with Trout Unlimited, my heart told me otherwise. The wild trout in the Delaware were non-stocked, producing on their own in the small feeder streams, and without friends the river would be subjected to man's encroachment.

The following year, Brian Wilson became a modern-day pioneer by being the first fishing guide to use a drift boat on the Upper Delaware River. Brian's endeavor was short-lived. The Hankins native, after a few years of guiding, relocated to the West Coast. It wasn't long, though, before others, including myself, followed his lead and started our own guide service businesses on the Delaware River. We were not, however, the first to float this historic river for profit. Three centuries earlier a man named Daniel Skinner had made his living floating large timber rafts to downriver markets.

The Colonization of the Catskills

The Hardenberg Patent, secured in 1708, contained nearly two million acres covering all of Delaware County east of the West Branch of the Delaware River. After the American Revolution in 1776, a new era dawned for the owners of the land. The Indians were all but banished from their haunts and it became white man's land.

Prior to the seventeenth century, the heavily forested land in the Upper Delaware region was inhabited by a group of Lenape or Delaware Indians who called themselves the Minsi. Historians differ in defining the territory of the Minsi, but it is generally thought they controlled the land downstream from the mouth of the Lackawaxen River. The Iroquois lived in upstream areas, and there was hostility between the Lenape (parent nation of the Minsi) and the Iroquois.

As early as 1614 the Minsi may have encountered early Dutch hunters who traveled west from the Hudson Valley and first settled the area.

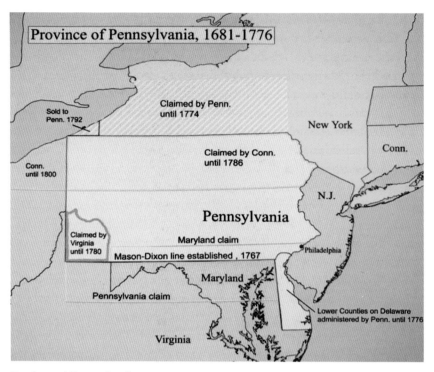

Province of Pennsylvania map. CREATIVE COMMONS

Here they found an ideal location on the banks of a river where, among other food sources, there was an abundance of wild turkey. The Dutchmen settled near a small stream and marked the location on their maps as Kollikoonkill, meaning "Wild Turkey Creek" (now called Callicoon Creek).

The Kollikoonkill settlement had very few structures until around 1848 when the Erie Railroad unlocked the area to others, renaming the growing village Callicoon. The year 1888 was a date etched in history, when a devastating fire nearly wiped out the entire Main Street. The resilient community immediately rebuilt, replacing every building by year's end.

In 1754, settlers from the colony of Connecticut began arriving in the Upper Delaware Valley with their families, where they purchased two ten-mile-long strips of land on either side of the Delaware River, between Ten-Mile River and Wild Turkey Creek. The area became a prime source

The river at Callicoon, New York, as it looks today. LEE HARTMAN

for fresh-cut timber, and the river served as a natural access to the populated coastal centers of the east. By the 1760s, timber rafting—where a few tree trunks of hemlock and pine were lashed together and floated to local sawmills downstream—had begun.

The founding colony was named Cushetunk (now Cochecton), from the Lenni Lenape word *ksch-itchuan*, meaning "a place of low land." The pioneers claimed the land for Connecticut. One of their first chores was to construct a blockhouse and stockade as a defense against marauding Indians, which they called Fort Delaware.

A few more courageous pioneers found their way, and by 1755 there were twenty families spread out over more than twenty miles of the river valley, from the mouth of Hollister Creek to the mouth of Ten-Mile River. One of those pioneers was Joseph Skinner, who came here with his son Daniel and siblings. Four years later, Daniel's father went missing. The family searched for more than a year, but he was nowhere to be found. Months later, a hunter found his skeletal remains with bible in hand in

46

the nearby forest. Joseph Skinner's name inscribed on the inside cover revealed his identity. He is believed to be the first white man murdered in the Upper Delaware region. After the discovery of his father, Daniel Skinner acquired twenty-five-acres of land on the Pennsylvania side of the river, referred to as Tammany Flats and later known as Bush's Point. By 1760 there were no native villages left in the valley, the Minsi having been driven out by militant Iroquois and their French allies.

Another Connecticut pioneer, Josiah Parks, may have been one of the first colonists to settle in the Upper Delaware Valley far above Fort Delaware near the junction of the East and West Branches of the river. Parks, a distinguished sailor, was awarded the rank of boatswain in the British fleet. His nickname, "Bos'n," stuck with him for the remaining years of his life. Bos'n was a bit of a nomad in his youth, exploring up and down the river corridor and finally settling on a plot of land in Pennsylvania in nearby Greater Equinunk Creek, called Safe Harbor.

Legend has it that Bos'n Parks was a likable sort, easily making friends with several local tribesmen. However, he was no fool. As a defense against the unfriendly Iroquois who were involved in the 1751 massacre at Minisink, New York, he built a permanent cabin for himself and his pregnant wife on a large island (now Frisbie Island) in the area called Safe Harbor.

A few months later, a trusted Lenape friend of Parks, affectionately called "Old Abe," came to his island home and told Bos'n that a band of native warriors were planning an extensive raid against the Connecticut settlers in the Wyoming Valley region. The Yankee pioneers rendered allegiance to Connecticut rather than Pennsylvania. Their claim was based on a land grant from Charles II of England, embracing all land not possessed by any other "Christian Prince." This venture led to a dispute that erupted into the Pennamite War.

Bos'n Parks wasted little time and walked to Wyoming Valley (now Wilkes Barre, Pennsylvania) to warn his Connecticut Yankee friends of the looming threat of war with the Seneca tribe of the Iroquois, who were allied with Penn's Quakers, known as Pennamites.

Parks's friends had few weapons. Being an ingenious sort, the British Navy veteran realized the need for effective fighting equipment and

The Pennamite–Yankee Wars, or Yankee–Pennamite Wars, were a series of conflicts consisting of the First Pennamite War, the Second Pennamite War, and the Third Pennamite War, in which the Wyoming Valley along the North Branch of the Susquehanna River was disputed between settlers from Connecticut and Pennsylvania. ALONZO CHAPPEL, 1828-1887

decided to build a cannon by cutting out a hollow log and bounding it with brass hoops. It appeared to be serviceable, but when loaded and fired, it burst—causing more damage to those firing than to the enemy. Though his cannon was a failure, the need for one impressed the officers to the extent that they raised money and commissioned Parks to go back to Connecticut and buy one.

Only a few of his Yankee cronies believed Parks's warning and left; the other settlers stayed on. Those that waited were eventually massacred during the skirmish known in history as the First Pennamite War.

When Parks finally came back home to Safe Harbor, he had a change of heart about his appointed job to buy a cannon. The much-worried Parks decided to leave his island home, and so he packed those of their worldly belongings that could be safely stowed in the canoe. Parks and his expecting wife were hardly out of sight of their island home when she went into labor. They stopped at a place called Oven Rocks, located one mile below Equinunk Creek, and hid in a small cave on a high river ledge until she gave birth to their baby son, William.

As soon as Mrs. Parks was able to travel, they paddled down the river to Minisink where he was detained by the British regarding the matter of money he'd received to buy the cannon. The British threw him in jail for spying. Eventually he was released.

The First Raft

Prior to the French and Indian War (1756–1763), Daniel Skinner spent time as a sailor on a merchant ship. The former seaman once made several voyages to the ports of New York and Philadelphia. Now entrenched in a new environment in the northeastern Pennsylvania woodlands, Skinner wanted to develop a profitable business. The tall virgin hemlocks and double-trunk white pines that graced the banks of the river looked like money in the seafaring eyes of Skinner. How to get the pine and hemlock to the port of Philadelphia became his dilemma.

The experimenting Skinner cut, trimmed, and rolled into the water several of the tallest pine trees and tried to guide them downstream with a canoe. The venture had disastrous consequences. The large, heavy pine timbers were uncontrollable. They either became lodged in inaccessible places or bogged down in the long, slow eddies. He abandoned that delivery method and began experimenting with a crude raft made out of four timber spars and held together by a wooden framework at each end. A block was fastened port and aft on the raft with wooden pins set in for the placement of each oar.

Historians say, as described in Leslie Wood's book *Holt! T'other Way!*, that he hired a "very tall Dutchman" to man the forward oar while he steered the log craft from the rear. In the spring of 1764, Skinner and the Dutchman, named "Cudosh," launched their maiden voyage with a fifteen-foot-wide and eighty-foot-long raft of lashed timber spars from the Catskill Mountain settlement of Cochecton, located forty miles north of Mahatmeck, what is now Port Jervis, New York.

The first trip was difficult and there were many delays. Both men were unfamiliar with the river and its changing flows, often relying on a canoe when they approached rough water and letting the raft take care of itself. The grueling two-hundred-mile journey to Philadelphia took over a week. After a long hike back home, the daring pioneers constructed a second raft containing ten spars, which made it five feet wider.

Dan Skinner soon learned of Josiah Parks and his abilities as a sailor. After discovering his whereabouts, Skinner convinced Parks to work for him and Cudosh. Bos'n had numerous credentials—as a sailor, a lumberman, and an Indian scout—and his knowledge of the waterways made him a good fit for Skinner's new river enterprise. Parks was to be used as the raft forerunner, with Dan Skinner and Cudosh as the steersmen. The three raftsmen made this trip to Philadelphia in just forty-eight hours.

The shipbuilders offered a rousing welcome for the three raftsmen when they came ashore in Philadelphia. Overjoyed with the fresh supply of timber, which was used for ships' masts, the shipbuilders honored Skinner with the title "Lord High Admiral of the Delaware." (Some say he later bestowed the title on himself.)

> *The forward end of the raft floated out a few feet in midair and suddenly plunged down into the water below, the raft bending in the middle from the force of gravity on both ends, and the forward oarsmen, who sometimes stood two feet in water when the raft plunged, were hidden from the sight of those on the rear end. A tremendous pressure was exerted on all parts of the craft when going over the dam, the whole framework creaking and groaning like a huge monster in terrible agony.*
>
> —*LESLIE WOOD,* Holt! T'other Way!

Dan Skinner was a pioneer whose inventiveness changed the face of a major waterway. His inaugural river voyage had opened a new trade route, later coined the "Delaware highway." The "New World" woodlands were now felled by the axe of colonization. For his remaining years Skinner had a lock on the title and the river's timber trade. He knew the task and the art of handling men. No man could be a steersman on a Skinner raft unless he paid the Admiral and Bos'n two full bottles of good liquor; no apprentice could serve as forehand, fending the raft from rocks on either side, unless the tribute price of one large bottle was paid beforehand.

The returns were well worth the small initiation fee, for the Admiral's men were handsomely rewarded in pay and gratuities. Perhaps the men had to be well paid to compensate for the heavy labor. Swerving long rafts around the dreaded point where the violent Beaver Kill waters enter the East Branch, rounding the hairpin turn at Pea's Island, and running the swirling eddies that swung the rafts in circles took unrelenting vigilance and courage.

Daniel Skinner was known to tie up his timber raft before entering the U-turn at Pea's Eddy to provide the crew with extra rum, enough to make each raftsman drunk. Then he'd send his happy crew forward through the danger zone, where they would pole and push the battered logs, often while wading in cold water up to their waists and shoulders. Those who emerged at Pea's Island often got drunk twice. It was high times!

Daniel Skinner, the High Admiral of the Delaware, died in 1813 at the age of eighty and was buried at Tammany Flats, next to his father. His friend and teammate Bos'n Parks became a river legend, later passing at the age of ninety-nine years old, according to Pierre DeNio in his book *The Winding Delaware*.

Bos'n spent his remaining years with his son, William, and daughter, Prudence, at the mouth of Tar Hollow Brook, later named Tyler's Switch. Though this hasn't been confirmed, it's said that Bos'n was buried in an unmarked grave on Partridge Island on the East Branch. He would later be joined there by William and Prudence, who lived to be 106. Many fellow timber runners also found their resting place on the river island, which is located near Fish's Eddy, New York.

The rafting industry continued throughout the Upper Delaware Valley region. The new age of rivermen learned that the best possible time for making the journey to downriver ports was during the spring freshets.

Entire families joined in the preparations at the first sight of rain, the men lashing down the raft timber while the womenfolk began preparations for sending their men on their way. The women baked a multitude of bread, pies, cakes, apple turnovers, and other delicacies for the huge dinner bucket from which the rafting crew would eat its noontime meal as they floated down the river.

Once the rain began to fall, meteorological conditions would be checked by setting out empty pails to gauge how fast the water rose in them. Some men notched a stick or cut a sapling, pushing it down into the gravel of the riverbed with the mark at the surface to measure the rate at which the stream rose. Like drivers at the start of a car race, they watched as the water deepened over the notch, signaling them to go.

It is not known whether timber rafting above Hancock occurred before the Revolutionary War. During the late eighteenth century, more Yankee settlers from Massachusetts and Connecticut arrived at the East Branch of the Delaware. Two were brothers, James and Ebenezer Wheeler

One method raftsmen used to gage when to float the river was a giant boulder near the middle of the river. Once the freshet (heavy spring flow) covered the rock, they were good to go. Today this area is called Skinner's Falls. GARTH LENZ

of Branford, Massachusetts, in search of new land. They found a suitable location on Partridge Island, named after the large flocks of partridge that came from the surrounding hills to graze on the island.

In 1793 the Wheeler brothers purchased 1,500 acres of virgin timberland on both sides of the river and built a sawmill, the first of its kind on the East Branch. The mill, with an up-and-down saw, produced thousands of board feet of the finest-grade pine lumber. Later generations said that the Wheeler sawmill at Partridge Island sent the best pine lumber to the Philadelphia market.

The entrepreneurial family built a frame house in the East Branch Valley that was the first of its kind. The home also served as a tavern for more than a half century. The second floor, which had an arched ceiling twenty-two feet wide, was used as a ballroom for dancing. All the local business and social activity centered at the Partridge Island Tavern.

With few social diversions the Wheeler clan got out of bounds on many occasions. Those pioneering individuals had the reputation of being rough, disreputable characters whose chief modes of enjoying themselves were swearing, getting drunk, and fighting. They would often party for a day or two before going back to their rafting jobs.

The third generation of Wheelers were no different than their forebearers. James III, a resident of Fish's Eddy, was also an individualist and nonconformist. He drank on Saturday, collected timber on Sunday, and steered a four-thousand-pound wooden raft on Monday. He was considered one of the best steersmen ever to pilot a timber raft downriver. A gifted mechanic, Wheeler built an aeroplane before one was ever built. He applied for a patent but was denied it since a combustible engine had not been developed. When the Wright Brothers flew the first plane in 1903, James Wheeler remarked, "There goes my dream." Before his death in 1906, he built fishing boats for the Delaware River. A setting pole rather than oars propelled the sixteen-foot-long, four-foot-wide flat-bottom boats.

When the ice had gone out and the spring freshet was in the offing, great was the excitement and activity along the river.
—LESLIE WOOD, HOLT! T'other Way!

During the nineteenth century the long river journeys were often accompanied by floating dining cars. EQUINUNK HISTORICAL SOCIETY

Only a small portion of the region's population was involved with river rafting in the late eighteenth century. After the death of the Admiral, shipbuilding began to increase, along with making wood furniture. By 1823, the young nation's lumber needs had boomed to unprecedented levels for making furniture and in the hand lining of large vessels. Sometimes dozens of rafts set sail downriver at the same time, which often resulted in traffic jams and runaway rafts. The stout logs became masts for warships like the USS *Pennsylvania*, a 120-gun frigate completed at a Philadelphia shipyard in 1837 for the fledgling US Navy. At the time it was the largest seagoing vessel in the world

During the mid-1800s raft composition changed because the best and tallest trees had been cut. This meant the rafts were composed of smaller logs. But with the increased availability of rope, the rafts became larger. By the 1840s sawmills were located on most major tributaries to the Delaware, and sawed lumber became an important commodity to send down the river. At the very least, one thousand rafts were at work on the Delaware with an annual volume of fifty million board feet of lumber.

Thomas Tyner, an Irish immigrant, born in 1816, found his way to Wayne County in the spring of 1849. He purchased 1,100 acres of land near Equinunk Manor (now Equinunk). The Irishman was no ordinary person. His reading and writing skills served him well as the new Wayne County commissioner. He also kept himself busy as a lumberman, farmer, and raftsman. Tyner's children, Oakley and Abner, also became raftsmen and were often seen going down the Delaware with the Tyner rafts of lumber heading for Philadelphia.

It was reported that many raftsmen, including Tyner and his crew, had a favorite stop at a certain bend in the river where the current slowed the raft down near the shoreline. There, a local whiskey peddler would row out to the raft and offer the cunning raftsmen a bottle or two of liquor. Abner and Oakley Tyner would show the peddler a twenty-dollar bill and take the whiskey at the same time. The salesman, who often had no change, said he would be back with change before they reached the bend, but he was foolish enough to leave the whiskey and money with them. By the time he got back, the raft would be around the corner and picking up speed with the bottle already being passed from man to man. The poor whiskey peddler would be left on shore waving his arms and shouting profanities.

Running log rafts of valuable timber down the river was seldom done at night, except in great emergencies. One incident was so unusual it became rather famous, especially along the West Branch. The Gregory boys of Carpenter's Eddy, on the West Branch, now known as Granton, had bought the last stand of first-growth hemlock in the West Branch Valley. The trees were peeled during the season of 1894, then the logs were hauled to Carpenter's Eddy to be rafted in the spring of 1895, making five double rafts. They were all started down to market on the same day. Each had a Gregory as steersman.

Four of the rafts went through Easton without trouble, but one raft with the largest logs was the last to be untied. This raft, with John Gregory as steersman, was 160 feet long and 40 feet wide and needed twenty-eight inches of water to float it. When John Gregory pulled out, he missed the channel and struck what was then Chamberlin's Dam, where the raft was stuck for many months.

On August 13, after a period of drought conditions, there came a series of thunderstorms, which caused the river to rise considerably. By the next day the heavy-laced timber showed signs of movement. The Gregorys prepared for leaving, taking the necessary articles on board to be ready when the stuck raft moved. The men remained on the raft into darkness. The moon, according to the almanac, was to rise at 11 p.m., and at about that time the raft left loose. The steersman shouted, "Jersey—all you have!" The raft plowed into the dam timbers, but no harm was done, and they were on their way.

A grandson of steersman Robert Gregory in his family memoirs told the story of his grandfather's trip with the timber raft that night:

Just as soon as the stern cleared the dam apron, the pilot called some of the forehands and they pulled toward Pennsylvania on the rear oar. This put us in the channel very nicely and we made Chubhole rift with no trouble. We ran into gravel at Canes Bend but swung off and Underwood's turn was made without incident. We slowed down several times passing Camp Meetin' Island but finally scribbled through. No more trouble was looked for until Craig's Digway and by then the moon was helping. We bumped the Pennsylvania side of shore but came through without damage at Craig's. From here we looked toward the old Fletcher dam and then the Stilesville dam. This dam was not a favorite with raftsmen and many were wrecked there in the past.

The pilot called some of the forehands aft and asked them what they thought we should make for. Peck and Frazier said, "The Old Orchard, now Port Jervis." All agreed. The opinion was that we could make Long Eddy by daylight. We drifted down to the dam and there it could be seen the river was still rising. We went over with little trouble taking only a few shale boards of the dam. Cold Springs Brook was still rising, and this indicated the river would keep at a high level for at least two days and show heavy rains to the west of the river.

We kept going and no incident occurred from Deposit to Little Falls, near Hancock, except a good wetting from a shower. As we glided down toward the Point, as the raftsmen called it, we could hear and plainly see a raft coming out of the East Branch. Drawing near them we hailed them, and it proved to be a Hubell with a double scantling raft. He made the big river just a raft length ahead of us. He said he was going to Old Orchard and would be there to help us land. We pulled up at the Point and the branch hands went ashore to return to Deposit by train. The pilot asks the crew remaining, now six of us, if we should stop at Long Eddy to eat. Charles Peck told the pilot they could eat in many places where you couldn't run a raft, so we kept going.

We passed Long Eddy just after daylight and the river was running high and rising. With daylight all the dangers and troubles seemed to fade; the pilot seldom spoke except to the forehands and kept looking ahead all the time. We had about a dozen logs on top of the raft that did not fit in and one of them was one of the largest that ever came out of the West Branch. It was 16 feet long and measured 1,544 feet by Scribner's log rule.

Just before reaching Lackawaxen everyone was alerted by a fisherman that the stream was running over everything. As we rounded the bend, we saw the worst; the creek was wild and the current, as it poured into the still water above the dam, carried nearly across the river and was full of driftwood. We hurriedly stretched all rope we had in case we pulled apart as we plunged over the dam. The resident pilot came out of his little shanty to take down the owner's name and amount of timber. He knew the pilot and said, "Gregory, you are in for a heck of a ducking. Hubbell went over a half hour ago and went all under but came through and those heavy logs of yours will do better yet." Standing on the big log I could touch the aqueduct.

Prior to the completion of the Erie Railroad, rafting crews were obliged to walk most of the way back to their homes after selling their logs at the Easton, Trenton, or Philadelphia markets. They collected their tools, axes, augers, and whatever else they had, then traveled by boat to New York City and up the Hudson River to Kingston. From there they

The Erie Railroad was incorporated in April 1832 and finished in 1851. It was roughly 446 miles long and built as a broad-gauge line, having six feet between the railings. MOUNT POCONO STATION, 1894

walked Rondout Creek, hiked over Pine Hill, and scurried to their homes along the East Branch.

Before the Civil War, raftsmen were paid ten dollars per trip to Easton and fifteen dollars to Trenton, plus the expense of returning home. Steersmen were paid fifteen to eighteen dollars to Easton and twenty-five dollars to Trenton but were not allowed expenses for returning home. Raft owners often paid from one to ten dollars to local men along the river who would take them through a difficult rift, such as Foul Rift just below Belvedere, New Jersey, and other bad rifts and turns on the river.

Another route home that was followed by the main-stem rafters was by foot up the valley through Pennsylvania. The young, hardy men often walked as many as fifty miles a day while carrying their equipment, crates of fruit, and tokens for their family. One of the Wheeler offspring living in Deposit had his own solution to get back in a more practical manner.

On April 16, 1835, the Erie & Ontario Railroad Company received a government charter to begin operation. At a general meeting on September 7, 1835, civil engineer James Archibald of Luzerne, Pennsylvania, was awarded the contract to build this railroad destined for Canada. ERIE RAILROAD ARCHIVES

When William Wheeler went downriver with the raft, he took his prized horse with him, and after he'd sold his timber, he'd mount the mare and ride back to his home on the West Branch.

Many other curious characters were employed as raftsmen and river hands. One of the most outstanding wits was a man named "Boney" Quillen. He was a lanky, raw-boned, fun-natured fellow who had the ability to readily make up a verse for most any occasion. His habits were sometimes not the best and he got in a good-many scrapes, but with his wit managed to get out of them. Once, Boney insulted a dining room girl at one of the taverns not far from a point on the river known as "Stairway Rift." The following morning the proprietor of the tavern met him at the top of the stairs and promptly threw him down them. When Boney picked himself up, he was heard to remark that it was the first time he ever ran Stairway Rift without a steersman.

Another time, Boney Quillen made a trip down the river, broke as usual, but was suddenly stricken with a fit of virtue and refused to allow his companions to buy him a ticket home on the train. "Not to worry," he said. "I will find a way to get home." Boney, with his eyes on the conductor, raised his window in the coach. When the conductor approached him for his ticket, he purposely stuck his head out of the window, knocking his hat off. Immediately Boney put up a terrific fuss, requesting the conductor to stop the train, and threatened to pull the emergency cord. "That was a good hat and my ticket was in the band of the hat, and I have no money for the fare." The conductor agreed that if he would quiet down, he would take him to his destination at no charge.

The timber-rafting industry was at its peak during the latter part of the nineteenth century. At the Lackawaxen junction watchmen counted more than three thousand rafts passing by on May 31, 1875, over the river dam where the Delaware and Hudson Canal crossed. One of those rafts, owned by Addison Francisco of Cooks Falls, had an incident with an elephant crossing the river.

The Barnum & Bailey Circus, while at Port Jervis, wished to cross the bridge to Pennsylvania. One elephant absolutely refused to set foot on the bridge and started to ford the river when Addison's raft appeared. The uncontrollable raft ran into the elephant as the raftsmen tried to get him out of the way with their poles. The trainer begged them to be careful lest "Jumbo" go on a rampage and break up everything in sight. Jumbo negotiated the rest of the way across without further difficulty, although his ear was nearly severed by a swipe of the raft.

Toward the end of the century, the rafting industry began to slow as the timber market diminished. The last raft to voyage downriver was in September 1923; it went from Stockport to the tidewaters of Philadelphia, manned by Lewis Realy Sr. and his two-man crew.

Pearl Zane Grey was born on January 31, 1872, in Zanesville, Ohio, a town founded by his mother's ancestors in 1673. Zane, the name he preferred to be called, was the fourth of five children whose parents were Dr. Lewis Grey and Alice Zane Grey. As a youngster growing up in Ohio, he developed interests in fishing, baseball, and writing. Zane wrote his first story, "Jim of the Cave," when he was fifteen. His father, resentful of his writings, tore it to shreds and whipped him.

Zane Grey Museum in Lackawaxen, Pennsylvania. Pearl Zane Grey (January 31, 1872–October 23, 1939) was an American author and dentist best known for his popular adventure novels and stories associated with the Western genre in literature and the arts; he idealized the American frontier. *Riders of the Purple Sage* (1912) was his best-selling book. LEE HARTMAN

Both Zane and his brother Romer were active, athletic boys who were enthusiastic and played baseball as much as they fished and swam. Zane's baseball prowess led to a scholarship to the University of Pennsylvania, where he graduated in 1896 with a degree in dentistry. However, he chose to play amateur baseball for several seasons before residing in New York City where he practiced dentistry intermittently.

Zane loved to get away from the city and began escaping from his Manhattan office to the Delaware (Boarding) House in Lackawaxen, Pennsylvania, where he fished and canoed the Delaware River with Romer. Important to him was the fact that the Erie Railroad stopped at Lackawaxen, which made it an easy trip from New York City.

One day during the summer of 1900, when Zane and Romer were canoeing down the Delaware, they were attracted by three young ladies standing on the bank at the boardinghouse. After a brief spontaneous flirtation, arrangements were made to meet that evening at the Delaware House. One of those ladies was seventeen-year-old Lina Elise Roth or "Dolly," as he would address her. She would call him "Doc."

Zane Grey enjoying the Delaware River, where he best like to fish.
NATIONAL PARK SERVICE

Dolly Roth was determined to finish college and earned a master's degree at Columbia University. She now was eager to equip herself so that she could better assist Zane Grey, her husband-to-be. Dolly became a positive influence in his struggle to become a successful writer. In 1902 Zane Grey first published his work "A Day on the Delaware," printed in the May 1902 issue of *Recreational* magazine, for which he received ten dollars. Her encouragement and belief in his abilities led him to continue writing despite rejection by publishers.

During his few years of courtship with Dolly, Grey still saw previous girlfriends and warned her frankly, "But I love to be free. I cannot change my spots. The ordinary man is satisfied with a moderate income, a home, wife, children, and all that. . . . But I am a million miles from being that kind of man and no amount of trying will ever do any good. . . . I shall never lose the spirit of my interest in women and fishing."

In September 1904, Zane Grey, apparently with matrimony in mind, purchased three acres of land in Lackawaxen from Frederick Holbert that included a farmhouse and barn, located at the confluence of the Lacka-waxen River where it empties into the Delaware. A year later, Zane Grey and Dolly married and settled near the river where he fished, hunted, and fathered three children.

Dolly, with a substantial inheritance, provided an initial financial cushion. She was her husband's best critic, as well as his business manager and editor. It has been said he could write one hundred thousand words per month and complete two books in a year, and yet had plenty of time to fish whenever he wanted.

With his success in writing, Grey traveled far and wide to fish around the world, and during this time he established a number of world records,

The Zane Grey Museum in Lackawaxen Township, Pennsylvania, is a former residence of the author Zane Grey that is now maintained as a museum and operated by the National Park Service. Located on the Upper Delaware River, it is on the National Register of Historic Places. The museum contains many photographs, artworks, books, furnishings, and other objects of interest associated with Grey and his family. LEE HARTMAN

many of which were mounted and sent home to the Lackawaxen house. Zane indulged his fishing interests in Australia, where he helped establish sport fishing. On his return home in Australian waters in his yacht, he wrote a story titled "Fly Fishing." The following is a quote from his article:

> *More than 20 years ago, coincident of my succumbing to the lure of literature, I began to learn to cast a fly. On the Delaware River and Lackawaxen for small-mouthed black bass, and later on for trout in the brooks of that lovely mountainous region. But I never really got very far until I came west and fell under the influence of Burnham and Wharton and other fly fishermen of the Rogue River. Every year I spent part of each summer in Oregon.*

Zane Grey died on October 23, 1939, at home in Altadena, California, and now rests in the Union Cemetery of Lackawaxen, Pike County, Pennsylvania, with Dolly beside him.

- 4 -

The Vanishing Brook Trout

The forests and their deep duff, with topsoil intact, covered surrounding mountains like deep sponge. Even the heaviest rain seldom raised the river's level appreciably or even clouded its waters. Flash floods were practically unknown. If they did occur, it was only in the late winter or very early spring, with the breakup of river ice or when frozen ground couldn't absorb snowmelt. The river was narrower because the banks were squared and closer together, not eroded by floods. They were well defined, sharp and steep. The Delaware was a classic example of a freestone river, its bottom filled with glacial boulders, graded stones, and gravel—silt was unheard of. The water was cooler. Dense

Brook trout thrived in the cold waters of the Appalachians for millions of years. However, as forestry and industrial development grew, the wild brook trout population severely declined. DON BAYLOR

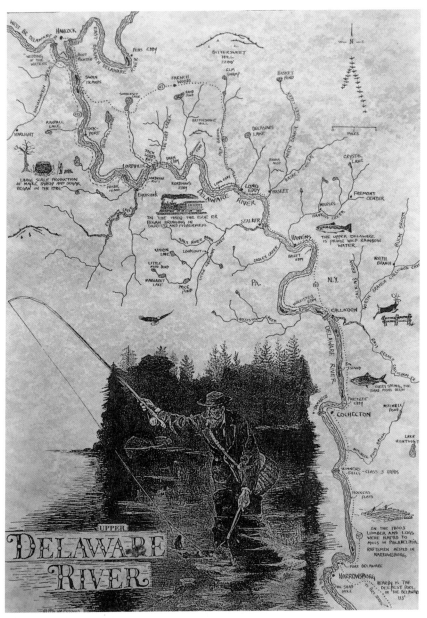

During the mid-nineteenth century, the Erie Railroad began bringing tourists and fishermen to the Catskill region. WILLIAM MONTOVICH, ARTIST

conifer forests interspersed with hardwoods kept tributary streams cool
and helped keep water temperatures low in the main stream. Even the
main river was better sheltered, because trees grew down to the banks
and overhung the river. Brook trout prospered.

—*NICK KARAS,* Brook Trout

The hardwood forests of pine and hemlock that covered much of the
Delaware River Watershed were unsurpassed in size, quality, and
beauty anywhere on the American continent. After the lumberman
came the tanner, and with this came destruction of trout everywhere.
Along the streams rose the ungainly buildings, and the water that
formerly flowed like liquid glass over its pebbly bed now ran as red
as blood and was fouled with lime and ill-savored "leach," while the
ground bark collected in the pools and sifted in among the gravel, driv-
ing the fish from their hiding places, destroying their spawning beds.

The trout continued to breed, however, in the numberless cold
springs in the higher mountains from which they descended into the
larger streams, and it was only when the headwaters were attacked
that they began to yield, until now the fisherman must penetrate to the
sources themselves, and even there long must be the line and light that
calls upon any but the unsuspecting youngsters, the fingerlings, whom
every honest angler returns to their native element with a few words
of good advice.

—FOREST AND STREAM, *DECEMBER 4, 1876*

The early pioneers used animal hides to make leather, tanned with hemlock bark that settlers found in endless quantities. Almost every farm
and homestead prepared their own leather from slaughtered domestic or
wild animals. With the rise of populous cities, leather-tanning industries
quickly developed across the Upper Delaware region.

Tannery operations needed water to process the bark and were constructed on nearly every artery in the Delaware River watershed. Hemlocks, many of them hundreds of years old, were cut down only for their
bark and the rest of the tree was left to rot in the forest. As demand

Eastern brook trout (*Salvelinus fontinalis*) was the first non-native species introduced in Yellowstone. They were stocked in the (then fishless) Firehole River in 1889. Brook trout are native to the eastern and northeastern United States from Hudson Bay down to the Carolinas and through the Great Lakes. NATIONAL PARK SERVICE, JAY FLEMING

By the late nineteenth century settlers saw denuded hillsides, with rotting hemlock trees stripped of their bark, and witnessed the destruction of the majestic hemlock forests that had stood for hundreds of years. The hemlocks and pine forest began to recover and today now stand tall reaching toward the sky. LEE HARTMAN

for timber increased in the mid-nineteenth century, the demise of brook trout habitat began in earnest.

The depletion of hemlocks stripped rivers and streams of their shade, leaving them with no stormwater buffers, and this led to rising water temperatures and silting river bottoms. Sawmills, with their high dams, impeded the passage of fish. Log drives clogged the waterways with timber, and tanneries spewed out poisonous chemicals, animal entrails, and lime solutions—polluting streams while fortunes were made.

By 1885, hemlock trees were nearly exhausted from the hillsides surrounding most tanning operations. According to the Northern Woods organization, seventy million hemlocks were harvested, leaving much of the formerly pristine forest without a single tree.

As sawmills and the tanning industries diminished during the late eighteenth and early nineteenth centuries, the acid wood industries (acid factories) became further established in the Delaware River Valley. John Turnbill, who in 1850 settled in Millburn (now Conklinville), Broome County, New York, built the first successful wood distillation plant to produce acetate of lime. The technology quickly caught the eye of others, and acid factories expanded on practically every major tributary in the Upper Delaware River watershed during the late 1800s and early 1900s. This new industry became the forerunner of today's chemical industry. A decade after the first acid factory appeared near Hancock, fish kills followed. The local newspaper *Hancock Herald* remarked, "More brook trout were poisoned than caught in local streams."

Bob Wood, a resident of Equinunk, with ancestry that can be traced to Josiah ("Bos'n") Parks, had this conversation with Melvin Emmet Parks, a relative of Bob's and a former acid factory worker:

I've always regretted that I didn't visit Melvin Parks earlier in life. He was a man of 89 years, frail and not too well, on that November 1983 day, I called at his home in Horton, New York. Someone commented that Melvin worked in acid factories all his life. I needed him to tell me how acid factories and chemical works operated. Long ago there were two acid factories in the vicinity of the village of Equinunk, Pennsylvania, where I have lived all my life. Melvin had still many family connections in the village. Knowing that he was interested in old photographs, I went loaded with pictures of Equinunk from those early years.

Oh, most of my life I worked around acid factories and the woods. I left Leighton's store to work for George I. Treyz at Russell Brook. The acid factory was right at the mouth of the brook. In the early days, you know, the wood was put into the retorts by hand. Two retorts would hold a cord and a half of four-foot wood. You fired up and sealed up with clay. On the back of the retorts was a cylinder that came out. It went to a condenser. The cold water was running on the condenser all the while, condensed the smoke. When the smoke came out, it was called pyroligneous acid. Well, it made wood alcohol, acetate of lime, coal tars, and acid. You took the tar out. It went through a copper still and lime stills. You added lime and made it acetate that looked like a gray kernel. It was dried in kilns on top of the retorts. It was so hot up there that the men had to take off their shoes and put on wooden shoes to spread it out on top of those retorts. A good cord of hard wood would make about 12 gallons of alcohol, 200 pounds of acetate of lime, and 50 bushels of charcoal.

—EQUINUNK HISTORICAL SOCIETY

The tanning operations and logging industries devastated the hemlocks, but the wood chemical industry was more brutal and less selective, stripping down every species of hardwood tree. Thousands of acres of maple, beech, oak, birch, cherry, and chestnut trees were chopped down and split into four-foot sections. Along with the loss of the hemlock, the mountainsides were left barren with little regard for the future.

According to Dan Myers, author of *The Wood Chemical Industry in the Delaware Valley*, wood consumption at its height in the early twentieth century was estimated to be 190,000 cords of wood in Delaware and Sullivan Counties, putting a strain on the region's hardwood resource. Entire hillsides became wastelands, which left many streams exposed to the hot sun, destroying critical spawning habitat for the native brook trout. Second-growth trees would take twenty to thirty years to mature and make it possible to harvest another crop.

Acid factories require an abundance of wood, fresh water, and an unskilled work-force to harvest the wood and work at the plant. Nearly every tributary attracted community development around the acid factories. A typical factory village contained simple frame homes mostly owned by the company, and a store for food and other goods that could be purchased with company-issued scripts. WILLIAM T CLARKE PENN STATE ARCHIVES

Working in the acid-producing plants was hard, dirty, and often dangerous. The factory odor clung to clothes and skin. Tar from the distillation process was dumped into lagoons, or directly piped into streams and rivers. The putrid discharges kept streams below acid factories permanently depleted of all aquatic life. Pollution laws that existed at the time were a joke. When a violation came to court, the fines were so small that owners continued doing business as usual. It was cheaper to run wastes into trout streams and kill fish than remove the cause of the problem.

Clear-cut forests and air and water pollution were not yet a concern of the local populace. The people who worked at the factories were heroes of the community and proud of their endeavors and the industry they worked for. Producing an important product and earning a paycheck while struggling to raise a family was an all-consuming activity.

Sport fishing for trout increased with each season despite the industrial onslaught that plundered defenseless Mother Nature. There were no size or harvest limits. Everyone who fished had a creel on his or her back. Few, if any, released fish. Daily catches were weighed, not measured. The combination of habitat loss and overharvesting of brook trout stretched matters to the limit. By the late nineteenth century, the native "brookie" had become increasingly confined to remote forest streams in higher elevations.

When I came home not a single acre of Government, state, or private timberland was under systematic forest management anywhere on the most richly timbered of all continents. . . . When the Gay Nineties began, the common word for our forests was "inexhaustible." To waste timber was a virtue and not a crime. There would always be plenty of timber. . . . The lumbermen regarded forest devastation as normal and second growth as a delusion of fools. . . . And as for sustained yield, no such idea had ever entered into their heads. The few friends the forest had were spoken of, when they were spoken of at all, as impractical theorists, fanatics, or "denudiacs," more or less touched in their head. What talk there was about forest protection was no more to the average American than the buzzing of a mosquito, and just about as irritating.
—GIFFORD PINCHOT, US FOREST SERVICE, 1898–1910

Gifford Pinchot

Gifford Pinchot was America's first environmentalist, establishing the modern-day definition of conservation as a wise-use approach to public land. Across the United States, land was being timbered, tilled, and harvested with destructive consequences. As a conservationist Pinchot believed in using the land sustainably to preserve it for future generations rather than allowing it to be exploited and lost forever.

Pinchot's ideas paralleled those of President Theodore Roosevelt, and together the two led a national conservation movement. Today, Pinchot's philosophy of multiple use continues to influence the mission of federal agencies like the US Forest Service and the Department of Interior's

Bureau of Land Management. Under Pinchot's control the number of national forests increased from 32 to 149 in the United States, totaling 193 million acres by 1910.

Pinchot's tremendous impact on American forestry earned him a forester's commemoration—public lands named after him to honor his legacy. The Gifford Pinchot National Forest (former Columbia National Forest), located in southwestern Washington State, was renamed in 1949 to bear Pinchot's name after his death. Gifford Pinchot State Park in Lewisbury, Pennsylvania, was also named to honor his contributions to the nation's public lands. Both parks commemorate a pillar in the American conservation movement whose legacy can still be felt today.

Gifford Pinchot, born in 1865, was an American forester and politician. Pinchot served as the first chief of the US Forest Service from 1905 until his firing in 1910, and was the twenty-eighth governor of Pennsylvania, serving from 1923 to 1927, and again from 1931 to 1935. WIKIPEDIA

Governor Pinchot, who lived in his ancestral home, which his father called Grey Towers, died October 4, 1941, at the age of eighty-one from leukemia. Grey Towers National Historic Site, also known as Gifford Pinchot House or The Pinchot Institute, is located in Milford, Pennsylvania, in Dingman Township.

The sportsman may indeed dream the olden dream, but the day 'id (of) overflowing game bags has departed; the runs and coverts, still alders grow, no longer throng with ruffed grouse and woodcock, while streams once abound in brook trout are of less attraction to the angler.
—Forest and Stream, *August 5, 1882*

Tale of the Rainbow Trout

Anyone who fishes the Delaware River often wonders where this wild, acrobatic rainbow trout came from. Spending time with bartenders, guides, and fly shop gossip, you frequently hear a popular tale of how the rainbow got in the Delaware River system. The fish story, by one often-repeated account, is that rainbow trout descended from fish that were released because of either a railroad train wreck or breakdown in the late 1800s. Milk canisters of fingerling trout— McCloud River rainbows from California, they say—were aboard the Erie Railroad train that chugged to an unexpected stop near Callicoon.

Dan Cahill, a brakeman, happened to be an avid fly fisherman. When the little fish began to go belly-up, Cahill could see they weren't going to make it to their destination in the Catskills. He grabbed a few canisters and released the fingerlings into the Delaware to save them.

The official version of the rainbow's introduction to the river is not quite as romantic as that of an accidental stocking. When early pioneers began migrating to the western United States, there were no catch limits

The rainbow trout, first introduced in the Delaware River system in 1881, is now considered by anglers as the crown jewel of the Delaware. LEE HARTMAN

on fish and no laws preventing people from modifying fish habitats to meet human needs for water, food, and safety. The country's abundant fish populations began to decline. By 1870, growing concern for such declines prompted fishery studies, which spurred the establishment of fish-spawning stations to stock small fish back into waters with weakening fisheries. Many of these early spawning stations later would become fish hatcheries.

The naturalist Samuel Latham Mitchill first scientifically described the brook trout as *Salmo fontinalis* in 1814. The specific epithet *fontinalis* comes from the Latin for "of the spring or fountain," in reference to the clear, cold streams and ponds in its native habitat. The species was later moved to the char genus *Salvelinus*. Though commonly called a trout, the brook trout is actually one of the chars, which in North America also include lake trout, Dolly Varden, and Arctic char. In 1878 fisheries scientists reclassified it and changed the Latin name to *Salvelinus fontinalis*.

The native brook trout once proliferated in the cold, clear, rapid streams of the northeastern United States and as far down as the higher elevations of Georgia. "Brookies" inundated the upper rivers, streams, and ponds throughout the Appalachia regions of Pennsylvania and New York, and in the upper tributaries of Ohio.

In the early 1800s every waterway contained excellent populations of brook trout. For the most part the brook trout lacked size—nevertheless, they were prized by early anglers. It was the only game in town, and anglers measured their success not by inches but by pounds, filling their creels until running out of room.

Artist William J. Stillman, an avid fly fisherman of his time, wrote, "I passed the whole day in the open . . . and my rod and fly book provided in a large degree the food of the household, for trout swarmed there. I caught in an hour, as large a string as I could carry a mile."

Stillman's fishing expeditions were interrupted by the Civil War, and when he returned a generation later, he complained that the woods were scarred by logging and fire and that "wretched dolts" had ruined brook trout fishing by introducing non-native fish. Things only got much worse.

Prior to 1853, fish culture in America was unheard of until Dr. Theodius Garlick and Professor H. A. Ackley of Cleveland, Ohio, were the first to succeed in artificially propagating brook trout. Dr. Garlick's experiment with impregnating brook trout eggs succeeded in hatching in January 1854. Although Dr. Garlick foresaw that the breeding of fish could be a new industry, he had no conception of the proportions it would assume.

In November 18, 1854, the *Cleveland City Fact* article on the "Growing Fish" exhibition at the county fair stated:

> *The most pleasing things exhibited was a lot of brook trout, artificially bred by Dr. Garlick and Professor Ackley, whose labors in this line we have heretofore noticed. They showed several broods of fish, in different stages of growth, and have demonstrated that it is just as easy to grow fish, as it is fowls, or any other descriptive of food.*

A few years later, following Dr. Garlick's work, fly angler Stephen Ainsworth constructed his own fish farm and began hatching and breeding trout for his personal recreation. The description of his work caught the attention of others.

> *The rise in commercial forestry coincided with other growing industries: tourism, tanneries, and acid factories. Railroads had opened the land to hordes of sportsmen. The result was the decline of fish populations in turn engendering a nearly maniacal hatchery and stocking program. The streams and lakes were overwhelmed with sport and commercial fishermen.*
>
> —BIOLOGIST CARL GEORGE, The Fishes of New York

Seth Green was born on March 18, 1817, in the Genesee woodlands near Rochester, New York. He was the son of a farmer and had one brother and two sisters. He grew up as an outdoor enthusiast in a primitive home located along the Genesee River and learned his fishing skills from his father and the local Seneca. His formal schooling only reached the fifth or sixth grade.

As an ambitious twenty-year-old, Green made a trip with a Canadian friend to Grafton, Ontario, to fish for Atlantic salmon entering Keeler's Creek. Green took an interest in propagating his own stocks of fish. His observations of wild spawning salmon led him to believe artificial propagation by man could work with trout species.

When the financial panic of 1837 severely impacted the economy of Carthage, Seth left home and decided to take up commercial fishing along the Genesee River. Soon after his marriage to Helen Cook, they established a fish and game market in downtown Rochester that Green operated with his brother and partner, Monroe Green. By 1857 it employed more than one hundred people and was the largest and most prosperous fish market in the region.

In 1862 Seth Green read an article about Ainsworth's hatching operation in the *Rochester Democrat and Chronicle* that piqued his interest. Green focused his attention on Ainsworth's fish culture work. After some tutoring from the amateur fish farmer, Green bought property along Caledonia Creek in Livingston County, New York, and constructed a fish hatchery of his own that resulted in the development of fundamental hatchery methods and mechanisms that are still in use today.

In 1868, while working with like-minded New York sportsmen, especially R. B. Roosevelt and ex-governor Horacio Seymour, Green encouraged the state legislature to form a fishing commission. He, Roosevelt, and Seymour were appointed the state's first fish commissioners and were charged with examining lakes and rivers to bring about a substantial increase in the production of fish in the waters of New York State. Their annual budget was one thousand dollars.

Seth Green and R. B. Roosevelt collaborated on *Fish Hatching and Fish Catching*, an early publication in fish culturing. As an American fish culturist, Green began working closely with European countries. In 1869, France honored his work and awarded him a medal. Soon after, both England and Germany similarly honored him.

Green was always willing to help and conducted volumes of correspondence, and he soon became widely known and quoted. Horace Greeley of the *New York Tribune* frequently published his exploits as a fly fisherman and fish culturist. He was the nation's fishery authority, and the White House was in constant contact with him regarding matters of fish and fishing.

The fish culturist became a full-time fish breeder, built a larger hatching house, and found that one pair of brook trout was able to produce thousands of eggs. The Caledonia facility was ready to produce a supply of trout fry for stocking New York streams. Green's ambition to replenish the depleted New York streams was now in reach. At the time, it was the only hatchery in the state of New York.

Seth Green later sold the hatchery to A. S. Collins, who then became a friend and partner. In 1870 Green resigned his position as fish commissioner, and the governor appointed him superintendent of fisheries. In 1875 the state bought the Caledonia hatchery (it remains as a functioning fish hatchery in New York to this day), and the state hatchery was now completely in Green's hands.

President Ulysses S. Grant was largely responsible for the first official government action to conserve US fishery resources for future generations. He established the US Fish Commission in 1871. The commission was the forerunner of the US Fish & Wildlife Service we have today. President Grant chose Spencer Fulton Baird, a self-taught naturalist and the first curator for the Smithsonian Institution, to manage the fisheries in the country, naming Baird commissioner of Fish and Fisheries. Baird, in turn, named Dr. Livingston Stone as the new deputy commissioner and assigned the fish culturist to find salmon and trout spawning areas and develop a National Fish Hatchery Station so that the eggs could be managed and shipped where needed around the country.

Dr. Stone and his scientific team explored northern California rivers as places for the hatchery's salmon and trout stock.

Dr. Livingston Stone was the leading fish culture expert in the nineteenth century. ADIRONDACK ALMANACK

The great salmon runs had all but vanished on many lower Sacramento River tributaries because of gold mining, but Livingston's team found an abundance of salmon in the upper Sacramento and at the outlet of the McCloud River. Stone, a keen observer of nature, realized that in addition to salmon the McCloud River contained native trout. He noted that two kinds were present in the river: the small red-banded trout, which resided year-round, and the large trout of five to ten pounds, which appeared in December.

Well, it matters if you are concerned about biodiversity. The first rule of intelligent tinkering is not to throw away a part because you do not understand where it goes or what it does.
—Robert J. Behnke, PhD, Colorado State University

Stone constructed holding ponds at the confluence and stocked them with caught trout (both types), then began the propagation of rainbow trout using the eggs of both residential trout and the larger rainbow trout, known as steelhead. Stone clearly stated in his 1872 report to the US Fish Commission that he mixed both forms in his egg-taking operation. He was advised to begin shipping eggs as soon as possible.

Dr. Livingston Stone became the modern-day Noah of his time. Things were different in 1872. The science was still young and the beginning of what a few US Fish & Wildlife Service veterans can fondly recall as the "Fish Car Era." The problem with the newly formed US Fish Commission was how to quickly move fish from hatcheries to far-off waters throughout the country.

Traveling coast to coast by train is not an easy trip even by today's standard. Back in 1874, just five years after the first transcontinental rail linkup, the journey was a downright arduous expedition—especially when tending thousands of fish eggs carried in open milk cans. The water in the fish containers required frequent aeration, and a suitable water temperature was necessary. Adding ice to the water was very important, as the colder water absorbed more oxygen and reduced the oxygen needs of the fish.

After days of such round-the-clock care, in the spring of 1875 Green received ten boxes of trout eggs. The trout, *Salmo iridea*, were a gift from the Golden State's California Acclimation Society. By early 1876 the trout had grown to three inches in length. The fast-growing juveniles lacked the characteristics of the eastern brook trout, so Green christened them "California mountain trout."

The McCloud or "Shasta" rainbow trout gained fame as the source of virtually all stocks of hatchery rainbows. But this legend is only partially true.
     —*ROBERT J. BEHNKE, PHD, COLORADO STATE UNIVERSITY*

A few years later, Green and his hatchery mates were exuberant when the now three-year-old mountain trout spawned, producing more than forty thousand eggs. He recognized the California brood to be a ruggedly strong, aggressive fish that could withstand higher water temperatures than its cousin the brook trout. Green requested another shipment of eggs.

In 1878, Green received additional eggs, which Dr. Stone had determined to be the McCloud strain of rainbow trout. The superintendent separated a few "mountain trout" for local stocking and kept the remainder for breeding purposes. These were soon to be the first rainbow trout stocked on the Atlantic coast region. Unbeknownst to Green, the stocking of California rainbow trout would dramatically revolutionize the culture of sport fishing on the Upper Delaware River.

Satisfying anglers' demands to stock more trout in streams would not be an easy task. But under Green's supervision the production of trout improved significantly, with over one million fry ready for distribution by 1878. The US Fish Commission began notifying the public that live trout fry could be obtained free of charge at the Caledonia hatchery during the month of February, but only to those who qualified by having suitable means of transportation. Milk cans were the perfect vessel, as suggested, and at the time were delivered only to public waterways. Additionally, they urged private landowners to plant trees and vegetation along the banks of their streams to improve shade and prevent soil erosion.

In 1878, in Caledonia Spring Creek, two thousand young rainbow trout were set free, and the following year an angler had no difficulty in landing a dozen with a fly inside of an hour. One fisherman wrote:

They remain in good condition for the table much longer than the brook trout, which spawn in the late fall or beginning of winter, and are lean, slab-sided and tasteless from September to February, while the California trout begins to spawn about two months later than the eastern brook trout. The female produces about 1,500 eggs. The males are ferocious. They fight with one another all the time. It is this aggressiveness that makes them take the hook so savagely.

Seth Green rightfully believed that the rainbow would fare better in the streams and rivers than would the brook trout. But not everyone agreed with Green's assessment, including Fred Mather, a noted fish culturist for the US Fish Commission, who believed that stocking smallmouth bass and rainbow would add to the demise of the brook trout:

The introduction of bass into brook trout waters was a grave mistake and is a source of regret to trout fishers. It was done some years ago by the New York State Fish Commission and they have been doing something equally as bad this spring by putting in rainbow into the stream, a fish much inferior to our brook trout, and one which will grow faster and eat up the food, if it doesn't eat the trout. Like the English sparrow, this fish may turn out a nuisance. No waters that will sustain our brook trout should be planted with bass and rainbow. The guides said many of the rainbow are dead, but I fear enough were alive to establish themselves.
—FRED MATHER, FOREST AND STREAM, *AUGUST 31, 1882*

The New York Fish Commission enlisted the Ontario & Western Railroad Company (O&W) to participate in stocking trout. Conductors were asking to stop the train whenever possible at any stream during their travels to plant fish. Over one million brook trout fry were stocked in streams, which soon expanded as far as the Catskills. It is believed the brook trout were first introduced into the Beaver Kill and its tributaries near Roscoe, New York.

Rail shipments of fish increased as the interest in "managing" streams and lakes spread. Containers were shipped in baggage cars, accompanied by government fish culturists who were called "messengers." Their task was to aerate the water and generally make sure their live cargoes arrived in sound condition. With the volume of such traffic steadily rising, the US Fish Commission decided in 1881 to purchase a "fish car"—a baggage car specifically equipped for carrying fingerling trout.

On June 24, 1881, E. D. Mayhew of Walton, New York, received twenty-five thousand rainbow fry and were first introduced into the East Brook tributary of Delaware's West Branch near Walton. Four days later fifteen thousand fingerlings went into Cadosia and Read Creeks in the Town of Hancock, New York. Over the next few years the rainbows adapted well to their surroundings and validated Green's claim that the rainbow would improve trout fishing in the Catskills.

At a meeting of the New York Association for the Protection of Game, President R. B. Roosevelt declared:

The rainbow trout of California are twice as strong as our Eastern brook trout and twice as rapid growers often reaching the weight of eight to ten pounds. In our eastern streams they grow to four and five pounds. Salmo fontinalis *grow to less than half this weight. . . . The complaint against them is that they are too gamey—they smash light tackle with their tremendous rushes, and the angler must be especially prepared for them. They can be easily introduced into our trout streams and will live where our trout will—in some places where they will not. They are perfection.*

The Baird Hatchery, established by Dr. Livingston Stone, continues to manage fish today as they did back in the 1800s. All rainbow trout eggs and salmon eggs native to northern California waters are still shipped across the world.

The Gaming Rainbow

The *New York Sun* sent a reporter down to Fulton Fish Market to interview owner and New York State fish commissioner Eugene J. Blackford about the latest importation from California. This is what Mr. Blackford said in an article titled "The Gaming Rainbow":

The beautiful Salmo iridea as a thrifty growing fish for the fish-culturist has long been known, but little has been said of its gamesome ways and its grit. We expect to display some large trout of this kind on our stand on April 1st; some will weigh five pounds apiece. As they run in California streams, they average about four pounds in weight. Ours will come from the United States hatching works on the McCloud River. Some trout will come too; from F.N. Clark's hatching works were produced from spawn brought from California.

It's only two years since fish culturists in the east have received the eggs of trout. This is to be the first year in which the United States Fish Commission is to turn loose small California trout in our streams. The culture of these fish has hitherto been carried on by private enterprise.

The California mountain trout takes its name, rainbow trout, from the beautiful band of color that runs along the side of the fish and is about a fourth as wide of the fish. There are no red spots on the body, as our brook trout, but there are a few black dots near the head. When the fish is first taken from the water it has all the tints of a rainbow. After it is dead it becomes a uniform red color but shading to a lighter color underneath. We had a rainbow trout about a year ago, sent by B.B. Redding, Commissioner of Fisheries in California, that was a male, over two and a half feet long and weighed five and three quarter pounds. It was well shaped and plump, with large black spots thickly sprinkled on the shoulders and tail. The operculum was decorated with bright red tint, blending into a greenish brown, or olive toward the eye. A broad red dash, or stripe of color stretched from the tip of the tail to the cheek. It was a gaudy-looking fish.

They are gamier, and they fight far more than the brook trout. At the fish hatching ponds in Caledonia, N.Y., last spring, I caught several rainbow trout with a fly weighing from a quarter to half a pound.

Each time that the trout struck my hook I thought I had a pound trout on my line. Why, they strike a hook like that Mr. Blackford, to illustrate, brought his hands together with vigor? Then they are off in a flash, with the line running out so rapidly that the reel nearly smokes with friction. While the average weight when full grown is about four pounds, yet, they have been taken as large as six pounds, while in a lake near Bellingham Bay, on the Pacific slope, the trout are said to grow to be ten or twelve pounds in weight.

Are they as handsome as the eastern brook trout? "No," the Commissioner replied; no fish is handsomer than the Long Island brook trout, unless it is the Dolly Varden trout. They are also a California trout, and frequently found in the same stream with the rainbow trout, and are of the same shape, plump, round and full. They differ from the rainbow trout in having all over their side's brilliant vermilion spots from one-eighth to three-sixteenths of an inch in diameter. This season, I think, there will be distributed in New York streams from 75,000 to 100,000 small rainbow trout. They mingle amicably with the eastern brook trout, but they will not be put in streams where these run in great numbers, because we want to keep these species distinct from each other.

As to their habits, they are, unlike our trout, fond of moderate currents of water or still places with the surface of the water shaded. The eastern trout, on the other hand, love to hover under a waterfall or to skip from ripple to ripple in the most dashing rapids. Fishermen who killed them on the Pacific Coast say that the rainbow trout is most plentiful along the Western coast of California, and northward. All the true brook trout West of the Mississippi River has black spots. Fishing is very fine in the rapid streams of the Coast Mountains and the Cascade Mountains in Oregon. At Fort Dallas, trout fishing is good in April, May, June and July. The rapid snow water streams that flow from Mount Hood abound in these trout, but the innumerable rattlesnakes often interfere, and in places prevent angling.

Forest & Stream, *February 24, 1894*

84

Before the turn of the twentieth century, the states, the federal government, and private enterprises constructed numerous fish hatcheries in the Northeast. Many state fisheries commissions began stocking black bass, walleye, and in some instances Atlantic salmon in large waterways. The smallmouth bass later became the predominant fish in the Upper Delaware River system.

A writer for the *New York Daily News* in the summer of 1897 wrote, "It is doubtful if greater success ever followed the transplanting of fish into alien waters than has resulted from introduction of wall-eyed pike (called Susquehanna salmon) into the Delaware River." He added, "How the fish came to be called salmon is one mysteries of piscatorial nomenclature, but that was the name it received in the Susquehanna River and by which it has been known ever since."

The Atlantic salmon is the key to one of today's great problems. Our ability to save the salmon will be measured by their ability to survive.
—*LEE WULFF*

In 1881 the US Fish Commission also had hopes of establishing an Atlantic salmon run in the Delaware River. In the spring of 1883, the commission sent 225,000 seven-week-old salmon to Hancock. The salmon from the Penobscot River were placed in the East and West Branches of the Delaware. According to the Monticello newspaper *Republican Watchman*, the experimental stocking was deemed unsuccessful.

However, an 1888 article in the *American Angler* stated that a seventeen-pound salmon was caught in the Delaware River near the Camden, New Jersey, Water Works. *Forest and Field* reported another New Jersey angler took two salmon the following year.

The Introduction of the Brown Trout

The fish culture experts in the United States looked at another trout to introduce to eastern waters—the European brown trout. Without much thought or science in the process, American hatcheries wanted to begin an exchange program that would send eastern brook trout and California

The early introduction of brown trout was criticized by many. Today it is considered one of the top gamefish for anglers throughout the country. LEE HARTMAN

rainbow eggs to England and other European countries in exchange for native European trout.

The first introductions into the United States started in 1883 when Fred Mather, a New York fish culturist and angler, under the authority of the US Fish commissioner, Professor Spencer Baird, obtained brown trout eggs from Herr Lucius von Behr, who was president of the German Fishing Society. The "von Behr" trout inhabited both mountain streams and lakes in the Black Forest region of Baden-Wurttemberg. The original shipment of German brown trout eggs was handled by three hatcheries, the Cold Spring Hatchery in Long Island, New York, operated by Mather; one in Caledonia, New York, operated by Seth Green; and another hatchery in Northville, Michigan.

Two years later, in 1885, brown trout eggs from Loch Leven, in Scotland, arrived in New York. These "Loch Leven" trout were distributed to the same eastern hatcheries. Over the next few years, additional eggs from Scotland, England, and Germany were shipped to many other US hatcheries.

The following year, von Behr sent another shipment of ten thousand brown trout eggs from England. The next winter, 116,000 fry were sent to New York hatcheries, later to be planted in Upper Delaware tributaries that included the Beaver Kill and the West Branch of the Delaware.

Dr. Robert Behnke, a renowned ichthyologist out of Colorado State University, believed all life forms of brown trout—anadromous, riverine, and lacustrine—were imported into the United States and intermingled genetically to create what he calls the American generic brown trout and a single subspecies, the North European brown trout (*Salmo trutta fario*).

Unlike Seth Green, who admired the rainbow trout, Fred Mather believed the brown trout, as he now described them, were destined to become the favorite fish of American anglers. Green's major concern about German and English trout was how they would interact with indigenous brook trout. By 1887 nearly every trout hatchery was stocking European brown trout in ponds, tributaries, and major waterways. Seth Green took a more cautious approach, choosing which waterways the fish should be placed in.

Many of us can remember how poor our sport was before the first of the brown trout came in. There were not many, but they were of good size and gave much sport, but they were called Dutchmen, and were accused of destroying the native trout. It seems the natural tendency of mankind is to throw bricks or stones at foreigners.

Brown trout fight desperately in cool water, and if heavily fished are often very crafty, dashing under rocks, logs, or driftwood as soon as they feel the hook. On larger eastern streams, the average size of fish is much larger than in the days when we had only native trout. Brown trout grow more rapidly and seem able to adapt to the climate change of recent years. They endure almost anything.

Again, and again conditions during the summer and autumn have been so bad that we expected poor fishing the following spring, but when the season opened the brown trout have appeared in strong force and given good sport to the multitude of anglers.

— *THEODORE GORDON,* ENGLISH FISHING GAZETTE,
OCTOBER *11, 1913*

The Legendary Seth Green

Seth Green, known as the "Father of Fish Culture," established the first fish hatchery and trout-rearing ponds in the United States, and also wrote three books on fish culture.

Seth Green was a humble man, a great teacher, thinker, and innovator. The valuable aquaculture industry that exists today had its roots in Seth Green's vision. Much of the credit for the introduction of rainbow trout into non-native waters east of the Continental Divide, brook trout and shad into the West, and brown trout throughout the United States can be attributed to the pioneering efforts of Green and his Caledonia Fish Hatchery in Rochester.

Seth Green from *Trout Culture* (1870).

In 1882 Seth Green was on a fishing trip off the coast of the Carolinas with his friend Robert Barnwell. During the trip he contacted typhoid pneumonia. He never fully recovered from the disease, and although he was still able to function, his physical and mental health deteriorated. In January 1888, Seth and his son William were visiting a museum when the carriage they were riding in overturned. Green severely injured his back in the accident and was confined to his house for the remainder of his life. At age seventy-one, senile and bedridden, he died on August 18, 1888, in Rochester.

The New York State Department of Environmental Conservation operates a forty-six-foot research vessel on Lake Ontario named the *Seth Green*. Seth Green Drive and the Seth Green Trail along the Genesee River, near the former location of Carthage, are named for him also. The Rochester Chapter of Trout Unlimited is named after Green. In 1987 the Fish Culture Hall of Fame, an institution of the American Fisheries Society, enshrined Seth Green as the "Father of Fish Culture in North America."

- 5 -

The Legacy of Tocks Island

The region around the Delaware Water Gap, sometimes called the Minisink, has a rich history going back to the seventeenth century, when this was America's frontier. In the time of William Penn, the Munsee kindled their council fires on Minisink Flats along the Delaware River above the Water Gap. The Dutch and English settled along the fertile banks of the river and later built forts to protect themselves during the French and Indian War. Villages at Walpack Center and Millbrook, New Jersey, were

The proposed Tocks Island Dam project, just north of the Delaware Water Gap, would cut the river in half and stop migrating shad and other seagoing fish.
LEE HARTMAN

gathering places for worship and commerce. But the area stayed sparsely populated for three centuries, though not by choice.

One wonders what it was like to be the first European to sail up the Delaware River. Most accounts give that honor to the English explorer Henry Hudson, who sailed for the Dutch East India Company while seeking a rumored Northeast Passage to Cathay (China). Hudson sailed briefly into the Delaware Bay before landing his ship in a northern river passage (now named the Hudson River) to explore the region that became a settlement known as New Amsterdam, now modern-day New York City.

However, in 1497 John Cabot, an early Venetian explorer under the commission of Henry VII of England, made the earliest known European exploration of coastal North America. The Italian sea captain claimed the land for England, setting the course for world domination in the coming centuries. John Cabot would mysteriously disappear in 1498.

A year after Henry Hudson's exploratory work, an English navigator, Thomas West, 3rd Baron De La Warr, sailed along the Delaware Bay on a food supply mission to save an early Virginia settlement that had been established in 1607. An English adventurer and naval officer named Sir Samuel Argall captained one of Lord De La Warr's ships to Virginia in a successful rescue operation that saved the colony from starvation.

Captain Argall attributed Lord De La Warr as the discoverer of the Delaware River in a letter written in 1612 to King Charles II. The bay, the river, the state, and consequently the Native American people were later named "Delaware" for the English navigator De La Warr.

Thomas West, better known as Lord De La Warr, was appointed governor for life and captain general of the colony of Virginia. WIKIPEDIA HTTP://WWW.TUDORPLACE .COM.AR/IMAGES/WEST,THOMAS(3BDELAWARR)

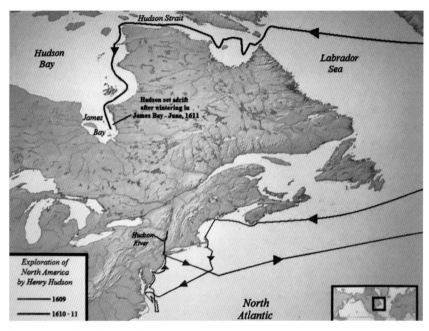

The many routes of Henry Hudson. WIKIPEDIA

The Delaware watershed was claimed by the English, based on the explorations of John Cabot in 1497. The Dutch also laid claim on the 1609 explorations of Henry Hudson, under the auspices of the Dutch West India Company. The Dutch were the first Europeans to actually occupy the land by establishing trading posts along the river, the first being at Hooghe Island on the Zuydt River (Burlington Island on the Delaware River). Peter Minuit, the Dutch director-general, called the early settlements the New Netherland. During this period he probably spent some time at the Burlington Island post, thereby familiarizing himself with the region.

Minuit had a falling out with the directors of the Dutch West India Company and was recalled from New Netherland. He quickly made his services available to his many friends in Sweden, then a major power in European politics. In late March 1638, Minuit led a group under the flag of Sweden landing at Fort Christina, the present-day site of Wilmington, Delaware. They soon participated in trading with the Lenni Lenape.

The peaceful American natives were seen merely as a source of fur as well as a hindrance to future settlements. Minuit now claimed possession of the western side of the Delaware River, saying he had found no European settlement there. Unlike the Dutch West India Company, the Swedes intended to actually bring settlers to their outpost, and they began a colony by purchasing land from the Lenape on the west side of the Delaware River, while the Dutch laid claim to the east side.

Peter Minuit was the Dutch colonial governor of New Amsterdam who is mainly remembered for his fabulous purchase of Manhattan Island (the nucleus of New York City) from the Indians for trade goods worth a mere sixty guilders. ENCYCLOPEDIA.COM

Peter Minuit drowned at sea in a hurricane on the way home that same year, but the Swedish colony continued to grow gradually. By 1644 Swedish and Finnish settlers were living along both sides of the Delaware from Fort Christina to the Schuylkill River. New Sweden's governor, Johan Bjornsson Printz, moved his residence to what is now Tinicum Township, Pennsylvania, where he intended to concentrate on the settlements.

While the Dutch settlement at Zwaanendael (meaning Swan Valley), or present-day Lewes, Delaware, was soon destroyed in a war with the Lenape, the Dutch never gave up their claim to the area. Under the leadership of Peter Stuyvesant, they built Fort Casimir, now New Castle.

Three years later, in 1654, Johan Resingh, the Swedish governor, captured Fort Casimir from the Dutch. For the Swedes this was a catastrophic miscalculation; the following summer, an enraged Stuyvesant led another Dutch expedition to the Delaware River, attacked all the Swedish communities, and forcibly ended the New Sweden colony—incorporating the whole area back into the New Netherland colony. It was not long, though, before the Dutch too were forcibly removed by the English, who asserted their earlier claim. In 1664, James, the Duke of York and brother of King Charles II, outfitted an expedition that easily ousted the Dutch from both the Delaware and Hudson Rivers, leaving the Duke of York the proprietary authority in the entire area.

The Lenni Lenape were not one single tribe but were made up of three bands. In the northern areas of their territory was the Munsee tribe, "the people of the stony country." In the middle, or central area where Philadelphia came to be located, was the Unami, or the "people down river." South of the Unami were the Unalactgio, or the "people near the ocean," who were also known as the Nanticokes.

This day my country was confirmed to me by the name of Pennsylvania, a name the King would give it, in honor of my father.
—WILLIAM PENN, FOUNDING OF PENNSYLVANIA

In 1682 the "royal charter" from King Charles II granted William Penn the land along the Delaware River to settle a debt owed to Admiral Sir William Penn, Penn's father. Penn's surveyors, located along the Delaware and Schuylkill Rivers, conformed to William Penn's ideals and laid out the first colony in Penn's charter. He called it Philadelphia (*philos*, "love," and *adelphos*, "brother"); it was to have a commercial center for a market, a state house, and other key buildings, and piers would be constructed for landing large vessels.

William Penn, a Quaker, believed in religious tolerance. Because of this conviction, Penn's land not only attracted his Quaker brethren but many other people including Germans, the Huguenots, and Scottish-Irish. As a pacifist, William Penn looked down on violence and felt that the Delaware Indians should be paid for their land. After reaching an agreement with the Lenape nation, Penn began to purchase other land by fair trade from the Native Americans. The first of these purchases occurred on July 15, 1692, and included the area north of the "Falls of the Delaware" to Neshaminy Creek (Neshaminy being the Lenape word for "place where we drink twice"). The land became known as Pennsylvania (Penn's Woods).

When William Penn suffered a stroke in 1701, he returned to England, where he died six years later. After his death Penn's son Thomas took over, but he did not have the same values as his father. Thomas Penn wanted to establish authority over the upper Delaware lands and began making treaties with the Iroquois, who held land to the north and west of the Lenape nation. Soon after, Thomas looked to exercise his right under his father's 1686 treaty with the Lenape.

William Penn (October 14, 1644–July 30, 1718), son of the admiral and politician Sir William Penn, was a writer, early Quaker, and founder of the English North American colony the Province of Pennsylvania.
WIKIMEDIA.ORG

In 1734 Thomas Penn falsely represented a document known as the "Walking Purchase," based on the agreement made between William Penn and the Lenape chief Tammany in 1686. The forty-eight-year-old "alleged" document reportedly stated that the Lenni Lenape would allow the English to have additional land for Penn's colony. This plot of land was to be determined by the distance a man could walk in one full day, starting at a given place on the Delaware and going northwest.

No River can return to its source, yet all rivers must have a beginning.
—*NORTH AMERICAN NATIVE*

The current Lenape, who had not been there during the drawing up of the original agreement, denied that such a treaty had ever been made and stated that the document itself had never been produced. The Lenape chiefs, however, trusted Thomas Penn and believed that the white men would take a leisurely walk through the tangled forest along the

Delaware. According to popular accounts, they assumed the walk would be forty miles and consented to the pact after three years of negotiations.

Unbeknownst to the chiefs, Thomas Penn had taken measures to ensure the distance covered by his walkers would be as large as possible. Penn's men spent weeks mapping out the route and clearing a straight path through the thick forest, then hired three of the fastest runners, offering cash to the one who could go farthest.

On September 19, 1737, James Yates, Solomon Jennings, and Edward Marshall started out on their journey at the chestnut tree in the present town of Wrightsville, Bucks County, Pennsylvania. All three men were in good shape and very athletic. Before the end, though, one runner dropped out and another lay near death from exhaustion. Only Edward Marshall ended his run, arriving the following midday at Mauch Chunk, the place now known as Jim Thorpe, seventy miles away.

The agreement was to draw a straight line directly east to the nearest point of the Delaware River. Thomas Smith, sheriff of Bucks County, had other ideas, and he drew the line northeast at a right angle toward the Delaware River. The deliberate violation meant that thousands more acres of land were taken from the Indians than if the line had been drawn to the closest point on the river.

The Walking Purchase tallied more than 1.2 million acres of Lenni Lenape land, which compares to the size of Rhode Island. The purchase encompassed the junction of the Lehigh River and Tobyhanna Creek located in present-day Carbon County—the very place my high school friends and I camped on our Lehigh canoe adventure. The additional land also comprised the Forks of Delaware River (Easton) and beyond.

> *The white runners should have walkt along by the River Delaware or the next Indian path to it . . . should have walkt for a few Miles and then have sat down and smoakt a Pipe, and now and then have shot a Squirrel, and not have kept up the Run, Run all day.*
> —*CHIEF LAPPAWINSOE*

The Munsee tribe, many of whom had been taught Christian beliefs by the Moravian Church missionaries, believed they had been scammed by the white man and refused to leave the Forks of the Delaware. This caused problems with settlers who had already relocated in the Munsee territory.

Thomas Penn, who remained friendly with the mighty Iroquois nation, called a conference in Philadelphia. The Iroquois leader, Canastota, supported Penn in forcing the Munsee out of the property the settlers had gained in the Walking Purchase. Penn made an alliance with the fierce Iroquois, who in turn began a series of military conquests that pushed Indian tribes out of the wide area between the Delaware and Ohio Rivers.

Lappawinsoe is chiefly known for signing the celebrated Treaty of 1737, commonly called the "Walking Purchase." LAPPAWINSOE PAINTING BY GUSTAVUS HESSELIUS, 1735

The Indians, furious with the colonists, sought revenge for their misdeeds. By the 1750s the French were encouraging the natives with arms and a promise of better treatment. Conflicts with the settlers erupted, one of whom was the runner Edward Marshall. He was wounded, his wife scalped, and his daughter killed. By 1758, after the French and Indian War, the Munsee had quit all claims to the Delaware lands at the treaty of Easton. Exacerbated by losses of their homelands, the disgruntled Munsee tribe moved to northern outposts, known today as the Delaware River Water Gap.

The Killer Storm of the Century

It was August 7, 1955, when Diane began chasing Connie up the East Coast at 105-mile-per-hour winds. On the heels of Connie, just four days behind, Diane moved inland and began to weaken, then suddenly turned eastward into the Atlantic Ocean. Fueled by the warm seas she became extra-tropical. Diane was a Category 3 hurricane that would last sixteen days following her sister storm Connie. The combined storms dumped nearly twenty inches of soaking rain onto northeast Pennsylvania.

Ten days later Connie vanished, while Diane suddenly turned westward, skirting New York City, to slam her fury on the Delaware River watershed, causing the region's worst flooding on record—largely in the Poconos and along the Delaware. The rushing river and its tributaries demolished about 150 roads and railway bridges, breached or destroyed thirty dams, and flooded homes and businesses.

The famed Brodhead Creek, located thirty miles above East Stroudsburg, Pennsylvania, submerged a summer youth camp with a forty-foot wall of water, killing 37 people. Throughout the state of Pennsylvania, the flood caused 101 residents to perish and an estimated seventy million dollars in damage to property. Additional flooding spread through the northwest portion of New Jersey, forcing hundreds of people to evacuate and destroying bridges in its path, including one built in 1831. Storm damage in southeastern New York was evident but less significant.

Twenty-three years prior to the 1955 flood disaster, in 1932, Congress had commissioned the US Army Corp of Engineers to conduct a river basin study to determine the viability of constructing dams along the Delaware. The study was kept on the back burner until the deadliest flood of the century brought attention to the issue at a national level. Congress responded swiftly and authorized the Army Corps to dust off the 1932 study to determine the viability of constructing a flood-control dam in the middle portion of the Delaware River.

> *Life, like the river, is always in motion. We don't know where it all began or where it will end. While we sometimes see farther up- or downstream, we can't see all there is in the vast scheme of things.*
> —*ANONYMOUS*

In 1960 the Army Corps completed the "Comprehensive Survey of the Water Resource for the Delaware River Basin." This eleven-volume study became the basis of evaluation for the Tocks Island Dam project. The House and Senate passed the compact legislation, and President

Kennedy signed the Delaware River Basin Compact into law on October 27, 1961.

The compact called for the formation of the Delaware River Basin Commission (DRBC), a multistate and federal coalition of four state governors—Pennsylvania, New York, New Jersey, Delaware—and the US government. A year later Congress passed the Flood Control Act of 1962, which included nearly two hundred public works projects across the nation. The queen of its projects was the Tocks Island Dam. Congress estimated the cost at ninety million dollars.

The Tocks project quickly gained the support of the Philadelphia and New York City mayors, who successfully lobbied the state commissioners for their support. The DRBC would serve as the planning, development, and regulatory oversight for regional—rather than individual municipality—management of the Delaware River.

Innocent river valley farmers tilled their fields and planted crops as the US Army Corps of Engineers silently mapped out plans in preparation for the development of a dam earmarked to be placed at the southern tip of Tocks Island, a small, uninhabited isle just north of the famed Delaware Water Gap, a picturesque gorge cut eons ago. The gorge extends five miles—flanked by Mount Minsi (Pennsylvania) on the western side and Mount Tammany (New Jersey) on the eastern side.

The Army Corps estimated that a 400-foot-high earthen dam would need about three and one-half million cubic yards of earth and rock to raise the water level from the riverbed 160 feet. This would create a thirty-seven-mile-long lake covering approximately 12,800 acres of woodland, practically flooding most of the Delaware River Valley. The billion-dollar dam, once built, would displace fifteen thousand inhabitants and submerge several towns, roadways, working farmlands, and many historical landmarks.

In addition to flood control, the reservoir would pipe its water to northern New Jersey and the cities of New York and Philadelphia. Surrounding the massive lake would be a 72,000-acre national recreation area to offer the public such activities as hunting, fishing, boating, swimming, and hiking—making it the greatest inland recreational resort east of the Mississippi.

The Tocks Island Dam project had the support of the public and business leaders who envisioned that the monstrous lake would be a fabulous place for year-round visitors and a boost to the economy in the region. There was one lone dissenter, a middle-aged housewife, who was born and raised on a generational family farm in Minisink Valley. Her name was Nancy Shukaitis.

Nobody cares how much you know, until they know how much you care.

—*TEDDY ROOSEVELT*

Nancy's family connection began long before her birth. George Michael, a thirty-year-old German-born immigrant, started the family tree when he stepped on American soil in 1754. He acquired eight hundred acres of land along the Delaware River in Northampton County, Pennsylvania, called Minisink Flat, named by the Paleo-Indians living in the Minsi region. A century and a half later, around the year 1900, Michael's grandson, Blanchard Michael, inherited the Michael farm and ran a family-owned business raising chickens and growing potatoes, melons, corn, and apples—selling his goods along the roadside and in nearby communities.

Nancy, one of the Michael children, worked on her father's farm for her first twenty-one years of life, helping with the family chores. Spring was Nancy's favorite time, when the shad began their annual migration journey upriver. The prodigious fish traveled three hundred miles or more, swimming uninhibited to their spawning grounds in the upper reaches of the Delaware River. April and May were the best fishing months for shad, referred to today as the "founding fish" because it fed the region's inhabitants for hundreds of years. Using Fyke nets that perform like scoop shovels, Nancy and her father collected shad—salting down each catch to preserve the fish for later use.

Nancy, at thirty-nine years old, was married and residing with her husband, Joe Shukaitis, on her father's farm near the proposed dam site. She and Joe feared the federal government decision that would take away nearly forty miles of centuries-old farmland and villages. Fifteen thousand people would be uprooted and a pristine valley turned into a massive watering hole. The river activist wanted no part of a broken river that would swallow up the farmlands in the historic valley.

Like a script out of the Jimmy Stewart movie *Mr. Smith Goes to Washington* Nancy Shukaitis packed her bags, left her four children with Joe, and went to a 1964 Congressional hearing in Washington, D.C., to testify against the dam builders.

Outnumbered and sitting alone with her dissenting statement in hand, she silently watched more than thirty organizations testify on the virtues of a thirty-seven-mile lake that would bring prosperity to the region. Tourism was the largest single industry in the Poconos, with seventeen thousand people employed by it. The owners of hotels, restaurants, and gasoline stations drooled at the prospect of the increased number of visitors who would be drawn to the lake area.

You never know your friends from your enemies until the ice breaks.
—*ANONYMOUS*

Nancy's testimony didn't faze the proponents. City people and newspapers scoffed at her, calling her position radical. With little support against the dam, President Johnson signed the bill the following year to authorize the Tocks Island Dam project. The homes and farms of the six hundred families who lived in the serene basin would be inundated by water. People, some of whom had lived in the river valley for centuries, were notified and given no choice but to sell their homes or face a costly court battle.

The sudden ultimatum only strengthened Nancy's resolve to oppose the dam project. Nancy Shukaitis became increasingly active as a volunteer in the Monroe County Republican Party and was elected the first female Monroe County commissioner in 1967.

The longtime resident of Minisink Valley needed allies to promote her cause and began soliciting other women and men—primarily people slated to lose their property to the government. Her efforts slowly gained support, and with the help of another local resident, Ruth Jones, owner of Kittatiny Canoe, organized the Delaware Valley Conservation

Association in 1966. The association gained the backing of hundreds of area landowners, a significant victory for the anti-dam group—the first of its kind to defend the free-flowing river.

The federal government continued to pursue construction of the massive reservoir at all costs. The Army Corps seized homes, farms, and entire communities—often by condemnation or force—that were located within the approved recreational boundary around the thirty-seven-mile dam site. The government seizure accumulated a collection of condemned houses, from shacks to historic landmarks, that extended across both sides of the river, offering owners who willingly sold their property a short-term lease to offset the cost of the project.

The government land grab included the peaceful village of Walpak, New Jersey, nestled along

The lone gravestone of Anna Symmes found near Old Mountain Road, Walpack, NJ. She died nineteen days after the Revolutionary War. Anna bore two daughters, one of which was Anna Tutill Symmes. She became the wife of President William Henry Harrison and grandmother of President Benjamin Harrison, nominally First Lady of the United States during her husband's one-month term in 1841. JEFF SUMBERG/ WWW.FLICR.COM/JEFFS4653

the Delaware, which dated back to the seventeenth century. The valley was part of America's frontier, from a time when the English, Dutch, and Germans settled in the area. One of its historical landmarks was the Old Mine Road, constructed in the 1600s by Dutch settlers after discovering copper in a ravine seven miles above the Delaware Water Gap, later named Paharquarry Mine. The 107-mile-long road, said to be one of the oldest continuously used roads in America, transported the ore from the mine to Kingston, New York.

Walpack Valley now appeared ghost-like, with dozens of unrented, abandoned farms and buildings left unattended, and youthful squatters were attracted, lured by the government's rental advertisements in various city newspapers. The squatters, referred to as "river people," occupied empty farm buildings and generational homes to make a new life for themselves, quite different from the more desirable life they'd left behind. Buildings that were unoccupied were vandalized. By the late 1960s the federal government began conducting a long campaign to remove the squatters, many of whom refused to leave.

Richard C. Albert describes it in his book *Damming the Delaware*:

As more and more land fell into government hands, new problems arose. The area became increasingly desolate, with declining road care, police and fire protection. As a result, many of the newly emptied houses were occupied by squatters or picked over by scavengers and vandalized. Arson became a widespread fear. Between June 1970

The Johnson Losey House was once the home of Enos Johnson. Born in 1825, Enos Johnson became the first mail carrier in Walpack Township, NJ. Prior to 1850, he brought the mail from Tuttles Corners to Walpack Center and Flatbrookville, NJ. JEFF SUMBERG

and June 1972, for example, about three dozen buildings in the valley were burned. Trespassing also increased because it was no longer possible to tell government land from private property. Adding to the fear were several cases in which government demolition teams accidentally destroyed the wrong house. The remaining residents, many of them elderly, became afraid to leave their homes for fear that something would happen in their absence. Many no longer had nearby neighbors. Many of these properties had been in the same family for many generations or represented the culmination of a lifelong dream.

Soon the support for the Tocks Island Dam project began to crumble. The estimated cost to build the dam increased to $214 million. The concern triggered Congress to call for a new evaluation of the project and again delayed funding. The General Accounting Office determined that the recreational benefits had been overstated by $8 million, while the water supply benefits were understated by $21 million by the Army Corps. All the while, the ongoing Vietnam War debt was escalating, as 534,000 troops fought an unpopular war. President Johnson began slashing his $4.6 billion public works budget and imposed a 10 percent tax surcharge to help pay for the Vietnam War efforts.

Shortly after Johnson left office, newly elected President Richard Nixon signed the National Environmental Policy Act, which led to amending the Clean Water Act in 1972 for regulating pollution discharges into the waters of the United States. Each dam project now required the Army Corps to file an environmental impact statement.

In the early 1970s the government's rising costs of the Vietnam War coincided with the nation's environmental concerns. Democratic activism at local and national levels was fostering public awareness, and the concern for clean water became a national priority.

Without the Delaware River, her bounty of shad, which fed our meagerly-clad-and-nourished officers in winter quarters, we would not have a nation.

—*John McPhee*, The Founding Fish

By 1972 Nancy Shukaitis, who spearheaded the Delaware conservation movement, now had the support of forty-five environmental and sportsman's groups, forming the Save the Delaware River Coalition. Harold Lockwood, chairman of the coalition, disagreed emphatically with the dam proposal. "The water in the reservoir is going to be polluted by the dumping of ninety-three million gallons of liquid waste per day into it," he said. "This will seriously impair any recreational benefit of the project." Lockwood also asserted, "The fluctuation of the water level in the reservoir would create mudflats and barren shores that would result in replacing an excellent game fishery with a trash fishery."

Other viable concerns were voiced by the US Fish & Wildlife Service and the National Wildlife Foundation as well as the Pennsylvania Fish Commission. The flooded land area would gobble up more than twenty thousand acres of wildlife habitat and hundreds of historic and archaeological sites, including evidence of Paleo-Indian culture as early as 10,000 BC. Shad runs would be cut off from their upper river spawning grounds, thus eliminating shad's primary remaining spawning area in the Delaware River system. The earthen dam holding back fresh water would increase the salinity in the Delaware Bay, possibly destroying a four-million-dollar oyster industry—and there was the safety issue of the dam itself.

Indirect assistance also came from a growing national environmental awareness and from new federal initiatives, including the creation of the Delaware Water Gap National Recreation Area in 1965 and passage of the National Wild and Scenic Rivers Act in 1968 and the National Environmental Policy Act of 1969.

The following year the Army Corps sent in an incomplete environmental impact statement fueling the anti-Tocks forces against the construction of the dam. In 1974 Congress appropriated funds for an impartial new impact study on the Tocks Island Dam with stipulation that no money would be spent on construction or land acquisition until the study was complete. Before the review was completed, the cost to build the dam had escalated to over four hundred million dollars.

In 1975 numerous studies confirmed the environmental arguments that the Tocks Island reservoir would be rapidly polluted by excessive eutrophication from drainage of agricultural effluent from Upper

Delaware runoff, which would seriously threaten the recreational quality of the reservoir, particularly swimming, boating, and fishing. Adverse impacts of an estimated 10.6 million annual visitors also would have disastrous consequences.

On July 31, 1975, the Delaware River Basin Commission broke ranks and voted four to one against the construction of the Tocks Island Dam. The vote left the National Park Service with a tangle of conflicting goals and management problems. With the prospect of shelving the project altogether, the Park Service did not have a clear mandate for managing the free-flowing river, nor the authority over the riverbank itself.

> *The countless studies and millions of taxpayer dollars that have been spent studying the middle Delaware have affirmed that this river is a treasure that should remain free flowing.*
> —AMERICAN RIVERS CONSERVATION COUNCIL

By 1977 the project had been the source of an intense sixteen-year battle of regional and national scope—in part due to its massive cost estimates (now approaching a billion dollars), and because of how Congress's pork-barrel system operated as an elaborate life-support system, keeping the project alive even after it had been almost universally rejected. De-authorization bills had been thwarted each time during the previous three years, and money had been appropriated for additional studies, even though no federal agency, including the Army Corps, the three basin states, and almost all local governments opposed the dam's construction.

A freshman congressman from Bucks County, Pennsylvania, named Peter Kostmeyer, who sat on the Interior Committee in 1977, introduced legislation in the House to incorporate both the middle and upper sections of the Delaware River into the National Wild and Scenic Rivers System. It was Senator Kostmeyer's hope that the act would provide a major roadblock to construction of the Tocks Island Dam and keep the Delaware a free-flowing river.

The young Democrat courageously took on his fellow Democratic rival, Frank Thompson (D-NJ), chairman of the powerful House Administration Committee and a longtime proponent of the project, in a lively debate. Congressman Thompson introduced an amendment to exclude thirty-nine miles of the middle Delaware from Wild and Scenic designation in the HR 12536 bill. When the smoke cleared, the vote stood at 110 to 275: The middle Delaware stayed in the bill. Two days later the House approved the final bill by a whopping 341 to 67, a tribute to the work of Pete Kostmeyer and his colleagues.

> *It is hereby declared to be the policy of the United States that certain selected rivers of the nation which, with their immediate environments, possess outstandingly remarkable scenic, recreational, geological, fish and wildlife, historic, cultural or similar values, shall be preserved in free-flowing condition, and that they and their immediate environments shall be protected for the benefit and enjoyment for present and future generations. Congress declares that the national policy of dams and other construction at appropriate sections of the rivers of the United States needs to be complemented by a policy that would preserve other selected rivers or sections thereof in their free-flowing condition to protect water quality of such rivers and to fulfill other national conservation purposes.*
>
> —CONGRESSIONAL PRONOUNCEMENT, *1968 NATIONAL WILD AND SCENIC RIVERS ACT*

The Wild and Scenic Rivers designation for 114 miles of river did not initially de-authorize the Tocks Island Dam project, but helped to foreclose the possibility of building the dam while ensuring the public's enjoyment of the free-flowing river within the Delaware Water Gap National Recreation Area.

It took fifteen years for Congress to finally de-authorize the Tocks Island Dam project, though the option to revisit the issue in future years was retained. In 2002, after more extensive research, the Tocks Island Dam project was officially de-authorized for good.

- 6 -

The Fish That Saved America

In the early years of settlement, confronted by famine and starvation, the colonists learned from Native Americans how to catch and preserve shad, an important food source, for the long, lean winter months. The migratory shad, arriving in March or early April, replenished the food shortages from the previous winter. Nathan Hale asserted that it was an uncommonly early run of shad in the spring of 1776 that saved George Washington and his near-starved troops camped along the Schuylkill River at Valley Forge.

It was the winter of 1993 when three dozen people crammed into the back room of the 1760 House restaurant in Trexlertown, Pennsylvania, to see my presentation, "Exploring Salmon Rivers on the Kola Peninsula." The program on Russian salmon fishing attracted a lot of folks and was a

Soon after spawning, shad will often feed on dry flies before returning to the ocean. LEE HARTMAN

peculiar way for me to promote my guide service business fishing for trout on the Upper Delaware River.

One inquisitive man, with a body made from eating too many strawberry cream cakes, stood out from the crowd and routinely asked questions. "How big are the salmon? What flies do you use? Tell me about the Delaware fishing. Are there any shad up there?"

After the program the chatty man introduced himself at the bar. His name was Richard Smith, a restaurant owner with a penchant for fly fishing, eating, and drinking lots of vodka. That evening he treated me to a Smirnoff on the rocks after my program ended. I immediately began warming up to the big fellow. "I don't want trout," he said emphatically. "I prefer catching large fish rather than small trout. If you promise me you can get me into catching shad on a fly rod I will come to your camp." There are never any guarantees in fishing unless you are using blasting caps or cherry bombs; however, I took him up on his challenge and booked him for three days in late May.

It was early evening when the former Marine veteran and his two sidekicks, Bill McNulty and his son Greg, completed the three-hour drive to Indian Springs Camp. The late evening temperature was ideal to fish during an evening hatch of Green Drakes—the most famous hatch in the state, maybe the country, for catching trout. The rainbow trout had finished their spawning rituals in the tributaries a month ago and now were satisfying their evening appetites eating drake duns and spinners.

"Wanna fish for trout before dinner?" I asked. Richard Smith, often called "Butterbean" by some folks, just frowned at me like an angry bear who wanted to eat. Without any hesitation I made dinner.

The Lancaster trio came armed with nine-foot, six-weight fly rods and floating lines to match—but no shad flies. "Couldn't find any in the tackle shop," Rick said with a troubled look. His experience was not unusual since most anglers on the big river fish for trout. But Rick was going to catch shad—nothing else mattered.

All Delaware River trout anglers have their own favorite patterns to use whether fishing for shad or trout. An earlier client of mine had given me a box of bonefish flies to take on a fishing trip to Belize I'd scheduled for the coming fall. Bonefish flies are simple ties that resemble many of the shad patterns I tie for the Delaware River. The metal bead-chain eye design was the same, only the hook size and tail and body materials were different. The body material was tied with mylar, and dyed breast feathers for the tail and beard in assorted colors were all that was necessary to complete my personal fly selection called "shad-a-lacs."

The red shad-a-lac, tied with a pearlescent mylar body on a #10, 3x long hook, using the fluff of a red breast feather for a wiggly-like action of the tail and beard, became candy for the springtime spawning shad.

The next day the early morning river fog lifted, turning the day bright, warm, and friendly. Taking three anglers in a three-man drift boat was not an option, as there'd be no room for the guide. Wade-fishing was the only choice. Armed with trout rods and a box of shad-a-lacs, we headed a mile and half downstream from the Lordville Bridge and found a stretch of river that was empty of anglers. A long, shallow riffle dumping its water into a wide, flat pool made an ideal space for three fly fishermen to cast and a perfect rest stop for shad.

Shad do not eat on their long trek from the ocean. The fish rely on stored energy to sustain themselves, as do Atlantic salmon. Though they don't feed before spawning, they will take a teasing fly that swings in front of their nose. I placed everyone one hundred feet apart to maintain ample room for a backcast. Rick and I went upriver while Bill and Greg spread out below.

Fly fishing for shad is not that complex. It's about the same as casting a metal lure across the river with a spinning rod . . . well, sort of. I had an excitable fly-fishing novice with a skinny trout rod hell-bent on catching a three- to eight-pound torpedo. No telling what I was in for. After a few demonstration casts and a brief explanation on how to control the fly across the three-foot-high riffles, my eager client appeared to be ready.

Rick finally solved his casting issues after fifteen minutes of unpoetic casting, a few tangles, and the foulest words that could put a blush on the face of the Boston strangler. After a few casts Rick drifted his red shad-a-lac nicely near the bottom, which teased a silver-sided fish to flash at his fly. "Did you see that, Lee?" he yelled excitedly. "I can't believe that bastard didn't take the fly."

Rick Smith holding America's "founding fish" taken on the Upper Delaware.
LEE HARTMAN

"They come in schools—make the same cast again." I answered. "If it doesn't intercept the fly this time, hang the line in the current and jig the fly back and forth—if the fish takes it let him run—but don't be discouraged if you lose it. Shad have a soft mouth and often will throw the hook."

The hefty fellow learned a mouthful of instructions well, and after a few lost shad the restaurant owner got his wish and landed the first shad of his life, a three-plus-pounder. The threesome caught many more shad that day, enough to turn their attention to trout the following day.

Over the years Rick Smith became a regular at Indian Springs Camp. On his many visits I watched him develop into an extraordinary fly angler, and most of all a great friend. He was no hatch matcher—didn't know an olive from a drake—but could he cast! Rick Smith could put the fly on a dime at sixty feet. During the following years, Rick followed me around the world: Russia, South America, Montana, Northwest Territory, and his most favorite place—Belize, for tarpon.

Size always mattered to Rick, and tarpon fishing became his first love. "They were like shad in the Delaware—only one hundred pounds bigger," Smith boasted. Rick eventually sold his Heidelberg family restaurant in Robesonia, Pennsylvania, and moved to Florida just for the tarpon. In 2015 my wonderful friend caught his one-thousandth tarpon on a fly, a notable feat that got him an award at the Melbourne Fly Fishing Club in

Florida. His fishing idol, the late great Lefty Kreh, presented the prized trophy to Richard Smith.

The American Shad (*Alosa Sapidissima*)

Charting the Delaware River in the winter of 1632–1633, Dutch explorer David De Fries wrote of waters so filled with fish that one drop of a seine net caught enough perch, roach, and pike to feed his crew of thirty for a day. William Penn was equally impressed by the natural abundance in the region, writing of oysters so large they needed to be cut in half before eating, giant sturgeon that leaped in the air in such numbers they often endangered small watercraft, herring that ran the shoals so thick colonists could easily shovel them into tubs, and rockfish (stripers) so abundant they were barreled like cod.

The fish that most impressed the early settlers were the shad, anadromous creatures, quite like the Atlantic salmon (also anadromous), meaning they spend much of their lives in salt water but spawn in fresh water. Shad are the largest member of the herring family. The slab-side fish can reach upward of twelve pounds. For a millennium they spawned in rivers along the Atlantic coast from Florida all the way to the St. Lawrence River in Canada. For most of their lives they are plankton feeders, swimming in large schools along the coastal waters as they feed on plankton and occasionally small shrimp and fish carried in on the ocean current.

During early March or April, rising spring temperatures reach the mid-50°F mark, which triggers shad to leave the Atlantic Ocean and return to the waters where they were born, often hundreds of miles upstream. Biologists tell us the fish find their natal beginnings through their uncanny sense of smell. Spawning shad prefer river channels dominated by flats of sand, silt, gravel, or boulders. Males arrive on the spawning grounds first, followed by egg-laden females. The spawning fish select sandy, pebble-like shallows between 60°F and 70°F and deposit their pale pink eggs between sundown and midnight.

Their spawning occurs primarily in waters with temperatures between 54°F and 69.6°F. Generally, water temperatures below 39.4°F cause total or partial cessation of spawning. However, American shad were moving into natal rivers when water temperatures were 39°F or lower. Additionally, peak spawning temperatures varied from year to year. For example, peak spawning temperatures in the Connecticut River were 71.6°F and 58.6°F in 1968 and 1969, respectively.

A female releases two hundred thousand to six hundred thousand eggs into the shallows to be fertilized by males as they roll about on the bottom in the current. In four to twelve days (dependent on water temperature and conditions), the eggs will hatch. The juveniles, which reach two to five inches and look like tiny versions of their parents, remain in the river feeding on insects until fall. Many river predators take their toll on the fingerlings—fish-eating birds, other fish, and mergansers—and when they enter the ocean they become prey to bluefish and striped bass.

Unlike Pacific salmon, and contrary to what happens in a lot of southern rivers, a good percentage of Delaware River shad survive breeding. Those that do not are gobbled up by the many bald eagles that inhabit the Delaware River.

Shad exhibit complex and little-understood feeding habits during spawning periods. Shad, which are plankton eaters when in the ocean,

Many shad die soon after spawning. Those that survive return to the ocean and come back the following year. LEE HARTMAN

appear to retain the ability to digest and assimilate food; often they are seen eating insects before their return to the Atlantic, and will come back to their freshwater home after maturity.

Historically, for Native Americans and, later, for Pennsylvania colonists, shad, often referred to as "poor man's salmon," delivered a badly needed source of protein and burst of flavor after a long, lean winter. Their roe was considered a delicacy.

The Indians of the mid-Atlantic region were skilled and resourceful fishermen who employed a wide variety of weirs, traps, scoop nets, spears, bow and arrow, gigs, hand poles, and other ingenious devices to capture their prey. The colonists quickly learned from the locals how to catch and preserve shad for use during the lean winter months. The fish quickly became the region's most important commodity and provided a considerable portion of the many river settlements' economy.

During each spring, people from the surrounding countryside would travel to the banks of the river, trading maple syrup, whiskey, tanned leather, and the salt that was always in high demand for salting their winter supply of fish. According to fisheries historian William H. Meehan, every frontier homestead and rural farm had a half barrel of salted shad sitting in the kitchen, with some choice pieces of smoked shad hanging by the kitchen chimney.

By the early 1700s the growing population was putting a high demand for shad throughout the Delaware Valley region, especially in and around Philadelphia. The Philadelphia fishing industry expanded to the Schuylkill River and other Delaware River tributaries to harvest the tasty fish. To maximize their catch, Schuylkill fishermen constructed racks across the river to collect the shad. Within thirty years the aggressive fishing and wasteful harvesting practices had created a serious decline in the numbers of shad reaching upriver settlements. The fish harvest was so reprehensible that in May 1724, the Pennsylvania assembly passed a bill requiring demolition of the racks and dams that were depleting the migrating fish.

Many colonists turned their eyes and ignored the government regulation. During the years that followed, tensions continued among the upriver communities over fishing rights and frequently turned violent.

114

At Long Ford, located near Valley Forge, local residents fenced the river and dug out deep pools, which they used to herd the shad, capturing and killing tens of thousands then salting and marketing them for winter use. Upstream residents, outraged by the greedy tactics, conducted raids using flotilla to destroy the illegal fences, racks, and dams.

Mob violence—even murder—followed the arrival of shad from 1738 through the Civil War. The warring parties soon reached an agreement in which the Long Ford fishermen agreed to lower the fences far enough for navigating and open them periodically so that shad could pass through upriver. According to Meehan, the fishing war of 1738, as it was called, not only ended rack fishing on the Schuylkill but also helped transform what had been a seasonable pursuit conducted by the entire neighborhood into the avocation of a handful of professional fishermen. The dispute also highlighted the need to assign rights to manage and preserve the regional shad fishery. The adjudication of fishery disputes would continue to occupy the colonial and state authorities for the next two and a half centuries.

Before the arrival of the railroad, rivers were the nation's primary arteries of inland commerce and transportation. Economic development relied on those waterways, and the colonies and later independent states invested tremendous amounts of money to improve navigation on rivers and canals. By the turn of the twentieth century, coal discoveries necessitated the construction of an elaborate system of dams and canals along the Lehigh and Schuylkill Rivers.

In 1815 the Schuylkill Navigation Company built two dams across the Schuylkill River at Reading and Shawmont (present-day Roxborough), drastically curtailing the great spring shad migrations. Schuylkill River fishermen, incensed that their legal rights were being threatened, took the Schuylkill Navigation Company to court and won, forcing the company to pay heavy fines for blocking the fish from migrating upriver.

The loss of shad migration (even temporarily) on the Schuylkill River was a major blow to the fishing industry and led to efforts to develop a more effective way to harvest shad. As coal operations increased, dams and canals grew throughout the eastern region's rivers and tributaries, blocking the shad's access to over 80 percent of its natural spawning grounds.

Unlike the Schuylkill, however, the Delaware River was too wide to span with a net, thus ensuring the survival of the fish upriver.

Before 1815, fishing operations operated in accordance with formulas brought over by the first European colonists. Many shorefront fisheries operations emerged along the river and took on a more modern capitalist approach that transformed the Delaware's shad fishery into an important regional industry. One of the larger of the new proprietary ventures was the Fancy Hill Fishery, located six miles below Philadelphia. The company supplied shad for the city market, and by the mid-1830s Fancy Hill employed nearly one hundred men to haul in heavy cotton nets that filled sixty to seventy wagons a day during the height of the spring run.

By the 1840s the increased demand for shad led to the use of more efficient techniques for harvesting. Two dozen large fisheries on the Delaware used shore-mounted windlasses, often turned by horses, and employed fifty to sixty men each. Collectively, during the height of the season, they employed one thousand men and could haul in twenty thousand fish every twenty-four hours. The efficient harvest system and the

Netting fish in the Delaware and Hudson Estuary was a common practice in the early nineteenth century. WILLIAM TYLEE RANNEY, *SHAD FISHING ON THE HUDSON* PAINT-ING (1846)

ideology that assumed the bounty of nature to be inexhaustible led to another serious decline in the numbers of fish.

In the early decades of the nineteenth century, a single shad had furnished a substantial meal for a laborer and his family. By the 1860s shad had become a luxury beyond their means. By 1872 fisheries above Milford, Pennsylvania, yielded only a single shad. The following year all the Delaware River shad fisheries failed to meet their expenses. The fish that were caught in the river continued to diminish in size. It had taken only about forty shad to fill a pork barrel in 1843. By 1873, due to smaller fish, it was taking more than one hundred, and a four-pound fish had become a curiosity.

The collapse of the Delaware River Basin shad fishery was not an isolated event. The overfishing of America's food fish had become a national crisis in the 1860s.

With price the primary means of regulating their harvests, America's commercial fisheries followed the invisible hand of the marketplace and left trails of devastation in their wake. The American oyster industry, by far the nation's largest and most profitable fishery, suffered the same state of crisis. Once the Civil War was over, both state and federal governments turned their attention to restoration of the nation's food fisheries.

Alarmed by the depletion of shad in the Susquehanna and Delaware and of sport fish in the state's mountain streams and lakes, the Pennsylvania legislature appointed James Worrell its first state fish commissioner, his principal mandate being to restore the state shad fishery. To that effect, Worrell engineered passage of laws that required fish ways and sluices to allow passage for fish on all the state's major river ways (1866), and forbade the use of fish baskets, weirs, and other traps (1871). In 1873 the Pennsylvania legislature set up a three-person fish commission to plan systematic restoration of the shad on the state's rivers.

Pennsylvania began an ambitious restocking program, planting 433,000 shad fry into the Delaware River in June 1873. The program continued yearly into the twentieth century. Other East Coast states stocked more than 92 million shad into their state rivers. Shad harvests increased steadily for twenty years, rising from a million pounds in 1880 to more than nine million in 1887—to a Pennsylvania history record harvest at

The overharvesting of American shad was a common practice as far up as Fish's Eddy, New York. DELAWARE COUNTY HISTORY

the turn of the century when more than sixteen million pounds of fish were hauled out of the river.

The US Fish Commission also worked to establish American shad in both the Pacific Ocean and Gulf of Mexico. A special train carried the first ten thousand shad fry to the Sacramento River. The release between 1876 and 1880 of more than a half million shad fry into California waters successfully established shad in Pacific coastal waters.

On the Brink of Disaster

After the peak harvest of more than sixteen million pounds, the catch plunged to only three million pounds in 1905. There was a small resurgence the following year, then it took another plunge. In 1916 fishermen took the last million-pound catch out of the Delaware. It was the second time in less than fifty years that the Delaware shad fishery collapsed. Fifteen years later the Uniform Fishing Laws, established by the US Fish & Wildlife Service, had concerns about the Delaware Bay and River and declared the shad industry was no longer profitable.

Landing a shad seine, Sutton Beach, Albemarle Sound, c. 1887. HUGH SMITH,
FRESHWATER AND MARINE IMAGE BANK, UNIVERSITY OF WASHINGTON LIBRARY

Efforts to restore the shad runs, however, did not end. Despite clear
evidence that stocking was ineffective in the long run, the New Jersey
Fish and Game Commission in 1927 yielded to the pleas of veteran
fishermen and built a small experimental hatchery at Pennsville, which
moved up to Hancock Bridge the next year. The New Jersey stocking program peaked in 1938 when the Hancock facility released six million shad
fry into the river. But the stocking programs at Torresdale and Hancock
failed to restore the shad runs.

To many older Pennsylvanians the shad's demise provided further
evidence that industrialization and urban growth were out of control,
destroying that essential balance between nature and civilization upon
which the nation had been founded and the future of the Republic still
depended. In the nineteenth and early twentieth centuries, Philadelphia exploded in size, soaring from 68,000 people in 1800 to more than
1,684,000 by the eve of World War I. Philadelphia's water use soared
from 58 million gallons a day in 1880 to 319 million a day in 1910.

Confident in the ability of its rivers to absorb and carry off waste, Philadelphia, by far the largest river abuser, continued to use the Schuylkill and Delaware as aqueous garbage cans. The city's water crisis erupted into a major health crisis. Pollution of the city's unfiltered water supply subjected Philadelphians to periodic outbreaks of waterborne diseases, including major outbreaks of cholera in 1891 and 1899. Philadelphia was compelled to restructure its water supply and sewerage systems. Completion of the Torresdale sand-filtration plant in 1908 and chlorination of all city water by 1912 ended cholera and typhoid's reign as a menace to public health. However, solving the sewage problem proved to be a daunting task.

In 1927 clean water advocate John Fred Lewis wrote, "Sewage in the lower Schuylkill has utterly destroyed its fishing and made its otherwise available banks unfit for human habitation and undesirable even for industrial purposes." The Great Depression and two World Wars postponed the city from building one of three authorized waste-treatment plants for decades.

Philadelphia and Trenton, New Jersey, continued to develop and flourish during the twentieth century. Steel mills, ironworks, oil refineries, chemical plants, and more were sited in and around the historical cities. The growing population and resulting runoff, sewage, and drainage problems associated with the growth added to the polluted state of this once-pristine river. Charles Hardy wrote in "Fish or Foul? A History of the Delaware River Basin":

> Philadelphia's sewers dumped more than 200,000 tons of solids each year, which combined with other solid wastes into deposits twelve feet deep. Exposed at low tides and churned up by incoming ships along the city's Delaware River wharves, they released an unbearable stench composed of sulfuric dioxide and other gases that assailed the nostrils of commuters using the Camden/Philadelphia ferries and drove sea-hardened sailors to jump ship rather than spend the night sleeping in their berths.
>
> By the end of World War II, the lower Delaware River remained an open sewer with fouled water devoid of oxygen needed to support

fish and aquatic life. The pollution block caught America's fish both coming and going and threatened the survival of the once-thriving shad that had fed Washington's soldiers. The passage of the 1948 Federal Water Pollution Control Act, which placed the pollution of interstate waters under federal jurisdiction, made available federal river funds for clean-up projects. With federal money, Philadelphia adopted an ambitious new 80 million dollar plan to construct three primary sewage treatment plants to be completed by 1953. The work project proceeded close to its schedule, with the last of the three plants being opened in December 1955.

Although the postwar pollution control efforts did not totally clean up the lower Delaware, they did succeed in decreasing the length and duration of the Philadelphia pollution block. Mother Nature did her part, too. The twin hurricanes in 1955 caused the worst flooding in the history of the river but did succeed in scouring out pollution-saturated sediments that had been accumulating for decades—washing them out to the sea. With Mother Nature's help the shad returned to the Delaware, reappearing in the upper river in 1960.

The migration was short-lived, however. Low rainfall produced record drought years in 1961, 1963, and 1965 that left the lower river pollution block intact, barring the shad from their spring migration and producing major fish kills. This was a blow to shad fishermen and the state and federal fisheries biologists who were working hard to restore shad in the Delaware Basin. "The future outlook for the shad in the Delaware presents a rather gloomy picture," warned Dr. Jay L. Harmic of the Delaware Fish and Game Commission in 1963. Fortunately, the bad spring weather in 1962 and 1964 increased river flows, which allowed fish passage through the Philadelphia pollution block into the upper river.

In 1968 the Delaware River Basin Commission (DRBC) was noted as one of the first agencies in the environmental movement when Stewart Udall, JFK's Secretary of the US Department of the Interior, stated, "Only the Delaware among the nation's river basins is moving into high gear in its program to combat water pollution." The DRBC was the first to impose load allocations on river dischargers, holding them to standards more stringent than the US Environmental Protection Agency issued years later. River historian Richard C. Albert wrote in 1988, "The cleanup of the Delaware Estuary represents one of the premier water pollution control success stories in the United States."

In 1972 Congress, led by George McGovern, overrode Nixon's veto and passed the Clean Water Act, a law that invested $1.5 billion in new wastewater plants along the Delaware River. Phosphate detergent bans by New York in 1973 and Pennsylvania in 1990, along with a 1994 halt on manufacturing phosphate detergent, prompted phosphorus declines by over 25 percent in many rivers.

> *I've looked in this river when the shad used to run full force. You'd stand on the bridge and look down and you could not see the water for the shad. It was just one solid mass of fish, and very dark. You wouldn't even know this was water. We don't get runs like this anymore.*
> —RUSSELL "DOC" HOMER, LORDVILLE, NEW YORK, DECEMBER 3, 1987, NATIONAL PARK SERVICE INTERVIEW

In 1981 Fred Lewis, who operated the only commercial shad fishery on the non-tidal Delaware River, netted 6,392 shad. Only twenty years earlier, the river had been so badly polluted that Lewis (who was then forty-five) did not catch a single shad. According to his records, the 1981 catch was the biggest at his family business location in Lambertville, New Jersey, since 1896. Catch reports rebounded in 1987; more than 56,000 shad were landed between Hancock, New York, and Yardley, Pennsylvania, during a nine-week period.

Over the following decade, the State of New Jersey, Division of Fish and Wildlife Management, in cooperation with the DRBC, the Fisheries Technical Committee, and the US Fish & Wildlife Service, conducted hydroacoustic sampling of American shad. Transducers strategically placed on the Lambertville Toll Bridge pilings emitted sound waves (sonar) that bounced off fish. Different species of fish reflect sound waves differently, so they are distinguishable from each other by the hydroacoustic echo pattern, school size, and unique behavioral characteristics. The

The Lewis family continues to operate the only remaining New Jersey commercial shad fishery on the non-tidal river. LAMBERTVILLE HISTORICAL SOCIETY

intercepted waves were then processed by a computer to give an estimate of the number of shad (and other fish) that passed by.

The Barnes-Williams Environmental Study report, at the New Jersey location for the selected years, revealed the following information:

STUDY PERIOD	SHAD PASSAGE ESTIMATE
April 7 to May 6, 1992	327,800+/-8,600
April 1 to May 9, 1995	289,900+/-9,600
April 1 to May 31, 1996	524,300+/-2,800
April 1 to May 31, 1998	392,700+/-2,500
April 1 to May 31, 1999	24,700+/-300
April 1 to May 31, 2000	382,200+/-2,700

The low count of migrating shad in 1999 had no reasonable explanation but plenty of unanswered questions. Was it due to low flows and higher water temperatures? Could it be the result of an earlier run? Was the monitoring flawed? Predation? Was it a mid-Atlantic commercial bycatch—or just a bad year for shad? No one could put a finger on it.

Like winds and sunsets, wild things were taken for granted until progress began to do away with them.

—*ALDO LEOPOLD*

By 2005 dissolved oxygen at Philadelphia exceeded four parts per million, the fishable water quality standard, and migratory shad and striped bass began returning to the river in increasing numbers. Bald eagles, a protected species that rely on a fish-laden diet, had been restored to the now-cleaner waters of the Delaware River and were growing in numbers, some even nesting in south Philadelphia at the Navy Yard. Historic water quality recovery occurred in the Delaware during an environmental era that coincided with the return of migratory fish populations.

In 2013 the federal Mid-Atlantic Fishery Management Council imposed a cap on the domestic commercial catch of shad and herring, meant to shore up the fish, which had been nearly exhausted by overharvest and poor water quality. Brian Neilan, a fisheries biologist with the New Jersey Division of Fish & Wildlife's Bureau of Marine Fisheries, said his agency has seen an upward trend in adult shad returns since 2011, as evidenced by catches taken by the Lewis Fishery in Lambertville. The commercial fisherman caught 1,032 shad, passing a total of 1,015 from the previous year.

In 2017 Don Hamilton, the twenty-five-year veteran research specialist for the Upper Delaware Scenic and Recreational River, led an August to October seining operation to document the number of young-of-year (YOY) shad in the non-tidal portion of the river. The sampling, using a three-hundred-foot, boat-employed beach seine, was carried out collaboratively with fisheries staff personnel from the Pennsylvania Fish & Boat Commission, National Park Service, New York State Division of Marine Resources, US Fish & Wildlife Service, and other volunteers.

The juvenile abundance provided data for comparison to a plan developed by the Delaware River Basin Fish and Wildlife Management Cooperative. Should the YOY shad fall below the predetermined benchmark, measures would be enacted to strengthen protection of the American shad population. The 2017 sampling set a new time-series high dating back to 1988. Encouraged by the survey results, Hamilton stated in his report to the public, "There is a ray of hope for the American shad."

One-Hundred-Pound Fish

On April 14, 2014, an early morning sun brightened the Saturday sky as Marty Crozier walked out to work on his boat dock. The sixty-year-old Forks Township resident glanced at the river below and spotted a huge fish carcass lying next to the bank. Not knowing exactly what the curious-looking species was, he called the Pennsylvania Fish & Boat Commission to determine its identity. A commission biologist, Greg Murphy, came out on Monday and confirmed the fish to be an Atlantic sturgeon, an

The Atlantic sturgeon of the Delaware River are listed under the Environment Services Administration as part of a distinct population segment, which includes all Atlantic sturgeon that spawn in watersheds draining to coastal waters from Chatham, Massachusetts, to the Delaware-Maryland border on Fenwick Island. Specimens weighing over eight hundred pounds and nearly fifteen feet in length have been recorded, but they typically grow to be six to eight feet and weigh no more than three hundred pounds. IAN PARK, FISHERIES BIOLOGIST, DELAWARE DEPARTMENT OF NATURAL RESOURCES AND ENVIRONMENTAL CONTROL (DNREC), DIVISION OF FISH AND WILDLIFE

endangered species that can grow up to fifteen feet long and can weigh up to eight hundred pounds. It's by far the largest fish swimming in the Delaware River, and perhaps the most elusive.

The fish identified as a male sturgeon measured six feet, three inches. Murphy, the regional biologist, speculated it was a young adult or possibly a juvenile. According to the US Fish & Wildlife Service, the American sturgeon reaches full maturity at eleven or twelve years of age and can live more than sixty years. "I've been fishing on this river for fifty years and it's the first time I've ever seen something like this," Crozier explained to Murphy. With no signs of trauma or injury, the commission never determined how the longest-living fish had died at so young an age. The juvenile sturgeon had somehow found its way upriver above Easton, not the normal place for it to be during spring spawning season.

Historically the Delaware River supported the largest population of American sturgeon along the Atlantic coast. Native Americans fished for the scale-less giant creatures, but early European settlers considered them a nuisance and less desirable than the preferred shad. During the mid-eighteenth century, after the Civil War, the commercial caviar industry emerged on the scene and made the sturgeon more valuable for its roe. In 1890, an estimated seven million pounds of sturgeon were caught on the East Coast.

The Delaware soon became the country's premier sturgeon fishery, gaining the title "caviar capital of North America." Fishermen crowded the river with their boats to collect the river-bottom feeders with deep nets and iron gaffes—slaughtering them one by one for meat and the hard, ripe roe during the spring spawning season.

By the early 1900s, numbers had declined dramatically, and roe prices soared. Fishermen continued to harvest even the smallest of sturgeon until near depletion. The once-abundant fish already faced an uphill battle for its survival, primarily due to saltwater intrusion, dredging operations, water pollution, and their river-bottom spawning habitat being covered with silt from the coal industry. It took man less than a century to nearly wipe out the seventy-million-year-old Atlantic sturgeon. It has been estimated that currently less than three hundred spawning adults are left in the Delaware River population.

The near-extinct Delaware sturgeon that remain today embark on a remarkable journey from their ocean water home to the freshwater spawning and nursery grounds of their ancestors near present-day Chester, Wilmington, Philadelphia, and Trenton.

The Delaware Riverkeeper Network's leader, Maya van Rossum, a longtime champion of protecting the critical habitat of the Delaware watershed's Atlantic sturgeon, filed a lawsuit in 2014 to get the federal government to comply with its obligation to designate critical habitat for this endangered species. On August 17, 2017, the National Marine Fisheries Service released its final rule designating critical habitat for endangered population segments of Atlantic sturgeon to help secure protection against any future threats.

Less than a year later, the Delaware Riverkeeper Network achieved another victory when the US Army Corps of Engineers proposed dumping sand and rock over a deep hole in the Delaware Bay, identified by scientists as critical for sturgeon for forage and growth and necessary for their reproductive well-being. An action alert sent to the Riverkeeper

DNREC fisheries biologists conduct a juvenile sturgeon abundance survey every year during the fall and winter, which allows them to create an estimate that is used to evaluate spring spawning success and to monitor long-term trends.
IAN PARK, FISHERIES BIOLOGIST, DNREC, DIVISION OF FISH AND WILDLIFE

membership secured seventy-five comments urging the State of Delaware to reject the project. In response to the strong show of opposition, as well as the facts and information, the Army Corps withdrew its permit application.

The sturgeon's offspring has a sort of a face only a mother sturgeon could love—the rubberlike lips over a toothless grin, with four sensory barbells dangling from the underside of its shovel-shaped mouth. For many of us, the fish's primordial appearance might be unsettling. But feeling akin to maternal affection might be the best way to describe the reaction of researchers who, in 2009, while sampling just downriver of Philadelphia, captured the first juvenile Atlantic sturgeon that has been found in the river in decades.
—TED WILLIAMS, OUTDOOR WRITER, "SAVING LAKE STURGEON, AN ANCIENT FISH WITH A BRIGHT FUTURE"

- 7 -

Birth of a Trout River

From General George Washington's acclaimed Revolutionary War crossing of the Delaware River near Trenton, upstream to the Delaware Water
Gap, and into the forests and farmlands of its headwaters, the river was
never intended to be a wild trout river until two water supply dams were
built on its uppermost tributaries, releasing clean, cold, trout-friendly
water.

    Fishing maps and boxes of winter-made flies cluttered the front seat
of my new 1973 Ford pickup camper as two of us rode through the Pocono
Mountains of Pennsylvania. It was May, prime time for good hatches,
cool water, and hungry trout. Our annual weeklong fishing adventure this
year was destined for no particular place. We planned this trip to rely on

An aerial view of the Upper Delaware River flowing around Frisbie Island above
the town of Equinunk, Pennsylvania. GARTH LENZ

our instincts to find new water to fish. Dick Lambert, a coworker at a pharmaceutical firm, and I were on the weeklong fishing vacation, prospecting for trout.

The afternoon sun began to melt behind the top of the mountain, signaling we needed to find a place to camp for the night. After driving a few more miles, I spotted what looked like the perfect place. A large, open cow pasture nestled along the Delaware River looked appealing to both of us. Across from the gated entranceway to the field, a beer sign flashed on a weather-beaten building. It was Pete and Lovey's tavern (presently MicBree's Crosstown Tavern). A quick brew and a lesson in local knowledge emboldened us to drive to the large white farmhouse one hundred yards behind the local watering hole.

Our unexpected presence alerted the owner, who emerged from the barn. The stocky, overalls-clad dairy farmer didn't miss a beat when I asked him if we could camp by the river for the night. "Sure can," he said politely. "Just give me two bucks and you can drive through the pasture and park next to the maple trees below the river junction." The farmer, glancing at our fishing hats, shared some words of warning. "If you are here to fish you ain't goin' to catch nothin' but trout. Ever since they put in those damn reservoirs the bass and bullheads have all but disappeared." Our jaws dropped as we gaped at each other like two kids in a candy store. Without uttering another word, we gave the man two bucks.

At the time, few people recognized the Delaware River as a trout fishery. The farmer's revelation that trout existed in the river was a welcome surprise. We drove through the open pasture and parked near the bank overlooking the two large tributaries that formed the Delaware River. It did not take long to confirm what the dairy farmer revealed to us. The evening sky was dusty with all sorts of bugs. Emerging caddis, mayfly duns, dancing spinners—and not a fisherman in sight. It was intoxicating!

Eventually, all things merge into one, and a river runs through it.
—Norman Maclean, A River Runs Through It

The main river bordering New York and Pennsylvania begins a half mile below Hancock, New York (once known by the Lenape name Chehocton,

The river's clean, cold flows produce an abundance of aquatic life. LEE HARTMAN

meaning "wedding of the waters"), flowing from the southern flank of the Catskill Mountains. We stood at the junction of the East Branch (Pohpakton River) and West Branch (Mohawk) looking for heads. The two of us stalked along the bank as the orange glow of the sun finally disappeared over the horizon. Trout noses bulged in the riffles, flowing into a long, wide pool, feeding their bellies. The mating rituals of dancing mayflies and skittering caddis put us into high gear to fish.

With so many flies on the water, my mind raced as to what to use. I don't remember exactly what fly I put on my tippet. It appeared not to matter. On the second cast a trout clobbered my imitation and put a buzz in my reel that echoed through the late evening sky. It was a football-sized rainbow with the fighting strength of a wounded bull, and it convinced us to stay the entire week.

The fly-fishing experience for a couple of Delaware River rookies was overwhelming. The three-hour drive to the river in my rust-colored Ford became routine on any available weekend. The few anglers that I met on the river bonded together and shared their fishing secrets with no one. You could fit the number of weekend anglers who fished the Upper Delaware into a school bus. The fly-fishing fraternity who visited the river respectfully fished where you were not, allowing each an intimate approach to a selected pool and its trout.

One of those loyal Delaware anglers was Ed Van Put, a serious Catskill fly fisherman, acclaimed to be one of the best, who may have been the first to fly fish the river after completion of Cannonsville Reservoir. The Livingston Manor resident fished the river almost every evening, spring, summer, and fall, and boasted it may be the best trout river in America.

Three years after Cannonsville Reservoir was in full operation in 1968, the fisheries expert began keeping accurate size and catch records of the trout he caught. His statistics were impressive. In the 1971 season

Ed Van Put is a champion for anglers not only in the Catskills but for the state of New York. As a former New York State Department of Environmental Conservation fisheries expert, Ed has secured more public access and special-regulation water for fly fishers than any other individual. KRIS LEE PHOTO COURTESY OF ED VAN PUT

The lower East Branch of the Delaware flows extend 33 miles to its junction with the main stem of the river. WILLIAM MONTOVICH, ARTIST

Van Put caught, taped, and released 449 trout in a ratio of seven rainbows to one brown. The average size of his fish was slightly below sixteen inches. A fish fourteen inches could weigh over a pound. His seven-year survey indicated that trout between ten and eighteen inches made up 75 percent of the catch, while 47 percent of the trout were from fourteen to twenty inches.

During a seven-year span (1971–1978), Van Put's catch count during his 438 trips was 1,112 fish. What is even more impressive, he used but one fly pattern almost exclusively—a Catskill-tied Adams dry fly in assorted sizes.

The dairy farmer who permitted us to camp and fish was John (Bunny) Gale. Bunny's terse remark about the flow changes was typical among local residents. What had been viable bass water in the upper twenty-seven miles of the river became a cold-water trout fishery directly related to the bottom releases from New York City dam impounds in the East and West Branches of the Delaware River. One can only surmise what this magnificent river was like when the early settlers came to the area.

The Early Settlers of the Catskills

In 1706 Johannes Hardenbergh bought the immense tract of land since known as the "Hardenbergh patent," which covered two million acres of the Catskill Mountains in what is today Sullivan, Greene, Orange, Ulster, and Delaware Counties, from Nanisinos, sachem of the Esopus Indians, for the small sum of sixty pounds. The purchase was subsequently confirmed, and a patent was granted to Hardenbergh and six others in 1708. There were some disputes as to whether Hardenbergh's acquisition of the property had been truly legal. Indeed, in 1769 another former British officer, John Bradstreet, filed a claim to fifty thousand acres based on that assumption.

In the early eighteenth century, the Mohawk tribe of the Iroquois Nation roamed peacefully in the Hudson River Valley region and along

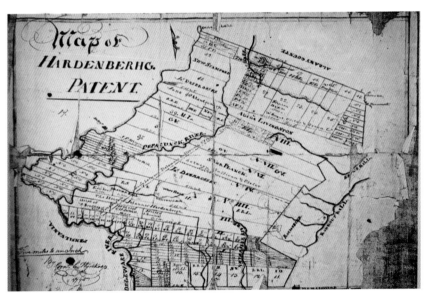

Johannes Hardenbergh was granted The Great or Hardenbergh patent, which consisted of approximately two million acres of land situated in Ulster, Greene, Orange, Sullivan, and Delaware Counties, New York. EQUINUNK HISTORICAL SOCIETY

nearby branches of the Upper Delaware River. By mid-century small groups of European settlers began moving into the Catskill region, constructing rough cabins conveniently on or near the many waterways. The Revolutionary War changed all that as the American colonists went to arms against their British rulers.

Near the end of the Revolutionary War, settlements in the upper reaches of the Delaware Valley were greatly scattered. What few families that lived in the area had little or no contact with each other, as there were no roads and communication other than tribal paths and horse trails.

Three years after George Washington's victory at Trenton, another battle occurred farther north along the Delaware River near Minisink, New York. The Battle of Minisink was led by the Mohawk Indian chief Thayendenegea (Joseph Brant) on July 18, 1779. Chief Thayendenegea and his raiding party massacred colonial soldiers and many villagers in a surprise invasion. The news of this violent uprising was slow to reach the early settlers.

Among the earliest pioneers who settled in the Catskill Mountains area was St. Leger Cowley, a native of Ireland. Prior to the Revolutionary War, Cowley traveled with his family from Albany, New York, and relocated on the West Branch of the Delaware (then named Papagonk and referred to as the Mohawk River by early settlers), forty miles north of what the Mohawks called Koo-Koose, meaning "a place for owls."

Three years after the commencement of the Revolutionary War, and notwithstanding the dangers to which the family was exposed, St. Leger Cowley, his wife, Mary, his sister's son Nicholas, and a relative named Adam remained at the settlement while Cowley, accompanied by his twelve-year-old son, Jonathan, and friend Isaac Sawyer, left on horseback. On their travels they were soon surprised and captured by four Schoharie (To-wos-scho-hor), a Mohawk word meaning "floating driftwood", two of whom were Christian, by the name of Seth and Ham Henry.

Immediately after their capture Seth fastened a warrior feather, which they'd undoubtedly procured from the hat of a fallen soldier in battle, to the front of the boy's cap and sent him on ahead, while they and their prisoners followed. The Cowley family was anxiously looking for St. Leger's return, and seeing a young lad approaching alone on horseback with a military ornament so conspicuous, they became filled with apprehension. The family was kept in suspense for a brief moment, and soon the father and friend Isaac made their appearance accompanied by their native captors.

The Schoharie warriors, allegiant to the British, offered no violence to any of the family but amused themselves by shooting their fowl and a churn partly filled with water, laughing heartily to see the water gush out of the hole made by the rifle ball. The next morning the Indians took Cowley and another man away as prisoners and left the women and the children at their settlement.

The party made camp the first night a short distance below what is now Delhi, New York, where the Mohawks, with assistance from their willing captives, constructed a rude but serviceable raft on which they all floated down the West Branch of the Delaware to Koo-Koose (Cookose—"cook-house," now named Deposit)—an Indian meeting place that intersected with the Oquago (Oquaga) Creek trail, which would lead toward the Susquehanna River. Once there they would resume their journey by land to Fort Niagara (controlled by the British), their destination.

Although unable to converse with their captors, the prisoners were far from being ignorant of Indian ways, and to conceal their plan to escape at the first favorable opportunity, they agreed to use signs as well as they could, all the while avoiding conversing together as much as possible so as not to invite the suspicions of their captors, who were watching their every movement.

The captives had already proceeded eleven days on their journey without seeing a favorable opportunity to make their escape. They had followed the blind Indian trail, traversed hills and valleys, crossed large streams, and were far beyond any white settlement—and all the horrors of a long captivity seemed inevitably their fate. The extremely dangerous feat of running the gauntlet was presented vividly to their imagination, with its long rows of hideously painted Indians arranged on either side, through which the life-race lay. Death seemed preferable to such a scene, and they mentally resolved to make one bold effort to escape or die in the attempt. It was their last ray of hope.

On the eventful night of the eleventh day's captivity, the party camped near Tioga Point. The captives on such occasions were ordered to make preparations for building a large wood fire (which they ignited in those matchless days by the aid of a large tinderbox) and to cut and carry to the encampment a supply of fuel for the night.

They had only one axe, which had been taken from Cowley at the time of their capture—one man would cut and the other would carry the wood to the spot where it was to be used. While Cowley was cutting and Sawyer was waiting for an armful of wood, Sawyer took from his pocket a newspaper and pretended to be reading its contents to his partner; instead, however, he was proposing a plan for regaining their liberty.

A quarter of venison that had been shot that afternoon was fire-roasted and eaten without the nutritious seasoning of salt and pepper. When all lay down to sleep, Cowley and Sawyer were each placed between two Mohawks, who were soon swept into deep slumber.

After waiting till near midnight, the mutual signal was given and the two friends cautiously got up. They shook the priming from the guns of their captors and quietly removed the remaining implements of death beyond the observation of the warriors. Then Sawyer, with the tomahawk of Ham Henry—who was recognized as the most savage of the four—took his station beside its owner, while Cowley with an axe placed himself beside another sleeping man.

The fire afforded sufficient light for the captives to make sure of their victims. At a given signal the blows fell fatal upon the two—the tomahawk sank deep into the brain of its owner, but unfortunately for Sawyer, he drew the handle from the weapon while attempting to free it from Ham Henry's skull. The blows that sent two to their final reckonings awoke the others, who instantly sprang to their feet.

As Seth Henry stood, he received a blow from Cowley, which he partially warded off by raising his arm, but his shoulder was laid open and he fell back, stunned. The fourth, as he came awake, Cowley hit with a heavy blow on his back; he fled and was pursued into a nearby swamp, where he finally died.

The two men returned to the fire and were deciding on what course to pursue when Seth Henry, who had recovered and feigned himself dead for some time waiting to embrace a favorable opportunity, sprang to his feet, dashed through the fire, and caught up his rifle, snapped it at his foes, then ran into the forest and disappeared.

The liberated captives were now the master of the bloody field and free of captivity. But after such an exciting scene, no sleep came for the remainder of the night. Their first precaution was to arm themselves with the implements of their fallen foes. They each took a gun, a tomahawk, and a scalping knife, together with all the remaining ammunition, and, thus equipped, anxiously awaited the approach of day.

At last the luminous sun rose from behind the eastern hills, with its rays peering through the overhanging branches of the forest trees, revealed to their eyes more fully the reality of the sad spectacle and gave the signal for the commencement of their march home.

Chief Thayendenegea, known as Joseph Brant, was said to be a full-blooded Mohawk Indian from Ohio, but others say he was a half-breed. Brant, who schooled at the Wheellock Moor's Indian Charity School in Connecticut, banded the Six Nations tribes and was a principal in the Treaty of 1768 with the British under the Providence of New York at Fort Stanwix. Brant also fought in the French and Indian War and in the American Revolutionary War.

Thayendenegea or Joseph Brant (March 1743–November 24, 1807) was a Mohawk military and political leader, based in present-day New York, who was closely associated with Great Britain during and after the American Revolution. GEORGE ROMNEY, ARTIST 1776

He was considered an intellectual man, but soon began to terrorize the colonials alongside the British soldiers. He even attacked other Indian tribes that did not support the British. Brant was chased by the colonial army but was never caught. He finally escaped into Canada, where he later died.

The Founding of the Village of Cannonsville

George Washington, the first American hero, was four years away from his 1789 inauguration when another young pioneer, Jesse Dickinson, a native of New Jersey, left his state on a long, treacherous journey through untrodden ground, exploring the "new country."

Once arriving on the western slopes of the Catskill region, Dickinson, lured by the sale of land patents, purchased several hundred acres at the confluence of Trout Creek, which the Indians called Gaddiwissy, and the West Branch (Papagonk) of the Delaware River. A year later, when New York was granted statehood, Dickinson traveled back to the property with his family and a few friends, several horses, cows, oxen, and other livestock. The purchase was praised by many of his colleagues—one being seventeen-year-old Benjamin Cannon who followed Dickinson from New Jersey.

After getting comfortably settled, Dickinson drew up plans for land improvements and laid out the town in regular squares, calling the small village Dickinson City. The following years he built a town hall, a grist-mill, and a sawmill, inviting all the male inhabitants within twenty-five miles to help in the construction efforts.

March 3, 1797, was George Washington's final day in office. Setting the precedent for a two-term limit and the civil transfer of power, he confessed, "I shall resign the chair of government without regret." This was the same year that Jesse Dickinson set his own fate when his debts far exceeded his income. Out of money, the young pioneer had no other recourse and was obliged to sell his estate to young Benjamin Cannon.

Benjamin Cannon followed in Dickinson's footsteps and built up the town he called "The City," including his own homestead on River Street, later called the Cannonsville House, in 1809. Benjamin, his wife, Persis, and his two sons were well respected in the community, and soon the townspeople changed the town name to Cannonsville in the family's honor. After Cannon's passing in 1839, his two boys, Benjamin Jr. and George, continued to reside in and operate the Cannonsville House, later converted to the Community House. The peaceful town of Cannonsville's only disturbance was an occasional explosion of dynamite from a mountaintop where bluestone was being quarried

The cut pine and hemlocks not needed for domestic use were logged and rafted downriver to Philadelphia. Sawmills and gristmills were numerous, as well as blacksmiths and cobblers. By the middle of the nineteenth century, enterprising settlers had rapidly cleared the surrounding valley. Later, the Erie Railroad opened the vast market for raw milk and other dairy products. Dairy farming soon took the lead in the growing community. A twin bridge spanned the river that led into town. A war memorial was on the left, and along Main Street sat the old Community House, Adams General Store, and a barber shop. There were three churches, two schools, three taverns, a cemetery, and a century-old covered bridge.

A Battle for Water Rights

Shortly after the Revolutionary War the problems of water supply for the region and navigation, energy, and flood control issues of the Delaware River began. These matters were shared by New York, New Jersey, Pennsylvania, and even Delaware, and led to more than two hundred years of disputes and poorly planned cooperative efforts, including the proposed Tocks Island Dam.

The Delaware River supplied early merchants with an inexpensive way to transport goods to downriver markets. The numerous tributaries also allowed for essential transportation of goods and supplies as well. People became so dependent on the streams and the Delaware that in 1783 Pennsylvania and New Jersey decided to appoint commissioners to decide ownership of each. The Delaware became equally free to use by each state, which meant that no state could build a dam across the river without the consent of the other.

In 1897 the state legislatures enacted a law allowing companies to be formed specifically for hydroelectric dams. In the 1920s the timber raft industry collapsed and opened the doors to dam building on the river system.

Finding clean drinking water had been a problem for settlers since the sixteenth century. When the Dutch settled in New Amsterdam

(Manhattan Island) in 1625, the inhabitants depended on surface waters from springs, ponds, and streams, including a forty-eight-acre, fifty-to-sixty-eight-foot-deep "Ketch-Hook" pond. A year later, Dutch merchant Pieter Schagen purchased the entire island (Manhattan Island) from the Lenape for a mere sixty guilders (twenty-four dollars).

When the English took occupation, the population rose to 1,500, and the first stone-lined wells became fouled with sewage. By 1748, locals claimed that not even the horses would drink the stuff. The first water distribution system was built in 1774 and consisted of a network of wooden pipes, wells, and a pond, which served as a reservoir. However, the Revolutionary War stopped progress and slowed the completion of the project.

The supply system became inefficient and later abandoned. In 1799, the New York State legislature passed a "water act" for supplying clean water. By 1800, the city's population had swelled to sixty thousand. The city council accepted the bill; however, it gave the authority for water resources to the Manhattan Company (now Chase Manhattan Bank), incorporated by Assemblyman Aaron Burr, which now had complete control over the city's water supply with a mandate to solve the problem within ten years.

Banking became more profitable for Burr, and little was accomplished except to lay wooden water mains that carried an inadequate supply of water to less than a third of the city's population. By 1830, New York City's population had grown to two hundred thousand, and it was still without a sewer system and dependent on a groundwater supply said to have been polluted with one hundred tons of daily excrement.

With cholera epidemics occurring and a devastating fire in 1835, the city was forced to find a new clean water source. Greenwich Village was settled by one hundred thousand residents who, fleeing the water-related cholera epidemic of 1832, moved their homes from south Manhattan in the search for clean water. Just three years later, when further groundwater contamination occurred, the Manhattan Common Council approved for the first time a plan to tap a new source of water outside the city.

By 1842, new technology and the use of iron pipes made the project to dam the Croton River of Westchester County possible. However, New Yorkers' celebration upon gaining the Croton water was short-lived: The city's population grew from 300,000 in 1842 to 1.2 million in 1883, making the Croton supply insufficient. Some improvements were made in the 1850s through the 1960s when flush toilets and a city-wide sewerage system was established. However, as the Croton system expanded, so did the city's population, reaching 3 million by 1910.

The city turned its eyes toward the clean waters of the Catskill Mountains to its north. Between 1907 and 1928, New York City built the Catskill supply system above the Hudson River, connecting the Schoharie and Ashokan Reservoirs by 144 miles of aqueducts. But even before completion, the city determined the water supply was already inadequate and predicted it would run out of water by 1930. The city engineers looked for an alternative source and considered the Upper Delaware watershed.

In 1923, the Delaware River Treaty was created by legislative action between the states of New York, New Jersey, and Pennsylvania. The state commissioner's job was to negotiate an interstate agreement that would govern any interstate water projects in the Delaware River Basin. Two years later New York City, the federal government, and the US Army Corps of Engineers conducted work on drafting a compact, which they adopted on January 24, 1925, that established a permanent regulatory interstate Tri-State Delaware River Commission. The proposed compact stipulated that Pennsylvania, New York, and New Jersey share equally the Delaware River water above Port Jervis. Below that point the water is shared only by New Jersey and Pennsylvania.

The three states continually ran into politically motivated hurdles while attempting to pass the compact bill. Pennsylvania and the powerful Lehigh Coal and Navigation Company lobbied vigorously against the bill's passage. The company had been given water rights to the Lehigh River one hundred years earlier and wanted to keep its Philadelphia customers. New York State, which had the most to gain, passed the compact quickly. New Jersey sided with Pennsylvania, and the bill was defeated.

A newer and less ambitious compact was approved by the commission in 1927, which gave each state an allocation of six hundred million gallons per day. Once again the bill was defeated by Pennsylvania and New Jersey in fear that the water flow would be restricted below Port

Jervis and turn the lower Delaware into a trickle. New Jersey was also concerned about the quality of restricted water and killed the bill.

New York City threatened to sue and made preparations to begin an independent water diversion project. New Jersey reacted quickly, and on May 29, 1929, the attorney general's office filed a lawsuit in the US Supreme Court against New York State and New York City to keep the city from diverting water out of the Delaware Basin. In the suit, New Jersey claimed that the diverted water would destroy the Delaware River Basin environmentally and claimed that the Secretary of War had to approve any diversions that would affect the river's navigability. New Jersey also claimed that NYC's use of water was extravagant.

The New York Board of Water Supply (now the New York City Department of Environmental Protection) submitted a plan to the Board of Estimate and Apportionment for the development of more water supply systems within the state of New York on the upper portion of Rondout Creek (Hudson River watershed) and certain Delaware River tributaries that included the East and West Branches of the river as well as the Neversink River.

On May 4, 1931, the US Supreme Court's Justice Oliver Wendell Holmes stated his case: "A river is more than an amenity, it is a treasure. It offers a necessity of life that must be rationed among those who have power over it."

The Supreme Court decree ruled that water must be "apportioned equitable." New York City could take 440 million gallons a day for its reservoir on the East Branch of the Delaware, and during any time the stage of the Delaware River falls below 1,535 cubic feet per second (cfs) at Port Jervis, New York, or Trenton, New Jersey, or both, being equivalent to a flow of 1,535 cfs at Port Jervis and 3,400 cfs at Trenton, water shall be released from one or more of the impounding reservoirs of New York City in sufficient volume to restore the flow at Port Jervis and Trenton.

Soon after the 1931 US Supreme Court ruling, New York City sent its engineers representing the Board of Water Supply of New York to the East and West Branch valleys, searching for suitable locations for dams to store the Catskills' clean river water.

The valley residents and other affected localities in Delaware County became resentful of NYC's incursions into their homelands and organized in protest. They held several contentious meetings in Delhi, New York, to prevent the encroachment of the Board of Water Supply. It was all in vain. A right of eminent domain was enforced that allowed the city to conclude the final purchase of land in the East and West Branch valleys.

Pepacton and Neversink Reservoirs

The city's first target to build a dam in the Catskills was in the least populated and relatively unspoiled East Branch Valley, displacing 946 people in 1942 in order to build it. Two decades later the eighteen-mile-long reservoir known as Pepacton was completed. Submerged in silence were four East Branch towns—Arena, Pepacton, Shavertown, Union Grove—all underneath 155 billion gallons of water, along with one-half of the Delaware Northern Railroad in the process.

The reservoir located above Downsville, New York, is most popular for its brown trout and smallmouth bass fishery; both species are caught annually at trophy sizes. Channel catfish have been caught with more consistency in recent years.
GARTH LENZ

In 1954, after completion of Pepacton Reservoir and the smaller Neversink Reservoir, the 1931 court decree became superseded when the US Supreme Court issued a decree in the case of *New Jersey v. New York*, which established an equitable allocation under federal common law. A lawsuit between states is one of the few instances in which the US Supreme Court hears a case that has not come up through the trial and appellate courts.

The 1954 ruling by the US Supreme Court, *New Jersey v. New York City*, set forth an allocation system (pending completion of Cannonsville Reservoir) for drawing out water from the river that each state and city was required to follow under federal common law under the following terms:

- Allocated to New York City the equivalent of eight hundred million gallons per day from the city's three Delaware Basin reservoirs, effective when all three of those reservoirs were fully constructed.
- Required compensating releases to maintain a minimum flow of 1,750 cubic feet per second at Montague, New Jersey.
- Required compensating flows to prevent saltwater intrusion that could contaminate Philadelphia drinking water.
- Granted division rights to New Jersey of up to 100 million gallons per day from the basin without compensating releases to maintain a minimum flow of 1,750 cubic feet per second at Montague, New Jersey
- Established an excess quantity, known as excessive release quantity, to be released from the reservoirs each year.

These five terms became the essential elements of the US Supreme Court Decree, equivalent to a court order, and those elements became the law of the river. The legislature, just as the US Supreme Court, has the power to provide for the allocation of water resources between states. The Supreme Court ruling ended a very important decade for the Delaware River and outlined the rules that would govern the river for many years thereafter. However, the states could not agree on other matters, such as pollution control, a long-range development plan, and how best to protect the natural river ecosystem in the Delaware Basin.

The solution to those tangible problems turned out to be the creation of a new water resource agency, unlike any interstate commission before or since. President John F. Kennedy signed the measure into law on September 27, 1961, creating the Delaware River Basin Compact (Compact). The governors of Pennsylvania, New Jersey, New York, and Delaware sit on the commission, and the US president's appointee usually is selected from the US Army Corps of Engineers.

"The rules for playing the water game have now been established," wrote Richard C. Albert in his book *Damming the Dam.*

The Taking of Cannonsville

After twenty-five years pending their fate in the peaceful West Branch valley, bulldozers, trucks, and flamethrowers came in force to the peaceful communities of Cannonsville, Rock Rift, Granton, and Rock Royal. It

The small farming community known as Cannonsville nestled between foothills at the confluence of Trout Creek and the West Branch of the Delaware River.
POSTCARD COURTESY OF EQUINUNK HISTORICAL SOCIETY

had taken a century and a half of dedicated work to build up the towns and farmland in the river valley only to see them destroyed in a matter of weeks—displacing more than four thousand disheartened residents.

Not a tree was left standing in the once heavily forested land. Every house, barn, business, church, and school that remained was demolished; many were burned to the ground. At night fires glowed eerily throughout the smoke-filled valley. During the day bulldozers finished off whatever stone walls, chimneys, and smoldering timbers remained. Trucks hauled away human remains disinterred from the cemeteries and family graveyards.

It was 1963 and the "taking of Cannonsville" by the City of New York was complete. Benjamin Cannon, the founder of this community, dead for 124 years, likely rolled over in his grave. Roger Fuller wrote:

There is nothing to indicate that this picturesque scene is anything other than pure, unadulterated nature. There are no clues to what lies 75 feet below the rowboats in dark submerged silence—roads untraveled for half a century, stone outlines of 200-year-old homesteads—of the Community House, Peg's Tavern, and scores of other former structures. Below the rowboats once-sacred sites lie dormant, long since stripped of graves and nine generations of residents lived and worked, and before that, unknown generations of American Indians called the confluence of these rivers home.

Truth be known, there is one clue to the existence of this secret world that can be still found. It is a road that branches off State Route 10 to the west. That same road that led to Cannonsville fifty years ago is still there, but now it slips beneath the gentle waves and disappears from sight. Watch for it when driving up route 10, but when you come to the fork in the road do not, as the saying goes, "TAKE IT." The City of New York already did!

In 1967, the 17-mile-long Cannonsville dam was the last of four city reservoirs to be completed, spreading its 95.7 million gallons of water over the sunken ghost towns where nine generations of residents once lived. A few landmarks survived the deluge, such as Mt.

Speedwell, reinterred gravesites, and a monument that is dedicated to the memory of those who once served their country.

Not far from Benjamin Cannon's 1809 homestead, reservoir water enters the world's longest gravity-fed aqueduct system 50 to 70 stories belowground to begin an 85-mile journey, eventually combining with the other Catskill reservoirs' aqueducts—Rondout, Neversink, Pepacton—leading to the cement-cased Delaware aqueduct, which flows its water below the Hudson River before reaching the kitchen faucets in the Big Apple.

The Ghost of Lordville

In 1804 twenty-seven-year-old John Lord and his friend Deliverance Adams found their way to Delaware County, New York, where John was granted 690 acres near Equinunk Island (Frisbie) and built the first home

The small hamlet of Lordville is well known for the Kilgour House, with its cold, lifeless, ghost-like mannequin staring eerily out the third-floor window over the town and all who travel through. Some say it is haunted by the ghost of Tom Quick, the self-proclaimed slayer of the Delaware Indians who roamed the banks of the Delaware. Those brave souls who walk the streets of Lordville at night often see a light flicker in a window, telling us that Tom Quick is still around.
LEE HARTMAN

The Lordville train station closed during the mid-twentieth century. EQUINUNK
HISTORICAL SOCIETY

in the area. He and his wife, Lydia, raised six children there, though one
died at an early age.

In the early days of the unnamed settlement, before a bridge had
replaced a ferry on the river, the pedestrian who wanted to cross was
offered a novel and exciting trip by ferryman George Lord. The passenger
was placed in a large basket hanging from a cable and then pulled across
the river safely. If he or she had a horse, it was pulled in a scow and poled
across to the village of Equinunk.

In 1835 John Lord sold land to the Erie Railroad for a right of way to
establish a train station that was completed in 1848. When this nameless

The bridge to the Pennsylvania side of the river connected to the village of Equinunk, Pennsylvania. EQUINUNK HISTORICAL SOCIETY

village got a post office and a railway station, it was christened with a
biblical name, Elam. A year later John's son Alvah became postmaster,
and the village's name was changed to Lordville in honor of his father,
John Lord.

The scow-ferry river crossing was soon outgrown. Local residents,
including John Lord and his sons, encouraged the construction of a
bridge to Equinunk. John Lord could only give moral support to his sons,
as he remained busy taking timber rafts downriver to Philadelphia. In his
seventy-ninth year, he made two raft trips and then passed away. John
Lord willed his interest in the bridge to his grandson John Henry Lord.

Alvah, who formed the Lordville-Equinunk Bridge Company
served as the president and treasurer of the organization. The bridge was
designed by E. F. Harrington of the John A. Roebling's Sons Company
and featured piers spaced farther apart than usual so that the difficult-to-
steer timber rafts could safely float through. The one-lane wire suspension

Roebling's Delaware Aqueduct, also known as the Roebling Bridge, is the oldest existing wire suspension bridge in the United States. It runs 535 feet over the Delaware River, from Minisink Ford, New York, to Lackawaxen, Pennsylvania. Opened in 1849 as an aqueduct connecting two parts of the Delaware & Hudson Canal, it has since been converted to carry automotive traffic and pedestrians.
LEE HARTMAN

bridge with its twin wooden towers and a toll booth opened on New Year's Day 1870.

The early life of the bridge was a busy one. The John Lord Hotel, situated next to the train station, was kept busy with itinerant lumbermen, bluestone miners, and railroad workers. The Lordville community now had seven stores, two hotels (Lord Hotel and Kilgour House), and three acid factories. By 1889 bottled milk shipments were being brought over to the special "milk trains" and shipped downriver to large cities. On October 10, 1903, the wire suspension bridge was destroyed by a devastating flood. It was replaced by an eyebar suspension bridge that opened on June 4, 1904. This second bridge lasted until February 1984 when it was closed due to an undermined pier, which caused one tower to lean and the bridge to sag. The bridge was demolished on November 24, 1986.

Construction of the replacement bridge started in May 1991, and the new bridge opened in 1992.

The Legend of Tom Quick

Thomas Quick Sr. emigrated from Ulster County in about 1733 and was one of the descendants of well-to-do and respectable ancestors who came from Holland to America in 1689. Quick relocated his family on some valuable land on the Pennsylvania side of the Delaware River, built a log cabin, and settled down with no one but the Munsee, a band of the Lenape, for his neighbors. He occupied his time hunting and fishing, together with clearing his acreage. In 1740, six years after his son Thomas Jr. was born, he built a sawmill and a gristmill on a bank of Van der Mark Creek, a tributary of the Delaware River near present-day Milford, Pennsylvania.

During his youth Tom Jr. took to the local Munsee, learned their language, and spent most of his days hunting and fishing with them along the river. While Tom Quick's siblings spent their days in school, he preferred the forest life and the companionship of young Native Americans. Tom Jr. became quite familiar with the Delaware River, exploring its branches, often tracing the headwaters to its very source. This was a huge benefit to him in later years.

Tom Quick Jr. EQUINUNK HISTORICAL SOCIETY

Tom Quick Jr., described by historical writings as having been six feet in height, and taken altogether, rather a raw-boned man; his cheekbones were high; his eyes gray and restless; his hair, before it had been balding by age, was of a dark brown. He was not in the habit of talking very much—in fact, was distant and very quiet in his demeanor. His features were grave and dignified, and seldom relaxed into a smile. He was quite temperate, and rarely drank alcoholic liquors, except cider, of which, like all of Holland blood, he was very fond.

The Quick family had very good relations with the Munsee and frequently spent time together, including occasional overnight stays at the family's cabin. As more settlers came to the area, and with the French and Indian War looming large over the region, the Munsee became apprehensive and began to fear the white man encroaching on their land and hunting ground. The annoyance triggered tribal leaders to plot for the destruction of all white people in the Delaware Valley.

Everything suddenly began to change for Tom Quick Sr. and his family. While he and his two sons and brother-in-law Solomon Decker were cutting ice on the Delaware River, they were ambushed by a warring party. The elder Tom Quick was mortally wounded by a rifle ball shot by an Indian named Muskwink. As Quick was dying, he told his sons to leave him and go save the remaining family. Tom Jr. and his brother escaped the gunfire, but upon returning to the area, they witnessed the Indians rejoicing over the scalping of their father.

Something snapped in young Tom Quick that day, and he now began to preach revenge for the death of his father. Once a friend to both the white settlers and the Munsee, he now carried a dual spirit—loving the settlers and loathing the Indians, most particularly Muskwink. Tom Quick Jr., who became known as "The Avenger of the Delaware," was determined to kill every Native American until he could freely walk along the Delaware River without ever seeing one. Quick became a one-man army, stashing weapons, powder, and rifle balls in the surroundings—such as in small dug-out caves and hollowed-out logs—to ambush the native people and kill them.

There are various tales told about how he tricked the Munsee to their deaths. One such incident occurred when Quick came across an armed tribesman walking in the woods. Tom, who was unarmed at the time, approached the Indian in a friendly manner and spoke to him in his language. He told the man that he could tell him where Tom Quick was and asked if he'd like to see him. The Munsee man agreed, saying that he had heard of him, as he was wanted for killing his people. Tom led him to a high ledge of rocks where he peered over the edge. After a few moments Tom motioned the Indian with his hand to take his place, ostensibly so the Indian could shoot him. As the man stood atop the ledge and asked,

"Where is he?" Tom grabbed his shoulders and hurled him over the edge to the rocks below.

When the French and Indian War ended in 1763, the local Munsee who stayed in the area made peace with the settlers. Around this time, people in the area would assemble to discuss neighborhood events at a county tavern run by a man by the name of Decker, not far from the settlement of Deer Park, New York. Among them were the Cuddebacks, the Gumaers, and the Deckers. Muskwink, who was a frequent visitor of the tavern, calmly appeared one evening. After a few rounds of drinks, he said to the tavern patrons, "Come and toast with me. Here's to all of you. The war is over and the hatchet is buried." Others warned him not to be too sure that the hatchet was buried with Tom Quick Jr.

In a story repeated often in the history of North America, Tom Quick entered Decker's tavern and a war of words ensued. "You, Indian dog!" Quick shouted. "You shot my father and you'll kill no more white men." Muskwink, somewhat liquored up, bravely replied that he was ready for him, and that he could handle him as easy as he did his father. Tom could not control himself any longer and seized a rifle that was hanging by hooks on a ceiling beam. He cocked the loaded and primed rifle and pressed it against Muskwink's chest, forcing him out of the tavern. The Indian had no option but to obey. After walking several miles on the main road toward a Huguenot settlement, Tom finally got his revenge and shot Muskwink dead.

In 1795, while on his deathbed, Tom Quick Jr. claimed the personal achievement of having killed ninety-nine Indians—all of them from the Munsee band of Lenni Lenape, including women, infants, and whole families—as a lifelong revenge for the brutal murder of his father. Legend says that before he died, he begged to have an old Indian who lived nearby brought to him for killing, so he could claim an even one hundred victims.

To many of the early settlers, who carried the mental and physical scars of war, Tom Quick Jr. was viewed as a hero, and they felt no desire to bring him to justice; in today's world his tendencies would more likely be diagnosed as those of a psychopath.

In 1889 the town of Milford erected the "Settlers Monument" and transferred Tom Quick's remains there from his resting place in the nearby town of Matamoras. Legend or not, people eventually questioned whether someone of Quick's reputation should be immortalized. Then, in 1997 someone took a sledgehammer to the monument, causing extensive damage. It was repaired, but not replaced. Several attempts were made to put it back, but the town repeatedly backed off under criticism. Tom Quick's monument currently stands in a storage shed. His bones are still buried in Matamoras, which once held his monument for over one hundred years. Much controversy has ensued, but for the meantime a plaque has been installed on top of the grave in the middle of Sarah Street, which reads:

> *This is a gravesite and should be respected as such. This monument and its inscriptions reflect a dialog and mindset of the era in which it was first erected, circa 1889, which was 94 years after the death of Tom Quick. Many stories have been written about Tom Quick, but there is not enough documented evidence to separate truth from fiction. However, research into his life continues to be encouraged by the Pike County Historical Society.*

The Making of a Fishing Camp

This was no ordinary driveway. It was more like the beginning of a steeply pitched ski slope, a rough and rocky incline that looked to be the point of no return. No wonder the local realtor declined to take me to the property—or maybe he didn't want me to see those ghostly looking mannequins staring out the third-floor window of an old hotel reportedly haunted by Tom Quick. This was Lordville, New York, population twenty-five. "How could I be lost?" I reasoned.

Sitting in the car, my fishing friend and I viewed the stony slope cropped with four-foot rock banks on each side of the one-lane road. I asked, "What do you think, Tom?" "Your car—your call," he answered bluntly. I had no choice but to go for it! The four-hundred-foot-long dirt roadway took us to an open field where a small, rough-shod building was tucked next to a dense patch of woods. It wasn't what I expected. The realtor had told me it was a rustic cabin. He was being kind. The entire structure was made of T-111 plywood with a steep tar-papered roof.

"Doc" Homer, a descendent of the Lord family and the architect of this well-hidden bungalow, greeted us at the door. As we walked into the cabin, the floor bounced like a swimming pool springboard despite being nailed to a foundation made of discarded railroad ties. Flake-board walls a half inch thick covered the entire downstairs area, which consisted of two long, narrow rooms separated by a thin flake-board wall with a thirty-two-inch-wide entrance door. There were no cabinets, no carpet, no nothing except for a beat-up electric kitchen oven and two chipped porcelain sinks—one in the kitchen and another in a tiny bathroom next to a leaky tub, both hooked to exposed PVC piping.

The newest part of the building was a pull-down ladder that led to the upstairs that Doc called the bedroom suite. The only heat for the upstairs sleeping quarters came from the downstairs woodstove's chimney pipe, which poked through the un-shingled roof.

Doc Homer, a self-described chiropractor, besides being a Lord descendant was also a longtime Lordville resident. "I built this place for

The two-story plywood building was perfectly concealed near the Delaware River.
LEE HARTMAN

my daughter," he said proudly. Homer's flake-board palace appealed to no one except me. I said to Doc, "What are you asking for the four-acre property?" Tom rolled his eyes and sneakily side-kicked my foot as if to say what the F#@%K are you doing? Doc, without hesitation, said, "Fifty-nine thousand dollars." After a few eye blinks I got my bearing and countered, "I'll give you fifty and no more." Got side-kicked again! Doc didn't relent on his price. Disappointed, I gave him my phone number should he reconsider the offer and walked away.

My twenty-five-foot Dutch Craft trailer, which I'd used for a fishing lodge the past ten years, sat on the bank of the river at the Equinunk Campground. The place was closing—eviction notices had been issued that put me in a bind to store the trailer somewhere. The Lordville property was the perfect place to start a full-time guide service business. The four-acre property had well water, spring water, electric and phone service, a sewage tank, and, most importantly, a railroad crossing that led to Doc's private river access one hundred yards away.

For two weeks I stewed nervously in my Pennsburg residence waiting for a Doc Homer phone call. A week later it finally came; he accepted my offer. After some last-minute haggling to gain use of the river access, Doc relented and included the deeded right-of-way to the river launch site. The Lord family resident became my new neighbor. Indian Springs Fly Fishing Camp was born—but not without a modern-day makeover. My weekends were spent under a leaky roof, sleeping fitfully on a bed with an old, squeaky spring mattress, which made for a tired workday.

For lodging purpose the cabin either needed to be torn down or reconstructed. My weekly paycheck decided the dilemma, choosing the latter. With the help of friends bribed with free float trips, we managed to shingle the roof, tear out the floor, refurbish the upstairs, and throw out the bathtub for starters, making the Bisbee lumberyard in Hancock very happy.

A new road, a replaced sewage system, an electrical upgrade, and reconstruction of the lodge and a new cabin completed the funky resort by its second year.

Guides in the early 1990s were but a few. River anglers who traveled from afar were on their own, spending their nights at campgrounds or motels. Indian Springs Fly Fishing Camp opened for business in 1992 and became the first fishing lodge located on a bank of the Delaware River. It wasn't the Taj Mahal for sure, but it did function well, providing food and comfort for up to six people.

The movie *A River Runs Through It* made its debut during the fall of that year, a story about a family living an idyllic life in rural Montana who spent summer afternoons fly fishing on a wild trout river. The average American embraced the hit film, and it brought attention to fly fishing, something many people considered to be a snobbish ritual.

Enchanted by the movie, urban dwellers left their claustrophobic offices to seek a breath of fresh air. They purchased rods, reels, flies, and any other necessary paraphernalia. The city folks soon put a spotlight on the river. In rented cars they traveled three hours to a cool-water trout river called the Delaware to emulate Brad Pitt's trout fishing on the Blackfoot River in Montana. Guide services on the Delaware, from Deposit to Callicoon, New York, began to sprout along the healthy waterway.

Indian Springs Fly Fishing Camp consisted of two cabins and a small river lodge.
LEE HARTMAN

In 1994 a second new cabin completed my piece of heaven. Indian Springs Fly Fishing Camp now had room enough to handle ten people.

You'll find them all here. Every major species and many of the sub-species of caddis, mayfly, and stonefly are found on this river. Small fish are here as well: minnows, shad, and the fry of spawning trout. Ann McIntosh is right when she writes that for trout, the Delaware is an extensive smorgasbord and, to be successful, anglers must match the hatch with precision that's rarely necessary elsewhere. Its rainbows and brown trout roam the waters of the river, migrating from deeper waters of the main stem up into its branches and feeders to spawn.
—*JOHN ROSS,* America's 100 Best Trout Streams

Being a first-time trout angler on a fickle river that's generally malicious to newcomers is as difficult a place to cut one's teeth fishing with tiny hair-spun flies as any. The Delaware, huge by eastern standards, with one hundred yards of fast, broken water flowing into lake-like pools, intimidates even the best of anglers. When the summer sun heats the air, producing sweat on your brow, anglers will reason there is not a fish in the river. Catching a trout in those conditions is like beating the house with a stacked deck. But when cool conditions prevail, trout become plentiful and so do the bugs—lots of them. Hordes of tiny olives, blizzards of caddis, and breathtaking size 10 drakes frequently carpet the water surface.

The Delaware is special and so are the rainbow trout: wild, fat, and feisty with lightning speed, rivaling that of an Atlantic salmon. Bug master Al Caucci christened the rainbow as the "Crown Jewel of the Delaware." *Sports Afield* magazine called the Delaware the greatest trout river in the East—a river equal to the Yellowstone, the Madison, and the Big Hole in Montana.

It was high times at Indian Springs. Wine was the guests' drink of choice and served at each dinner. The wine bottle corks, speared with old trout-caught flies, lined the lodge walls and were christened "corkers." Fish over eighteen inches were immortalized with the angler's name and the date and location where it was caught, giving credit to the angler, fish, and water conditions. There were many corkers, but only a few revealed a

The initial dining area served each guest a hearty dinner after their day of fishing. LEE HARTMAN

twenty-inch-plus rainbow trout that had unusually surpassed the normal trout life span of four to five years. The big-bruising browns, less abundant in the main stem but inches bigger, were more often caught during nasty days. If you wanted to catch a two-footer, you prayed for drizzling rain or you fished till midnight.

The river's popularity, despite unpredictable summer flows, escalated with each new season. By the end of the decade, more than three dozen guides, all licensed by the National Park Service, were required to submit catch reports. Rainbow trout, most prominent in the Wild and Scenic corridor, outnumbered brown trout by six to one. The West and East Branches, blessed with wild brown trout, dominated these river sections.

The Delaware River, listed under the Wild and Scenic Rivers Act, became a great resource and a financial boon to an economically depressed region. Managing reservoir releases for water supply and the cold-water fishery with downstream temperature and flow targets employed a complex set of rules that required full-time vigilance.

Casting Blind

Sight fishing for surface-feeding trout is an addiction for many fly anglers. They become purists—dry flies only—trying to "match the hatch," often referring to the fly hatches by their scientific names. For hours, anglers will sit and stare at a pool surface or riffle waiting for the right moment to cast to a sipping trout. When they finally see the ring of a rise, only then will they make the cast. If there's no hatch, they go to the nearest bar or fly shop and philosophize about why they hadn't caught or seen a fish.

There are others who don't give up that easy. They are the roamers on the river, who constantly change flies and blind cast to every conceivable spot, hoping for a fish to take their offering. I suppose I am in that category and very often go without a bite, nibble, or tug. But when you do get surprised with a take of your offering, you frequently break the fly off and lose the fish.

Blind casting took on new meaning when I met Bob Runge, a cofounder of the Family School (now French Woods Sports & Art Center), a boarding school for high-risk teenagers that was located five miles outside the village of Hancock. Patricia (Sam) Decker, who guided for Indian Springs, introduced me to Bob, who actually was blind. His son and grandson had bought him a float trip for his seventy-second birthday.

After picking up lunches and making formal introductions, Sam and Bob's son, Larry, followed us to the East Branch with her drift boat in tow. Bob explained that he quit fishing at the age of forty when he'd been declared legally blind. Looking at his antiquated equipment I knew he wasn't lying. He brought with him an ancient fiberglass rod equipped with a thirty-year-old automatic reel loaded with a god-awful weather-beaten dry fly line that would sink like a rock. "Let's put this rod to rest for now," I said politely. "You can use my rod."

Bob sat in the front of my fourteen-foot raft, while his fourteen-year-old grandson sat in the back. I rigged up his leader with a stonefly nymph and large strike indicator. After some roll casting lessons of no more than twenty feet, Bob felt comfortable enough to fish. We anchored a mile above the hamlet of Fish's Eddy, and his strike indicator sank quickly in a three-foot-deep run that telegraphed a fish was on. The well-hooked rainbow leaped skyward as the line raced upstream. "Reel in the slack,

Bob," I exclaimed anxiously. He did, only backwards. The line spilled onto his lap like a pile of spaghetti. The fish never stopped and soon the line tangled into a "bird's nest" trying to rip through the rod guides. The fish was gone along with the leader. Bob asked, "Was that a trout?" "Yup," I answered. It was time for lesson number two: how to reel properly.

Bob sat back on his seat as if nothing had happened. The fish had hooked itself—he never felt the strike and never saw it jump. It was a lost memory. After another lesson on how to properly reel in the line, Bob was ready to try fishing again.

The mid-May weather and river conditions were perfect both for floating and wading. The grandson, content just to watch his grandfather fish, helped when needed. Very soon we approached Partridge Island, where the river split. On the left side a row of tall, overhanging hemlocks looked enticing to me. The broken pocket water, no deeper than two feet under the branches, looked perfectly suited for trout and became my target.

Fearful of Bob making a cast into the trees, I anchored the raft and instructed him to make a cast. Nothing happened. His repeated presentations were short of their target. While lifting the anchor I told him to make another cast. Bob's cast was dead-on and drifted naturally under a tree branch where a big fish grabbed his fly. I yelled, "Lift!" and the hooked fish quickly turned downstream, peeling off line. Bob followed instructions perfectly, keeping a tight line as the big brown trout fought recklessly in a hundred yards of swift current.

The trout tired as we approached the quiet pool where I could safely land the beastly thing. No sooner had it come into the net than Sam Decker and Bob's son arrived to witness his father's catch. The only person who didn't appear excited about the catch was Bob Runge himself. He had no idea what he'd caught despite being told how big the bragging-size fish measured—twenty-four inches!

A week later I delivered a photo of his catch to the Family School, where Bob worked as a director. His coworkers raved about his success and placed the photo in their monthly newspaper, the *Family Times*. It was only then that Bob Runge realized what he had accomplished.

A hefty East Branch brown trout caught on a home-spun stone fly imitation.
LEE HARTMAN

Bob Runge cofounded the Family School at French Woods, New York. Today it is
now a sports and arts summer camp for young high school students. LEE HARTMAN

The Perfect Storm

The Northeast Floods of January 1996 were the result of a very rapid snowmelt punctuated by a short but intense rainfall. What made this event so unusual was the nature and the intensity of the snowmelt, combined with the intense rainfall for this time of year, over such a large geographical area. The flooding was compounded by ice movement and jamming in many of the rivers and streams. The floods were described by some as a "flash flood" for main-stem rivers due to the unprecedented rates of rise recorded during this event.

—US GEOLOGICAL SOCIETY REPORT

Heavy rain of more than 4.5 inches during January 18–19, 1996, combined with unseasonably warm temperatures, fell on at least forty-five inches of melting snow in the Catskill Mountains region. Damages to highways, bridges, and private property exceeded one hundred million dollars.

The storm and flooding claimed ten lives, stranded hundreds of people, destroyed or damaged thousands of homes and businesses, and closed hundreds of roads. In Delaware County, forty miles east of Binghamton, a roadway collapsed and four cars plunged into the Cannonsville Reservoir in the town of Tompkins. A family of five was killed that included Donald Cobb of Lakewood, Pennsylvania, and Melvin Cobb of Cadosia, New York, and another man went missing. But several people were rescued in the incident, including a police officer who spent twenty minutes trapped in an air pocket in his car before getting out.

The most severely affected area was in the Catskill Mountains region where three Delaware River tributaries run through the villages. Damages and losses within Delaware County alone exceeded twenty million dollars. In the nearby village of Walton, hundreds of homes and businesses—almost every structure in town—were five feet deep in floodwaters. "The heart of the village is in really bad shape," Walton's Mayor Jack Kelly said.

Trout Movement Study 1995–1997

A large pulse of cool Cannonsville water bound for the Montague flow target filled the river perfectly for late season fishing. My raft sat at the edge of the river awaiting Dr. Dave Langan for an eight-mile float trip to Long Eddy. The Whitesboro, New York, native had never fished the lower section before—a section of the Delaware haunted by rainbow trout.

At the time, New York State Department of Environmental Conservation's (NYSDEC) fisheries manager Norm McBride was in his second year of a three-year study titled "Radiotelemetry Study of Trout Movements in the Delaware Tailwaters and the Beaver Kill." Dave Langan, a fellow Delaware River Committee leader for New York State Trout Unlimited (NYSTU), supported the effort for the three-year program, which began in 1995. His mission to Indian Springs was to coordinate fund-raising efforts with Pennsylvania Trout Unlimited and help fund the radiotelemetry program.

The hard-working Trout Unlimited-er, who'd witnessed the wrath of the January 1996 blizzard and flood devastation on the Catskill tributaries, was somewhat concerned about the NYSDEC's remedial work taking place on many of the cold-water tributaries that entered the East Branch watershed, and he filled me in on the details of the stream work:

Throughout the spring season I saw heavy equipment working in the Catskills. Like many other TUers, I felt the work was necessary and appropriate with proper NYSDEC oversight. Well, the dredging didn't stop. By July I became restless and grew concerned and reported what appeared to be questionable work. Nothing happened—then came August.

During one August morning last year, my daughter Sonya and I were joined by a NYSDEC staff person to help radiotag a rainbow trout on the lower East Branch near the mouth of Read Creek. After tagging the trout we returned to fish Read only to find it turned into pure mud. The NYSDEC representative concurred with us that this was a problem and drove back to the Stamford office. I followed up with the regional office, and they assured us it would be handled properly. It wasn't. Over 1,000 permits were given out to overzealous bulldozer operators—turning dozens of streams into ditches.

This isn't trout versus people. There is nothing more frightening or fatiguing than a flood. But what happened afterward was beyond what was reasonable and necessary.
—JOCK CUNNINGHAM, NATIONAL TROUT UNLIMITED ECOLOGIST

The 'dozer onslaught impacted sixty-five miles of Catskill trout streams, on which there also was twelve miles of illegal landowner activity. The NYSTU Delaware River Committee members teamed up with National Trout Unlimited (National TU) and all hell broke loose. In early December the NYSDEC commissioner left office and was replaced by a more pragmatic administrator. National TU pressed a more cooperative commissioner for proper restoration, education, and a review of government process to ensure that such an event next time would be handled more responsibly.

The tributaries and trout habitat below Lordville were fairly intact after the 1996 winter flood. One nice rainbow rewarded my NYSTU Delaware River Committee counterpart on that gorgeous day in September. A year later, a well-deserved Trout Unlimited award honored Dr. David Langan for his gallant conservation efforts in the state of New York.

The primary goal of NYSDEC's feasibility study was to track trout migration related to seasonal spawning and to determine the extent of their use of Delaware tributaries for refuge and spawning. Locating prime spawning areas within the river system allows management practices to be tailored to protect these areas.

The tailwater sections lie below New York City–owned reservoirs. Trout in these areas are dependent on the bottom releases of cold water, whereas the Beaver Kill is not influenced by dam releases. To properly track trout movements within the Delaware River system, radio tags were surgically implanted in 111 trout, including 77 brown trout and 34 rainbow trout. The fish tagged with transmitting units were found in the East

Branch below Pepacton Reservoir, the West Branch below Cannonsville Reservoir, the main stem, and the Beaver Kill tributary, a freestone river.

Elevated summer water temperatures that create stressful and/or lethal conditions are a common occurrence in the Upper Delaware River. During stressful periods, trout must seek thermal refuge to survive. In particular, in the Delaware River below Hancock and the lower East Branch below the Beaver Kill, trout will often migrate toward the West Branch or upper East Branch, while others seek out cold-water tributaries and seeping spring holes.

In 1995 fifty-five tagged trout were released throughout the Upper Delaware system, thirteen of which moved out of the area in which they were initially tagged and went into another river.

Throughout the warm summer and fall, trout tagged in the West Branch remained there, as cool water kept temperatures suitable for survival. The inter-river moves were the most common by Delaware River and lower East Branch trout and the least common by trout in the West Branch and upper East Branch, where water remained cool.

The West Branch trout, known to stay stationary throughout most of the year, changed their target area in 1996 and focused on lower sections of the river system. A greater number of tagged trout were monitored in the Beaver Kill, the lower East Branch, and in the main stem of the river. The emphasis was on studying the movements of each tagged fish in the three river sections that often remain warmer during the summer months.

Twenty-five of the fifty-six tagged trout in 1996 moved from their respective tagging location. Higher reservoir discharges and rain events maintained suitable water temperatures for trout in each section. However, rainbow trout, the most mobile of the two species of fish, showed much more varied movement patterns than was expected.

One female rainbow, tagged on March 13 at the junction of the West Branch, migrated to Callicoon Creek, some thirty miles downriver, and spent the entire summer there. The sixteen-inch, three-year-old fish then left the lower refuge area in late August and settled for two months in Ten-Mile River, located a few miles below Narrowsburg, New York. In early spring the fish then returned to the Upper Delaware confluence to live out her four years and later died in the fall of 1997. The round-trip covered 127 miles of water—the longest distance traveled of any tagged fish in the three-year study.

Another four-year-old rainbow trout, tagged at Balls Eddy, Pennsylvania, in the early spring of 1996, exited the system entirely. This movement, from the West Branch to the main stem of the Delaware, was believed to be due to the time of season that the fish was tagged. It was assumed that this trout was originally a main-stem resident and that it was tagged during its migration to spawn. After the tag was implanted, the rainbow returned to its residence in the main Delaware River and remained stationary throughout the study period.

Rainbow trout seek tributaries in which to spawn during the spring season, while brown trout are fall-spawning fish in local tributaries and upper river sections of the East and West Branches. There are many tributaries in the lower main stem that are accessible to trout and capable of supporting the various life stages, used as spawning tributaries and nursery water.

There were twenty-one hatchery brown trout tagged during the three-year period, with only two entering a tributary, presumably to spawn. Rainbow trout in the Delaware system were found to spawn twice in their short four- or five-year lifetime, returning to the same stream in which they were presumably born. The brown trout, whose life span is a few years more than its rainbow cousin, can either spawn within the upper West Branch or enter a local tributary for this purpose.

The NYSDEC trout study proved to be a valuable tool to manage the Upper Delaware tailwater fishery. The monitored trout spawned in at least fourteen of the ninety-six tributaries located within the drainage basin. The Beaver Kill trout-tagging study gave fisheries managers another perspective. The low frequency of movement by Delaware tailwater trout into the Beaver Kill and Beaver Kill trout seeking refuge in the upper East Branch indicated that the Beaver Kill should be managed independently of the Delaware tailwaters.

The Upper Delaware River has gained significant notoriety during the past ten years, despite erratic flows, torn-up tributaries, and a winter flood. Anglers, guide services, boaters, and outfitters increased in numbers, which continued to strengthen the economy of the Upper Delaware region.

The American Sportfishing Association and Trout Unlimited, in a jointly sponsored 1996 study titled "The Economic Impact of Trout Fishing on the Delaware River Tailwaters in New York," found that angling for Delaware's wild trout resulted in $17.69 million in local revenues and generated some $30 million in local economic activity.

- 9 -

Fishing When the Sun Don't Shine

The impoundments of water in the city's reservoirs river flows were now the responsibility of lawyers, politicians, engineers, and state and city commissioners, taking it out of Mother Nature's hands. The US Supreme Court did not take into consideration that bottom releases would fuel the river with cold, fertile water that would manufacture a dramatic change of aquatic life in the Delaware River. The warm-blooded fish population began diminishing in the Upper Delaware system only to be replaced with brown and rainbow trout. The tributaries would become a vital part of the Delaware system, producing the wild fingerlings that mature into the spirited-fighting trout the Upper Delaware is known for today.

Cannonsville Dam. GARTH LENZ

When It Rains, It Pours

My six-month-old Labrador retriever, Bandit, alerted me with a loud bark when Kurt Berry pulled into the driveway at 6 a.m. It was mid-May, perfect weather for our planned one-day fishing trip to the Upper Delaware. Quickly, we loaded our fishing gear into the trunk of a 1977 Oldsmobile for the three-hour ride for a day's fishing. "I am not going to watch a dog and two kids all day—you are going to take him," my wife told me in no uncertain terms. There was no way I wanted to take a six-month-old pup fishing. Nevertheless, to keep peace I relented to her last-minute demand.

Kurt Berry, a newly hired employee at the pharmaceutical firm where I was employed, immediately became a friend when I learned he was a fly fisherman. My work partner had never fished the Upper Delaware before and was excited to try new waters.

We arrived mid-morning and parked the Oldsmobile next to Ralph Delmarter's summer fruit stand located by Route 191. Bandit anxiously got out of the car to get relief from the three-hour drive and headed to a grassy field adjoining the West Branch. As we prepared ourselves for the day's fishing, a lone Jeep sped toward us, and Bandit began to scurry across the field. The dog didn't stop running, nor did the car, suddenly sideswiping him and ripping open the skin, which rolled halfway down to his paws, on both his front legs.

Helpless, we carried the pup to the car and laid him on the backseat. I drove to the Circle E restaurant in Hancock, not knowing where a veterinarian could be found on a Sunday morning. Luck was not on our side. The nearest veterinarian was a horse doctor named Hank Nebzadowski, located near Pleasant Mount some twenty-five miles away on the Pennsylvania side of the river. After a forty-minute drive we arrived only to be told by his wife that he was out on a house call. An hour went by before "Doc" finally showed. The young vet sedated Bandit, stitched him up, and told us we could now go fishing. "Bandit should sleep for the rest of the day," he said.

Kurt and I arrived a few miles below the river's confluence eager to get a few hours to fish as Bandit continued to sleep peacefully in the backseat. Not more than an hour went by when threatening storm clouds appeared and soon spewed out a torrential downpour. The rain didn't stop.

Soaked to the bone we crawled up the riverbank to wait out the storm in the car. In a rush for cover we quickly threw our broken-down rods and wet gear into the trunk and slammed it shut, not realizing I'd laid the car keys inside the trunk.

The front driver-side window was cracked open no more than an inch or two. With no tools, the situation looked hopeless. A lone truck parked forty yards away had two fishermen inside the vehicle waiting for the rain to stop. Our luck soon changed. They had a coat hanger and a set of tools we could borrow.

After unlocking the car door with the coat hanger, we then struggled to remove the backseat in order to get to the small access panel and expose the trunk. The keys were lying on the back ledge but out of arms' reach. Carefully guiding the coat hanger onto the key ring, I was able to pull them out. Drenched from the rainstorm, we called it a day. Bandit continued to sleep, and after a warm coffee and a bite to eat, we headed for Pennsburg.

Two hours before midnight we arrived home. Bandit, now wide awake, looked in good spirits, like a kid in a playground. Kurt said his goodbyes, got into his car, and left. Tired, soaked, and hungry, I struggled through the garage with wet gear and a broken-down fly rod, unknowingly dragging a nine-foot leader attached with a size 10 Woolly Bugger across the floor. The dog chased the buggy-looking artificial fly and quickly grabbed and crunched it like a dog biscuit. The fishing trip from hell continued.

Fearful of hooking him in the throat with the fly, I cut the leader. Off we went ten miles to the emergency clinic in Quakertown. The doctor's X-ray revealed that the Woolly Bugger was in his stomach and seemingly unattached. He suggested I check his bowel movement in the morning to see if it passed. Sure enough, the green-grizzly Woolly Bugger was there, leader and all, topping off a shitty weekend.

For the next sixteen years, Bandit was my fishing companion. Born in the fall of 1982, he collapsed unexpectedly at Indian Springs Camp in June 1999. That very day, with my daughter, Nicole, and lady friend, Sara, I drove the ailing dog to the same Quakertown Animal Hospital, only to have him euthanized while in my arms.

The Building of Cannonsville Dam

No reservoir system in the country, possibly in the world, is as complicated to manage as that of the NYC Delaware Basin. The constraints determined by the 1954 Court Decree are set in stone. The yearly water needs of four states and a city too often leave little water to protect the fishery. Yet these prominent wild trout have managed to survive despite the most unlikely conditions.

The Pepacton Reservoir on the East Branch in Delaware County was built between 1947 and 1954. The 2,400-foot-long dam at Downsville impounds the largest of the city's reservoirs. Eighteen miles long, it covers nine square miles and has a fifty-five-mile shoreline and a capacity of 140 billion gallons.

When US Supreme Court justice Oliver Wendell Holmes made his decision, he took the flows out of nature's hands and put them in the lap of state, federal, and city politicians. The decree contained no provisions for minimum conservation releases nor did it address the ecological necessities of the river's newly created cold-water habitat, but it did specify that the water must be shared in an equitable way.

Pepacton Reservoir. GARTH LENZ

174

After the completion of Cannonsville Reservoir in 1967, the Delaware flows were never the same. The river's own fluctuations in weather and rainfall, coupled with eight years of often-erratic summer releases, played havoc on the fish. The bass became depleted, and trout began to thrive. By the mid-1970s both brown and rainbow trout were abundant, offering some of the finest trout fishing in the Northeast.

In 1975 the attempts by the city to control the flow and random dumping of excess water got the attention of Maurice Hinchey, a member of the New York State Assembly.

Hinchey took notice of the debacle and introduced legislation in 1976 to gain control of reservoir releases from the City of New York. The bill passed, granting the authority to New York State Department of Environmental Conservation (NYSDEC) for control of releases under the Environmental Conservation Law (Article 15, Title 8). The New York State attorney general's office and local environmental groups called it one of the greatest victories ever.

As part of the legislation, specific regulations (Parts 671 and 672) were implemented under the state fisheries reservoir release program. The State of New York, with an agreement with New York City, began a two-year (later extended one additional year) "experimental" monitor and evaluation release program, headed by field technician J. Douglas Sheppard, known as the Sheppard Study.

The objective of the program was to develop a statistically reliable relationship between water temperatures and flows in the Upper Delaware River system to develop a temperature/flow relationship that could consistently maintain the daily water temperature at 72°F, and no higher than 75°F, at selected US Geological Survey sites downstream from the three basin reservoirs. The purpose: so thermal stress would not pose a threat to the trout.

According to scientific literature, water temperatures above 68°F have significant impact on trout growth and survival. Scientific literature observes that brown trout experienced almost no grow and a loss of weight at 71°F while the weight of rainbow trout will begin declining at water temperatures above 68°F. The recorded upper lethal temperatures

A trout that goes into long periods of thermal stress will rarely feed until it finds suitable water temperature. LEE HARTMAN

for these species ranged from 71°F to 82°F depending on acclimation temperatures and exposure time.

Cannonsville Reservoir releases provided flow for the temperature/flow relationship for the West Branch and main stem of the Delaware River—likewise Pepacton releases for the East Branch and Neversink releases for the Neversink River. During the Sheppard Study, Ray Youngblood, a friend and fishing companion, supported the study and agreed to co-chair with me the newly formed Delaware River Committee for the Pennsylvania Council of Trout Unlimited (PATU).

Sheppard's preliminary temperature/flow relationships indicated that a flow of 325 cubic feet per second (cfs) would maintain a satisfactory temperature regime on the West Branch. However, for protection of the designated trout management section on the main Delaware River (Hancock to Callicoon), the West Branch summer conservation releases would have to be greater than 325 cfs. For this purpose, a thermal bank of water (augmented conservation release bank) set at 4,000 cfs-days (100 cfs release/day x 40 days) would be necessary to maintain the temperature/flow relationship for the West Branch and main stem of the Delaware.

The initial focus of the Sheppard Study was to protect the trout and its habitat in respective downstream river sections that included the East and West Branches and upper main stem of the Delaware. The thermal-stress-day results for 1977–1979 indicated that the experimental releases out of each reservoir were highly effective in meeting the stated thermal regime in the East Branch between Corbett and the town of East Branch. The percent frequencies of thermal stress days in this section were practically eliminated. The entire West Branch had complete elimination of thermal stress days for trout in all three years of the study. On the main stem of the river, thermal stress days were reduced over 75 percent of the time as far down as Hankins, New York, with the help of court-obligated decree water.

The farthest temperature monitoring site was at Callicoon, located 27.2 miles downriver from the junction of the East and West Branches of the Delaware River. This area of the Delaware River maintained numerous rainbow trout; Doug Sheppard wanted to continue with the study in this area and requested another year of the program. The young fisheries manager's request was denied, and that ended the program for the main stem.

In 1980, after completing the three-year study, New York City rebelled against extending the control of releases by the NYSDEC and petitioned the New York State Supreme Court to set aside Parts 671 and 672 rules and regulations dealing with augmented conservation releases on the three city-owned reservoirs. At year's end a bipartisan agreement was reached between the City of New York and the NYSDEC, called the Stipulation of Discontinuance. The somewhat underhanded maneuver, which many believed to have been illegal, was not challenged, and allowed the city to retake control of the reservoir release program.

The quietly affirmed 1980 court ruling, Stipulation of Discontinuance, with the two principal parties having agreed, gave sovereign control of all NYC-owned reservoirs back to the city—and along with it, the city's ability to block any new resolution or proposal presented by any representative of the four basin-state commissioners. However, the State of New York could continue the 325 cfs summer release out of Cannonsville from June 15 to August 15 of each year.

The city, however, does not have any superior rights to manage the water in the Delaware Basin reservoirs nor do they own the water. The four states in the basin watershed have an equal and sovereign right to make beneficial uses of these waters. Rondout Reservoir, for example, receives water from the three Delaware Basin reservoirs that make up a component of the city's water supply system.

It didn't take long before a water crisis ensued in the Delaware Basin. On Tuesday, December 2, 1980, warning flags went up as a four-state drought triggered a drought warning from the Delaware River Basin Commission. Philadelphia water commissioner William Marrazzano, at a hearing at Independence Hall Visitors Center, asked the commission to declare a drought emergency immediately. He was extremely critical of New York City's efforts to reduce their water use, as it was not experiencing a drought.

Drought conditions often occur needlessly despite near-full reservoirs.
LEE HARTMAN

By June the calamity continued as Cannonsville releases were abruptly halted by the city, squeezing it from 45 cfs (minimum flow) to 15 cfs into the West Branch waters—a mere trickle. River temperatures rose, fish perished, and tempers flared. Conservation organizations such as Pennsylvania and New York Trout Unlimited, Fontinalis Fly Fishermen, Catskill Rivers Coalition, and Theodore Gordon Flyfishers banded together in protest of the city's action.

The Philadelphia water commissioner called New York City's 190-gallon-per-person allowance "extremely large" considering most of it goes to residential consumption. The commissioner stated, "The first step in dealing with it should be a further reduction in the allowable diversion of basin water to NYC."

> *The fact that we can predict in March what our water situation will look like in June is the result of twenty-five years of technical development. We have a plan. We don't wait until there is an emergency.*
> —LT. GOV. MARK SINGEL, HEAD OF DROUGHT TASK FORCE

Phil Chase, president of Fontinalis Fly Fishermen, spearheaded a public meeting in Callicoon with the concerned organizations and anglers. This was a storage drought, not caused by a severe precipitation deficit, but by NYC's inability to restrain their usage during a prolonged heat wave. The river was coming into prominence, but now the habitat of the river hinged on the whims of the releases. Without a loud voice from the group to sustain the cold-water fishery, its future could be in jeopardy.

Edward Shad was one of those concerned Delaware River anglers. He went to the Callicoon meeting independent of any organization. The dedicated river angler wrote the following letter to organization leaders to contribute his personal findings regarding temperature and flow conditions on the main stem and West Branch of the Delaware River:

> *I am writing to clarify some of the temperature readings we discussed at the Callicoon meeting of July 11th-81.*
> *The temperature readings started an upward trend in the last week of June when we started to record readings of 70 degrees in*

Maple Pool on the Delaware (Junction Pool). At that time, we witnessed no releases from West Branch. East Branch had been maintaining better than average flow for this time of year.

Coming into the first week of July, we began reading in West Branch. The procedure was to read at four points:

> *Deposit Bridge*
>
> *Hale Eddy*
>
> *Balls Eddy*
>
> *Pa. Bridge—Hancock, NY*

We also watched water levels within the Basin above what is known locally as the Weir. The Weir is a dam at the first entry to reservoir property going upriver on West Branch. During a release the Weir will show signs of overflow. If no release is in progress the Basin will be drained through three pipes of approximately 12 inches in diameter.

The reason for an explanation of the Weir is that it is a good measure of a release. We have witnessed what we call marginal releases where the Basin is filled—the release cutoff—and the Basin allowed draining itself through the 3 pipes. We have seen this procedure a half dozen times in a two-week period.

The structure of the river above Hale Eddy is good for maintaining temperature. The river runs narrow with deep water, 3 to 5 feet, and somewhat shaded. Below Hale Eddy, the river widens out in many areas to some 2 to 2½ times the upper river. A pool could be 20% riffle and 80% shallow flats to the tail.

With these points identified, let me relate my experience under various conditions of flow in the first two weeks of July.

One morning (first week) I detected a small release below Hale Eddy, went to Deposit, read 54 degrees, investigated the Basin (not quite full) 2 pipes spewing water. When the water reached Balls Eddy it was 74 degrees; Pa. Bridge—74 degrees. Back to Basin four hours later water was going down. Release was over. That evening we read 74 degrees in Maples Pool. In the second week we experienced, at Pa. Bridge, temperatures of 74 and 82 degrees.

The problem on the West Branch is that we are now getting less water than we had in the river at its historic drought period lows of the pre-Cannonsville Dam period. I qualify the above statement by what has been related to me by old time residents from Deposit.

With no releases the river below Hale Eddy exposes at least 50% of its bed to sunlight. When a minor release is made it will take at least 12 hours to drive the temperature down to static position.

To prove a point, allow me to take you to the 85-degree reading I mentioned at the meeting. This temperature was read on a moderate release Thursday late afternoon at Maples Pool, Delaware, Pa. side East Branch—Fireman's Park—78 degrees. The slug of water was 1½ hour past Pa. Bridge.

My conclusion was that the releases came down over a two-day-old dry bed and rose in temperature by the time it arrived at Maples. In fact, the East Branch's 78 degrees was beneficial to the lower river at this point.

In the first two weeks of July we had only two releases of value. The first, a moderate release, was viable not because of size but because of continuity. The second, who started Fri. A.M. July 10, had both size and continuity. In fact, it was the largest release of the year. At Hale Eddy my log shows that to bring a 64-degree release down to 59 degrees required some five hours.

Pa. Bridge at Hancock:

> *3:45 – 74 degrees*

> *4:45 – 73 degrees*

> *7:15 – 69 degrees*

That Friday night in Maples Pool, temperatures fell from 72 degrees to 62 degrees and remained at 62 degrees thru early Sat. morning.

Before I close, I would like to relate a mild encounter I had with an employee of our adversary. One afternoon in the second week of July, while taking a reading at Pa. Bridge a Mr. Baxter from NYC Dept. of Water Supply came over and introduced himself. He was complete with badge, uniform and truck. His function he told me was to record temperatures at Pa. Bridge and Balls Eddy. I could not get any information from this fellow beyond "It's my job" and his dismay as to why he was always getting high temperature readings. He was even suspect of his thermometer until we both drew an inside 82 degrees on a moderate slug of water. I wonder what motivates their (NYC) interest in temperature readings?

The letter from Ed Shad triggered a public outcry. Craig Billingsley, the Pennsylvania Fish Commission's area fisheries biologist, also noted that some two hundred dead trout had been found as far down as Equinunk, Pennsylvania. "The low-flow/high water temperature combination is deadly, reducing oxygen supplies so essential to fish life," reported Billingsley.

Both the Pennsylvania and New York State Councils of Trout Unlimited and a few local conservation groups rallied to protest NYC's decision to end the summer releases. The Delaware River Basin Commission (DRBC) quickly called a hearing in Philadelphia of all involved parties.

At the July meeting, PATU Delaware River co-chairmen Ray Youngblood and I, representing by proxy the New York State Trout Unlimited Council, and many other agencies testified against NYC's failures to not abide by New York Department of Environmental Resource regulations requiring a 325 cfs summer release out of Cannonsville. A few days later the commissioners held a hearing and announced that NYC would resume proper releases under the New York State summer fishing regulations, which ended the 1981 water crisis.

In 1983, after many hearings, the DRBC adopted the water supply provisions for the Pepacton, Cannonsville, and Neversink Reservoirs and approved the first revision (Rev 1), which provided a storage-based rule curve using trigger points for drought watch, drought warning, and drought emergency. Under Rev 1, Cannonsville continued to maintain 325 cfs release levels and raised court-appointed releases from 1,750 cfs to 1,850 cfs from June 15 to August 15.

In 1994, NYC began replacing the gated valves (fixed releases incapable of controlling exact release volume) with new regulating valves at

Pepacton (1994) and Cannonsville (1997). The management of the reservoir releases dramatically changed. It was now possible to release water in the exact amounts called for. Previously, for example, if 200 cfs was needed to meet downriver flow requirements, a 325 cfs release had to be made.

The DRBC had regulated flows based on the fear that a drought of record would start tomorrow. With the new release valves in place, the commission agreed to cut minimum summer release rates from Cannonsville in half, from 325 cfs to 160 cfs, now regulated by "how little rather than how much" water can be devoted to sustaining some level of the fishery. The release process substantially saved additional water in NYC-owned reservoirs. However, the reductions in conservation releases, without the aid of the mandated summer releases, would adversely impact the wild trout in the river.

The court adopted the recommendation of an independent Special Delaware River Master in the amended 1954 decree. The River Master's job is to determine the allotted amount of excessive release quantity (ERQ) of water provided for the down-basin states in accordance with the court doctrine of equitable apportionment, and required NYC to release water from its impoundments to let out the necessary flows.

The ERQ is calculated as the highest year's consumptive use by NYC, plus an additional 7.25 billion gallons to account for possible growth in the following year. Then subtracting from the total combined systems' safe yield, the remaining quantity is then multiplied by 83 percent. The excess quantity of water is to be used by the down-basin states as agreed upon each year.

The Second Water Crisis (2001–2002)

The way that water is managed in the Delaware is inflexible and irrational, and needs to be reformed.
—LEON SZEPTYCKI, NATIONAL TU

I couldn't believe my eyes! The reservoir practically had gone dry, all ninety-five billion gallons of Cannonsville water turned into a creek bed.

The Cannonsville Reservoir nearly went dry during the winter of 2001.
LEE HARTMAN

I pulled my car off the road to get a better look. With camera in hand and the light fading, I found my way through the brush to a high ridge and quickly snapped a picture of the near-empty reservoir. Fear set in when red-flashing lights bounced into the darkening sky. It was the New York State Police along with a follow-up New York City Department of Environmental Protection (NYCDEP) car. I should have known better. Trespassing on a city-owned reservoir just thirty-three days after 9/11 (the 2001 Twin Towers disaster) made me want to crawl under a rock and hide.

The trooper wasted no time asking who I was, where I lived, and why I was trespassing on city property. He then confiscated my camera and placed me in the backseat of the police cruiser where I waited for a verdict. My fear of being arrested, and my worry. . . not making it to the Delaware River Coalition meeting that night in Deposit, New York. Ten minutes passed when suddenly the car door opened and the officer told me to get out. To my surprise he gave me the camera back with a stern warning: "Don't let me see you here again!"

184

It was a drought year, a drought that did not want to go away. The shortage of water had its beginnings in the hot, dry summer months. Average rainfall in the Catskill region is normally forty-five inches per year. Rain had totaled just ten inches for the entire year. The US Supreme Court decision in 1954 did not specify any type of flow regime or which city reservoir to use. Despite lower-than-average reservoir levels, releases from Cannonsville continued full-throttle to satisfy the Montague and Trenton flow targets, which left Cannonsville Reservoir in its near-empty state.

While the down-basin states suffered from thirst, New York City continued to lavish in water, pumping 570 million gallons a day through leaky aqueducts to city faucets, garden hoses, and fire hydrants—gushing out water without any restrictions or conservation measures.

A river that forgets its source will surely dry up.
                                                    —*YORUBA PROVERB*

Cannonsville Reservoir—higher in nutrients than its sister reservoirs—was the city's choice to maintain the minimum flow targets at Montague and Trenton, and dumped a total of 120 billion gallons of water, which reduced its storage to 3.4 percent by year's end despite pleas from Trout Unlimited and the Delaware River Foundation (DRF) to moderate all Delaware Basin flows equally.

On December 18, 2001, the commission declared a drought emergency. The river became miserably low, choking out the aquatic life. "The drought emergency caused fish kills and a loss of an entire year-class of brown trout eggs and fry," declared National TU representative Nat Gillespie. "Brown trout have just completed spawning, and reduced flows will leave their eggs stranded on a dry river bed."

The entire Delaware River fishing communities were livid by the actions of NYC. Phil Chase, an Upper Delaware River councilman, wrote the following editorial in the weekly *River Reporter*:

The NYC Department of Environmental Protection (DEP) certainly does not deserve such a lofty disguise for a name. The destruction of

Cannonsville and possibly a $50 million trout industry of the West Branch Delaware by mismanagement of the Catskill watershed by the DEP holds all the legal cards due to the 1954 Supreme Court Decree and the Stipulation of Discontinuance and that the woodchucks of the Catskills can go to hell.

The '54 Decree allows NYC to divert 800 mgd (1,200 cfs) while we get 1,750 cfs at Montague (Milford). In 1976 the Catskill Rivers Coalition with a great deal of local political support was able to pass State legislation taking control of the reservoir releases from NYC into the hands of the NYSDEC. The Attorney General's office called it one of the greatest conservation victories ever. It didn't last long.

By 1980 NYC had sued the DEC and the case was settled out of court; it was over a decade before environmentalists knew of the voided legislation. The Stipulation of Discontinuance insured the City got to divert the best quality water. It also stipulated that financial payment occurred for loss of any electrical power due to increase of downstream releases from the reservoirs. At that time power plants were located on the Neversink and Pepacton tunnels to Rondout Reservoir, the holding reservoir that sent the 800 mgd of Delaware watershed flows to the City. Cannonsville, due to its lower elevation, initially had no generators on its tunnel, which made it ideal to dump large quantities of water to Montague while making electric money from Neversink and Pepacton water.

In the early '80s the three reservoirs received a tripling of tiny releases (Neversink 15 cfs to 45 and Pepacton 25 cfs to 75) so that the DEP claimed they lost that amount of electric revenue to the tune of $250,000/year. NYS has been paying this amount since the early '80s. Recently Warren Lavery, representing the Governor on the DRBC, told the NYCDEP "we are not paying the $250,000 any more to NYC."

Just what this means in the long run is questionable. Does it mean that the DEC will go back to court over the Stipulation of Discontinuance that many believe was non-legal as it was secretive or now that Cannonsville has a low head (low efficient) generator on its tunnel there is no loss of revenue for the City, and what will happen to the tripling of releases?

It is doubtful that the mayor of NYC, Rudy Giuliani, even realizes the mismanagement of his reservoirs—this summer when Cannonsville was dumping huge 1,000+cfs quantities of water and the East Branch was getting 100 cfs and the Neversink 50 cfs that a small percentage of the 1,000 could not have been sent down the East Branch and Neversink, preventing the destruction of Cannonsville and improving all three rivers and reservoirs.

Rudy knows how the people of the Catskills poured their hearts and pockets out to the City of New York in their day of disaster. Where is the turn-around from the City when we need help?

Temperature and flow targets are not mandatory requirements. They require the good-faith willingness to be met. Failure to meet such determined targets carried with them no consequence other than the impact on the habitat. To be effective, such a system needs to bear the force of law with penalties for failed adherence. Any system that relies on day-to-day monitoring will unlikely gain the authority of law or regulations.

Since the mid-sixties eight droughts have been declared in the down-basin states all-the-while the City has remained drought free. Drought Management Plans and Rules were negotiated and agreed to by the Decree Parties in 1982 pursuant to the Good Faith Agreement. The need for refinement was necessary to create an equitable solution for all users of water from NYC Delaware River Basin Reservoirs.

Water management release practices from the three Delaware River Basin reservoirs became the subject of intense public debate. Realizing the many obstacles for improving the flows to maintain the cold-water habitat in the Delaware system, National TU, in 1999, commissioned Cornell University's Piotr Paraziewicz, PhD, of the Department of Natural Resources, to do a study on the release/temperature problems and find pragmatic solutions for the Upper Delaware River system.

The Piotr Study

Out of all three branches, the damages to the West Branch are the most obvious. Trout are relatively abundant in the upper reaches because of

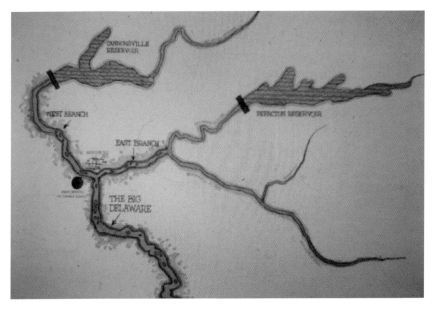

Cannonsville Reservoir is the primary source to satisfy the flow targets mandated by the US Supreme Court. When releases are called upon, erratic flows often occur in the West Branch. The East Branch flows below Pepacton generally remain cool and stable throughout the year as far down as the entrance of the Beaver Kill. LEE HARTMAN

higher release flows, but lethal temperatures lead to fish kills, creating a fishery that is very inconsistent from year to year. Low winter flows and anchor ice create a long-term habitat bottleneck for fish and benthic fauna.

During summer, releases from Cannonsville Reservoir more effectively reduce the temperature of the main stem because the distance to the confluence is shorter and the temperature of the East Branch is elevated by the inflows of the Beaver Kill. For this reason, to accommodate the cold-water fishery (mostly using the West Branch and the main stem) it would be necessary to increase the Cannonsville releases to 300 cfs in winter and 600 cfs in summer.

Because of the high vulnerability of the system to sudden temperature increases during low flow, the releases when drought periods occur should be reduced to a ratio lower than for other users, and should never go below 50 percent of the identified minimum.

It is important to avoid sudden flow and thermal fluctuations due to excessive ramping rates. The maximum amplitude changes should be identified based on the Walton hydrograph. Ideally, the ramping rate should be more gradual than the extreme values occurring at the Walton gage. The shape of the Walton hydrograph is narrowed due to the location of the gage higher up the drainage and because the watershed suffers from lack of forest cover.

The situation for the East Branch is also severe, with very low flows and consequent rapid warming. Although the water released from Pepacton Reservoir is cold, the channel is wide and shallow, and the volume of warm water entering from the Beaver Kill largely exceeds the downstream thermal capacity. The Neversink seems to be more resilient, probably due to a dense canopy cover and higher morphological diversity.

Paraziewicz, the Cornell University professor, indicated that significant year-round changes are necessary to restore the aquatic health of the Upper Delaware system. On the West Branch he advised increasing winter minimum flows from 45 cfs to 300 cfs to avoid anchor ice, and summer flows from 160 cfs to 600 cfs to maintain proper thermal conditions.

On the East Branch, his study recommended increasing winter minimum flows from 45 cfs to 200–250 cfs, and summer flows from 95 cfs to 500 cfs. On the Neversink, the report advised increasing winter minimum flows from 25 cfs to 150 cfs and summer flows from 53 cfs to 100 cfs.

The professor's well-defined twenty-page summary, titled "Strategy for Sustainable Management of the Upper Delaware River," completed the two-year study in September 2001. He noted that frequent thermal stress causes long-lasting damage to fish despite the mitigation efforts using a thermal stress bank. Unpredictable weather conditions and a time lag of flow over long distances also make precise temperature control difficult (just one catastrophic event can undo a multiyear effort).

The study enlightened many environmental organizations that were concerned about the eroding ecology of the Upper Delaware River system. However, to adopt Dr. Paraziewicz's release plan to maintain a cold-water habitat without disturbing the court-mandated flows would be a daunting task, though many believe there is enough water in the three Delaware Basin reservoirs (558 billion gallons) to improve ecological flows without sacrificing water needs.

The latest release program incorporated three separate "banks" of water. One of those banks was a habitat protection bank of 20,000 cfs-days (200 cfs for 100 days) of water to help meet thermal and in-stream flow objectives on the East Branch, the West Branch, the main stem, and the Neversink River. Rev 7 also included a study program for the following three to five years to define ecological flow needs for the tailwater fisheries. The study plan caught the attention of environmental groups, though some continued to remain skeptical of the program.

Enticed by the increased water allotted to the habitat bank, the National Trout Unlimited (National TU) leadership agreed to support the new revision, with a slight modification—replacing the 225 cfs minimum flow with a 325 cfs flow as measured on the West Branch flow target at Hale Eddy, New York. The suggested changes by National TU were later rejected by the DRBC prior to Rev 7's formal approval at the April 2004 meeting.

Although National TU and DRF leadership recognized the need for more water flow from Cannonsville, surprisingly they abandoned the Piotr Study sponsored by National TU and formally announced their support for the latest three-year experimental release program despite the looming Pennsylvania Power and Light power releases. The decision to back Revision 7 disappointed many in the environmental community at a time when unity was important.

- 10 -

Unnatural Flows

The future of Delaware's cold-water flows became uncertain when water politics threatened to curtail the historic summer releases out of Cannonsville Reservoir. Pennsylvania Power and Light's (PPL) application to relicense their hydroelectric operation on Lake Wallenpaupack included an amendment to the Comprehensive Plan and Water Code that would directly impact the West Branch and Upper Delaware flows. The utility company was asking to raise the dam level and release higher volumes of water into the Delaware River, via the Lackawaxen River, during critical

The lower East Branch near Pea's Eddy during dry conditions. LEE HARTMAN

summer periods. These releases would be credited to the Montague flow target, which would cut back mandated releases from Cannonsville Reservoir.

Finding clean, clear water with wild trout and dancing mayflies during the 1970s was not an easy discovery for those living in the coalfields of Schuylkill County, Pennsylvania. Many of my coal region friends and I traveled for hours during this time to find an unspoiled stream or river to fish. We often slept in cars, found a cheap hotel room, or camped in a tent near a stream just to catch an early morning fish by the crack of dawn.

One of those places was Long Eddy, New York, formerly called Dickson City, a once small and prosperous nineteenth-century settlement nestled along the Delaware River. The Sullivan County village, founded on April 9, 1867, was a lumber town. Historians say it had nearly 1,500 souls and one hundred saloons that were popular one-night resting stops for the weary and thirsty lumberjacks while taking their timber to downriver

A pair of anglers enjoying life on the Delaware. LEE HARTMAN

ports. It was not uncommon to see the eddy there so full of rafts that you could walk across the river on them and not get wet.

By the late 1800s timber rafting began to slacken. Long Eddy turned its attention to local commerce, becoming an industrial community. Factory and mills produced board lumber, furniture, rolling pins, rake handles, spindles, porch posts, cornmeal, buckwheat flour, wooden cheese boxes, and excelsior. Large "acid factories" in Pea Brook and Hoolihan Creek burned wood in big ovens to produce charcoal, acetate, and wood alcohol. To maintain their manufacturing, the village built several utilities that included water and a telephone company. The Hydraulic and Manufacturing Company constructed a dam across the Delaware River to provide water power. Unfortunately, the impoundment lasted just one year, as a flood destroyed the dam and it was never rebuilt.

The century-old community of Long Eddy was a favorite fishing hangout during the 1970s. Young and energetic, my fishing pals and I took hikes along a lengthy two-mile pool to undisturbed riffles inhabited by feisty rainbows that fed in the river around a group of islands. We named the place Fly Rock after the huge boulder that marked the tail end of the broken pocket water that entered the long, wide pool.

A river is the coziest of friends. You must love it and live with it before you can know it.
—G. W. CURTIS

After spending a pleasurable day fishing, we'd trudge back to the village to pay a visit to its few conveniences. The Sportsman's Bar (now Chestnut Inn) was one of those places where the bartender made us guess how a pickle got into a coke bottle before serving us a drink. After laughs and a few beers, we'd take a short walk to Ginger's roadside diner to complete our day.

The cool water of the West Branch was also an acceptable place to fish for trout, particularly during midsummer. The trout-cool river had very limited overnight camping areas. The campsite anglers most often used was situated on a large flat of land located just south of the Hale Eddy bridge. The spartan campground, owned and managed by an elderly man named Rocky, came with just a water spigot and an electric receptacle at each tent site.

The short, muscular fellow with a gravel-like voice and a disposition to match lived comfortably on the site in a white clapboard building. He charged five dollars per night to camp and offered each angler a newspaper to wrap your fish in while giving you a friendly reminder that it was free of charge.

Rocky's little piece of heaven was later bought by New York contractor Harry Bachelet, in 1992, and he soon turned the campground into a resort, naming it West Branch Angler, that now features a dozen one- to three-bedroom cabins, a restaurant, a conference center, river access, and a fly shop.

The recovery from the drought of 2001 had a residual effect on the river in the spring of 2002. The fishery continued to be in peril despite Cannonsville filling to 80 percent near the end of May. By August, mandated releases out of Cannonsville were called upon throughout most

Drift boats have become very popular for fishing in the Upper Delaware system.
LEE HARTMAN

of the month, which dropped the reservoir to 54 percent capacity by mid-August.

The August 13 release of 700 cfs from Cannonsville provided a "Day on the Delaware," a notable event that was held each year sponsored by the Delaware River Foundation (DRF). The purpose of the annual event was to make people aware of the importance of the river and its fishing.

The many political dignitaries and local business owners who floated the well-attended event held at the West Branch Angler Resort did so under the most ideal conditions. The reservoir valve at Cannonsville was turned up so boats could float, anglers could wade, and trout could feed. The occasion was quite impressive for those who'd never experienced fishing and floating the river.

After the brief taste of perfect flow conditions, the week following the event, releases were throttled down to less-than-adequate flow levels, and drifting a boat became near impossible. Power releases into the Lackawaxen River had been raised in late August, lowering the water to minimum levels in the Upper Delaware.

The Day on the Delaware event in August 2003 proved to be quite different. Total flows as measured on the West Branch gage at Hale Eddy averaged 229 cfs in the month of July—less than half of what they were for the same month during the preceding twenty-five years, and not nearly cool enough to maintain good fishing conditions on the West Branch during the hot summer, let alone the Wild and Scenic corridor.

It was Cannonsville cold-water bottom releases that helped create a highly recognized world-class wild trout river. To protect this vital fishery, since 1983 countless of concerned groups and individuals have in good faith attempted and failed to negotiate something as seemingly simple and worthy as regulated minimum releases. The natural West Branch flows before the dam was built were twice as high as the 225 cfs offered under the new plan. Clearly it was time to find a new strategy without replicating the mistakes of the past.

On September 25, 2002, PPL Holtwood, LLC filed an application to the Federal Energy Regulatory Commission (FERC) for a new license on the Lake Wallenpaupack Hydroelectric Project. The intention of the license renewal was to increase the dam height one foot to gain additional power releases that would be counted toward the Montague flow target. The PPL project, though not as yet sanctioned by FERC, was tentatively approved by the Delaware River Basin Commission (DRBC). In the spring of 2003, PPL Holtwood, LLC presented its flow plan at a public meeting. The license application called for a fifty/thirty-five-year relicense for the Lake Wallenpaupack Hydroelectric Project with FERC.

A Gathering of Friends

New York City uses Cannonsville water to satisfy the mandated flow targets almost exclusively because of its eutrophic characteristics in most summer months. The historic cold-water releases that provide the river's cold-water habitat would be in jeopardy should a PPL relicense request gain approval for increased flows out of Lake Wallenpaupack. Without proper safeguards the low-water situations would become frequent and could spell disaster for the Upper Delaware trout fishery.

It was a cool September morning in 2003 when a small, wiry man with eyes of steel stepped into the screened porch at Indian Springs Camp, extended his arm, and introduced himself with a firm handshake. His name was Craig Findley, and he had come to the fishing camp on my invite after reading an email sharing my own personal feelings that flow and release requirements were falling far short of what was needed to preserve the Upper Delaware cold-water fishery.

Craig Findley, a former campaign manager for the Democratic Party in the state of New York, lived in the suburbs of Syracuse, New York, where he was a member of the Iroquois Chapter of Trout Unlimited. We both had concerns with National TU and the DRF supporting the proposed Revision 7 release plan.

Born and raised in Watts, a high-crime, low-income neighborhood of Los Angeles influenced by street gangs, Craig candidly told me about his childhood upbringing. "There were no pillow fights, just fists, guns, and switchblades to settle any differences," he said somewhat proudly. "For self-preservation, I always keep a six-inch switchblade in my possession," he added, boldly displaying the knife, which he pulled from his pocket while telling of his boyhood.

An aerial view of the West Branch Angler Resort next to the West Branch of the Delaware River. GARTH LENZ

His astounding childhood story wasn't in my comfort zone, but his vision for the flow necessities to protect river life was that there is plenty of saved water in the Delaware Basin reservoirs to safely release enough water for fisheries protection without jeopardy to the water needs of others.

The Upper Delaware River and its equally renowned West Branch have become the leading wild trout rivers in the Northeast. But the rivers are much more than that. They have created a dynamic tourism mecca that generates the region's economic engine; however, it may never reach its potential under the current management policies.

The decades-old revision changes were nothing more than using the same "pot of water" camouflaged in the complexity of the ever-changing release banks. The court-mandated releases are frequently erratic and cause unnecessary harm to the river ecology. The discharges need to be harnessed in a way to benefit the environment, the fishing, and the local business enterprises.

197

The California native and I set out to find other advocates to help formulate a less complicated plan that could convince the managing authorities to change their perspective on trout-friendly releases. Our efforts to find supporters didn't take long. Within two weeks a lodge full of river friends showed up at Indian Springs, including Delaware River fishing pioneers Phil Chase and Al Caucci.

Watching the DRBC and Decree Party members juggle revisions for the past few decades they often termed as fishery plans always came up woefully short. Anyone believing you could gain additional water from New York City (who took back control of releases from NYSDEC in 1980) either was naïve or believed in the good fairy.
    —PHIL CHASE, UPPER DELAWARE COUNCIL REPRESENTATIVE

Changing a multifarious reservoir release system bound around the constraints of the US Supreme Court decree and regulated by four states and a thirsty city would not be easy to overcome. Notable rivermen such as Phil Chase, Upper Delaware Council representative; Al Caucci, longtime river advocate and owner of the Delaware River Club; and fly shop owner Jim (Coz) Costolnick were all proponents of the Piotr Study.

Our group, called Friends of the Upper Delaware River (FUDR), officially formed in November 2003 and appointed Craig Findley as president. A year later FUDR incorporated in the Commonwealth of Pennsylvania as a nonprofit corporation. FUDR's purpose: to protect, preserve, and enhance the cold-water ecosystem of the Upper Delaware River system and to address any environmental threats to our area for the benefit of local communities, residents, and visitors to the region.

Waste not, want not, is a maxim I would teach. Let your watchword be dispatch, and practice what you preach; Do not let your chance like sunbeams pass you by, for you never miss the water until the well runs dry.
    —ROLAND HOWARD (1876)

At the inaugural January 2004 meeting, the PPL issue burdened our thoughts. All eight elected board members feared the worst should the utility giant get its way. Under the current release guidelines, the minimum 225 cfs summer flow target on the West Branch could put the Upper Delaware literally in "hot water." Trout Unlimited (TU) and the DRF, which earlier sought to reform existing water management problems, supported Revision 7. Many FUDR board members were affiliated with the TU and DRF organizations and also hoped that we could take a realistic and honest stand together to gain proper releases for the benefit of the cold-water fishery.

The history of reservoir releases and spills is well documented. Cannonsville alone released, with occasional combined spills, a summertime average (July and August) of 645 cfs. During the month of August, mandated releases would commonly reach over 1,000 cfs per day, which cooled river flows to comfortable levels for wild trout as far down as

Aquatic life becomes exposed and often dies during sudden release drops.
LEE HARTMAN

Callicoon. However, there was a downside to these sudden releases. Once the Montague flow is satisfied, releases can drop abruptly and rise again suddenly when the mandated flow target is repeated—commonly called the yo-yo effect. The unnatural fluctuation of water levels exposes the riverbed, which then traps small fish, endangers the federally protected dwarf wedge mussel, and suffocates many macro-invertebrates important to the ecosystem of the river.

Should the utility giant get its way, FUDR, taking a lesson out of the Piotr Study, adopted the conception of a steady summer release protocol of 600 cfs out of Cannonsville Reservoir from May 15 to September 15, and a winter release of 300 cfs. The concept was a practical way to manage the releases in a more natural manner during the spring and summer season. The simplified management approach would eliminate temperature targets and help curb yo-yo–like releases.

More water being released from Lake Wallenpaupack means less water that needs to be released from three New York City reservoirs.
—WILLIAM DOUGLAS, UPPER DELAWARE COUNCIL DIRECTOR

The controversial PPL plan, if granted, would increase Lake Wallenpaupack releases into the Lackawaxen River, a major tributary in the Wild and Scenic corridor, by large amounts, particularly in the crucial summer months. The Lackawaxen flows inevitably would be "credited" to the Montague flow target and thus reduce the directed releases from Cannonsville.

At the public meeting in Hawley, Pennsylvania, on May 1, 2003, the PPL representative stated, "The plant discharges about 1,750 cfs when generating forty megawatts with the lake at normal full pool. The minimum discharge from the plant is about 125 cfs, corresponding to single-unit operation at an output of two megawatts."

His revelation was easy to comprehend, that one release alone from Lake Wallenpaupack would have the potential to meet the minimum 1,750 cfs Montague flow target—a sure threat to de-water the self-sustaining wild trout fishery and its cold-water habitat in the Upper Delaware.

Lake Wallenpaupack is long and wide but considerably more shallow than the Delaware Basin reservoirs. LEE HARTMAN

We can't run a river by average—it is extremes that kill.
—PHIL CHASE, UPPER DELAWARE COUNCIL REPRESENTATIVE

PPL's own computer modeling demonstrated that during drought conditions, August flows in the Delaware River above the Lackawaxen confluence would significantly be reduced and boating would be degraded. As a member of the Pennsylvania Council of Trout Unlimited's Delaware River Committee, I could not support the PPL/FERC license request unless water released from the dam *not* be credited to the Montague target.

The relicense request created a conflict of interest between the Stanley Cooper Chapter TU and the Pike/Wayne Chapter TU. The Pike/Wayne Chapter favored the PPL release plan, believing it would improve their home water of the Lackawaxen River. Ironically, the proposed power-generating releases on the "Lacky," operating five days per week

The Lackawaxen River is a 31.3-mile-long tributary of the Delaware River in northeastern Pennsylvania. The river flows through a largely rural area in the northern Pocono Mountains, draining an area of approximately 598 square miles. LEE HARTMAN

and shutting down its flows on weekends, would produce the same de-watering (yo-yo) effect as on the West Branch of the Delaware.

Faced with the quandary of two state TU chapters opposing each other, a three-hour car trip to State College was necessary to address the Pennsylvania State Council on the dilemma and possible de-watering of the Upper Delaware River. At the meeting, Dr. Robert A. Bachman, chairman of the Wild Trout and Salmon committee for Trout Unlimited, quickly recognized that the power release credits would negatively impact the Upper Delaware and West Branch wild trout fishery.

Bob Bachman is no ordinary man. He is to trout what Mario Andretti is to car racing. He holds a doctorate in behavioral ecology from Pennsylvania State University, a Bachelor of Science degree in oceanography from the University of Washington, and a Bachelor of Science degree in marine and electrical engineering from the US Naval Academy. During his twenty years of service in the US Navy, Dr. Bachman served on two diesel-powered and three nuclear-powered submarines, including the USS *Nautilus*, America's first nuclear-powered sub. As a young man, his pioneering behavioral study of brown trout at Penn State University won him the American Fisheries Society's "Best Paper Award," and he has been widely recognized in national publications such as the *New York Times* and *Newsweek*. His article in the 1985 winter issue of *Trout*, "How Trout Feed," won him the Best Published C.E. Orvis award.

Dr. Bachman, after his distinguished military career, served as director of the US Fish & Wildlife Service in the state of Maryland, supervised Maryland's cold-water fishery for thirteen years, and established environmental and regulatory changes that resulted in the creation of four nationally recognized trout fisheries in the state of Maryland.

Dr. Robert Bachman with his catch using his favorite fly he so named the "Whatsit". LEE HARTMAN

Meeting Dr. Bachman and gaining the support of the state council was a gratifying experience. The trout expert has been a positive influence in my life since he joined FUDR to serve on the board of directors in 2004. Bob Bachman wrote the following dissertation related to the flow management issues in Upper Delaware wild trout fishery:

The Problem with Habitat Banks, Thermal Banks, Temperature and Flow Targets
by Robert A. Bachman, PhD

Any fisheries management plan for the Delaware River tailwater trout fishery that is based on habitat banks, thermal banks, temperature targets, and flow targets depend on the accuracy and timeliness of the bewildering numbers of assumptions, predictions, and monitoring ability. To be effective, such a plan needs to accurately monitor, on a continuing basis, water and air temperature and flow conditions at several locations AND be able to predict, far enough in advance, the effect that a certain amount of water at a temperature and flow will have on living resources tens of miles downstream, tens of hours later. Even more problematic is the ability to estimate, a year or more in advance, how much water should be allocated to these banks.

Effect of Non-Monitored Tributaries and Weather
The temperature and flow of tributaries and springs within the three main tributaries have a profound but unmeasured effect on the temperature and flow in the designated trout management sections. The Delaware River system spans hundreds of miles. Local weather conditions have important, unpredictable, and often unrecorded effects on the waters under consideration.

Monitoring and Location of Gages
Water temperatures and flow change rapidly as a function of the amount of water being released from the reservoirs and local weather conditions. On any summer day, one tributary may be receiving mostly cold-water from releases whereas another tributary may consist of almost entirely of flow from unmonitored tributaries to that stream.

For the system based on temperature and flow targets to be effective, the location of key temperature and flow gages must not only be calibrated frequently for accuracy, they must be in places that accurately reflect conditions that are of significance to the resources to be protected.

Prediction and Lag Time
Relying on a bank or portion thereof to be released to prevent undesired consequences to a living resource requires a daunting requirement to be able to predict the time, duration, and amount of water that needs to be released, and is dependent upon many unknown or unpredictable conditions and effects. For example, if a reservoir is spilling and water is being withdrawn (diverted) from the system, the manager needs to be able to predict the effect such withdrawal will have on the amount being spilled and the rate at which the amount that is spilling will change during the release. He needs to be able to predict how much the water will be heated by exposed rocks during transit time (a function of existing flow and weather) and how long it will take to reach the target. Releases from major tributaries such as the Lackawaxen River and Mongaup are highly unpredictable but profoundly affect the flow at Montague, New Jersey.

Air Temperature and Cloud Cover
Although air temperature is an important factor, the greatest heat gain to the river system occurs by the absorbance of sunlight by the rocks in the bottom of the stream, especially on shallow riffles. Even on comparatively cool days, when the sun is high in the sky, as in June, a great amount of solar energy is absorbed by the rocks through the relatively transparent water and then conducted from the water from below. Although part of this prediction can be inferred by weather forecasts, there can be considerable variation from day to day and is highly unpredictable. The amount of heat that is absorbed by the substrate changes throughout the summer, being greater in June when the sun is higher in the sky and then decreases throughout the remaining days. Consequently, the water temperatures in the designated trout management sections also rise and fall rapidly throughout the summer.

Assumptions

A system based on temperature and flow targets assumes that the temperature and flow targets chosen are biologically important to the target organisms and that these targets reflect optimum conditions for the entire system, not just at the target location. Because the trout can move, and their behavior is strongly affected by water depth, velocity, and temperature, all of which vary widely throughout the entire system, the ability to calculate a specific set of temperature and flow criteria best for the trout fishery, let alone the complex array of aquatic organisms that may have important ecological significance, is highly problematic at best. It is by no means given that in a system as large and complex as the Delaware River that any such combination of temperature and flow targets could ever be judged as being best for the system.

Temperature targets of 72°F and 75°F are based on mortality rates of individual trout held in isolation. They are not intended to nor do they adequately reflect the impact of the ecosystem much less the various populations of wild trout. Temperature strongly affects not only the physiology of trout but their behavior as well. Above 68°F, trout can no longer feed efficiently. At this temperature trout begin to move in search of cooler water. This movement affects the social hierarchy of the trout and causes excessive expenditure of energy just at the time at which the fish can no longer feed efficiently. If temperatures can gradually increase and flows are not artificially changed over an unpredictable and erratic period, the trout will instinctively move upstream, or even downstream if cold-water refuge exists downstream at nearby springs or tributaries.

Assumption: Pulsed Releases Are Beneficial to Trout

If flow is temporarily raised and temperatures temporarily lowered, the behavior of the trout is unnaturally altered to the detriment of the population. Instead of moving to cooler water, the trout may be induced to stay in a potentially lethal location. Then, when the flows are reduced and once again temperatures begin to rise, the trout may not be able to negotiate shallow riffle areas in search of cooler water.

Sudden and brief pulses of cold water in a stream environment are unnatural and are found nowhere in a natural system. No natural organisms have ever been exposed to such an environment naturally and therefore have never become adapted to cope with such conditions. Pulses of cold water cause fish and invertebrates to behave in a manner detrimental to both.

Assumption: Drought of Record Starts Tomorrow

The easiest way to reduce the risk of running out of water is to assume the drought of record starts tomorrow. But a fisheries management plan that is subject to such constraint essentially constrains the ecosystem to permanent drought conditions. In natural streams, aquatic organisms undergo periods of scarcity and abundance depending on the weather that year. A system based on the most extreme drought conditions condemns the ecosystem to perpetual drought regardless of the actual climate conditions.

Enforceability

Temperature and flow targets are just that—targets. They are not mandatory requirements and require good faith willingness to be met. Failure to meet such targets carries with them no consequences other than the impact on the resource. To be effective, such a system needs to carry with it the force of law with penalties for failure of adherence. It is unlikely that any system needs to carry with it the force of law with penalties for failure of adherence. It is unlikely that with any system that relies on so many variables, unknowns, day to day monitoring and un-testable assumptions could ever gain the authority of law or regulation.

An Alternative

A system based on the availability of water on a real-time basis and acceptable risk, in which a specified amount of water is released as a function of storage and time of year (probability of refill) eliminates virtually all of the "problems" discussed above. Such a system need not increase the frequency or probability of "drought," is much more beneficial to the aquatic organisms in the river, and is easy to implement.

His dissertation in a few words: Give aquatic organisms the amount of water that is available today and they will take care of themselves.

Revision 7 Fails to Meet Its Promise

The winter snowpack of early 2004 and an early spring rain produced a historic flood in April, causing Cannonsville spillage to exceed 9,000 cfs, and helped produce the highest river levels in half a century. By late May the large amounts of uncontrollable spillage stopped, and bottom releases were held to minimum flow levels. June air temperatures soared to unseasonably high levels and river flows became as warm as bath water, enough to slow hatching activity, practically shutting down most of the fishing in the West Branch and the scenic corridor on the main stem. Anglers responded by staying home, which was terrible for Delaware County commerce.

The problem was neither drought nor a lack of reservoir water. It was two separate events that occurred downriver, fueling a summer water crisis. The heavy spring rain events damaged a hydroelectric dam on Swinging Bridge Reservoir owned by an electric company located in Sullivan County, New York. To repair the dam, vast amounts of water had to be released into the Delaware. In the meantime, PPL at Lake Wallenpaupack began releasing more water than it had done in years past. The dual summer releases were enough to satisfy the court-obligated Montague flow target. With the target met, New York State was not obligated to release compensated water from its reservoirs.

In June 2005, with plenty of water in basin reservoirs, a terrible decision was made by the State of New York. Gerry Barnhart, director of the New York State Division of Fisheries, gave the order to stop thermal releases and abandon the Hankins gage temperature target altogether, located fifteen miles below the junction of the East and West Branches of the river. "Instead," he said, "the state would concentrate on only the cooling for the East and West Branches as well as the Neversink River."

No one should relinquish their responsibility to the fishery.
—Dr. Peter Bousum, FUDR board member

"Abandoning the Hankins target will have a substantial impact on the Delaware," Barnhart said in an interview. "However, in my judgement, it's not going to be catastrophic. It is something that the river system can recover from in better water years." His astonishing declaration made little sense to everyone in the environmental community. You could walk across parts of the river without getting your knees wet.

The extra water downriver and the partial abandonment of an important component of the plan created a catastrophe that could have been avoided. When temperatures rise above 68°F, trout become stressed and begin crowding together near cool-seepage and cold-water tributaries. By July the water-starved scenic corridor reached upward of 78°F—a sure death for trout. By mid-August, Swinging Bridge Reservoir stabilized,

The West Branch of the Delaware is approximately twenty-two miles long to its confluence with the East Branch. GARTH LENZ

and with Lake Wallenpaupack releases nearly depleted of water, the mandated releases out of Cannonsville were once again restored.

Leaky Aqueducts

The city's major water supply is diverted from the NYC Delaware Basin
reservoirs and the Rondout holding reservoir through a complex Delaware aqueduct system that was constructed between 1936 and 1945. The
water from these reservoirs is drawn through the East Delaware Tunnel,
West Delaware Tunnel, and the Neversink Tunnel to the Rondout reservoir, from which the water is sent through the eighty-five-mile-long
Delaware Aqueduct.

For many years the antiquated infrastructure in the tunnels has been
in critical condition. Dilapidated shaft houses, crumbling aqueducts, and
antique machinery all contribute to the city's eroding ability to deliver

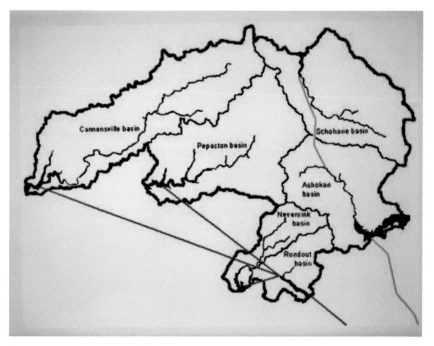

Cannonsville, Pepacton, and Neversink Reservoirs feed into the Rondout, a holding reservoir, before entering the Delaware aqueduct that supplies the city with
drinking water. NYCDEP PUBLICATION

reliable quantities of safe drinking water. As a result of these maladies, infrastructure maintenance has suffered decades of economic starvation. The full extent of leaks is not known. What is known is that the city is losing millions of gallons of water a day in the sixty- to seventy-year-old tunnel system.

The loss of thirty-five million gallons or more of water is not included in the many millions of gallons of water the city already takes out of the river, which provide the city and its suburbs with some of the best unfiltered drinking water in the country.

"That's a major loss to the river system," said FUDR board member and fisheries specialist Bob Bachman, who sat on the Pennsylvania Fish & Boat Commission for eight years. "I think this whole issue is a matter of New York City throwing its financial weight around. The lost water could go down the Delaware instead of creating a 'bubbling spring' in someone's backyard. This would go a long way to help preserve one of the best trout rivers in the country."

The real issue is proper management of New York's reservoir system—how to regulate flows to not only protect the river's ecology, but also provide continued recreation and some measure of flood control.

In 2017 the New York City Department of Environmental Protection (NYCDEP) launched the largest repair project in the history of New York City's water system. The eighty-five-mile Delaware Aqueduct supplies more than five hundred million gallons of water per day to more than 9.5 million New Yorkers—approximately half of New York City's water.

The NYCDEP for the past twenty-five years has been monitoring two leaky sections of the Delaware Aqueduct, one in the Orange County town of Newburgh and the other in the Ulster County town of Wawarsing. The leaks were estimated to be twenty to thirty million gallons of water per day. According to the data gathered in its report, the leak rate has remained constant and the cracks have not worsened since the NYCDEP began monitoring the two leaks.

In 2010 the city announced a plan to address the leaks by building a permanent 2.5-mile bypass tunnel around the leaking section of the aqueduct in Newburgh. The bypass would be constructed six hundred feet below the Hudson River, from Newburgh on the West Shore to Wappinger Falls on the East Shore.

Work on the bypass tunnel began on September 8, 2017, and will continue twenty-four hours a day, five days a week, for approximately twenty months. At this rate the tunnel should advance at the rate of about fifty feet per day. The Delaware Aqueduct will stay in service while the bypass tunnel is under construction. Once the bypass tunnel is nearly complete, the Delaware Aqueduct will be taken out of service and the bypass tunnel will be connected to structurally sound portions of the Delaware Aqueduct. The leaking sections will then be plugged and permanently taken out of service.

During the six-month shutdown of the Delaware Aqueduct, scheduled for October 2022, water supply augmentation and conservation measures via the city's Croton and Catskill systems will provide a reliable supply of water to meet the needs of the city. The project is expected to be finished in 2023.

The aqueduct repair project was long overdue. Millions of gallons of river water have been wasted over the course of twenty-five years. Every river stakeholder should have an equitable right to the lost water from year's past. Can we get a return of the displaced water for the Delaware River? Only time will tell.

Water, Water, Everywhere

The Upper Delaware River is "special." The wild brown and rainbow trout that exist in the river today are a hardy strain of fish. For over one hundred years they have survived the most volatile conditions of nature and man. The rigors of producing offspring have made their descendants one of the strongest trout of our time. The combination of cold-water tributaries used as nursery waters, the river's hatches, and cold bottom releases from Cannonsville contribute to the success of the Upper Delaware ecosystem. It is everyone's responsibility, including the state, local, and city agencies, to recognize the plight of Delaware's wild trout and begin working together to protect the environment so we can continue to provide economic growth and guarantee another century of good fishing. The question is can it last?

Guiding in God's Country

Although I'd fished the Upper Delaware River for fifteen years, I never had any intention of being a guide. While serving as the banquet chairman for Perkiomen Valley Trout Unlimited in 1987, I donated a two-day guided fishing trip on the Upper Delaware as an auction prize. Dr. Hamsey, a seventy-four-year-old retired doctor from Bethlehem, Pennsylvania, won the bid. He had heard that the river had a decent Green Drake hatch, and it was his lifelong ambition to witness it. To trout-loving fly anglers the Green Drake is considered the dream hatch, and I wanted to provide him with the best opportunity to fulfill his wish. I suggested he schedule his two-day float trip on the last weekend of May, a likely time for the hatch to occur. I warned him—it could be hit or miss.

Fly fishing from a canoe is by no means safe nor is it practical for an elderly person. Fortunately, the weather and flow conditions were perfect for a leisurely float. After launching at the Shehawken access in the early morning hours, we were immediately surrounded by dancing mayflies flying elegantly above the water. How lucky could we be? They were Green Drake spinners putting on a show. The adrenaline began rushing through our veins like two kids seeing Disneyland for the first time.

At an appropriate stop to wade-fish, Doc Hamsey's eyes glistened while watching the graceful mating rituals of the drakes in the cloudy sky. Soon the spinner flight began to drop near the water surface. After a brief wait a trout nosed in the river. Soon trout dimples were seen everywhere. Doc needed no instruction on how, when, or where to cast. He made a perfect presentation of his fly imitation a foot or two above the fish and hooked into a pretty fourteen-inch rainbow. He held the fish tenderly for the moment and carefully released it, completing his lifelong mission.

Doc Hamsey fell in love with the river that day. He landed a half dozen more fish and accomplished his goal of catching a trout on his homespun drake spinner. After a cozy evening eating dinner next to the campfire, he said to me, "You should do this for a living. Is it possible for

The green drake fly hatch is popular with fly fishermen who fish Delaware River system. DON BAYLOR

me to stay and fish for the week?" How could I turn him down? A phone call to my boss sealed Doc's request that would launch my guiding career on the Delaware.

A friend of mine told me that I would never make it as a guide simply because I like to fish. His declaration that I love fishing is certainly true. Even after many years of guiding, there was never a day I thought of quitting. Guiding is a seasonal sport on the Delaware. When your backyard is the river, you can find plenty of time to go fishing.

However, one aspect of managing clients you need to overcome is frustration—"You can lead a horse to water but you can't make him drink." This happens frequently with inexperienced anglers and those who think they know how to fish but really don't. When they do hook a fish and lose it, quite often they will blame you for their incompetence. You just nod your head and smile.

The best part of guiding is teaching how to cast properly, picking out the customers' flies, pointing where to cast, and cheering when they hook and land a fish. Any reasonable guide will tell you that the feeling is like catching the fish yourself. And as for memories, there are lots of them, both good and bad and rarely forgotten. One such memory of mine fits both categories.

April is a great month for fishing before the guide season kicks in. It helps to satisfy my fishing addiction and is also a good way to check out any new fishing gear and the early season hatches. One of my friends that I fish with is Barry Weinperl, a dry fly purist who, like many anglers, enjoys fishing the Hendrickson hatch.

It looked like a perfect day to float, and we launched around noon hoping to find a mid-afternoon hatch. While floating leisurely I entertained myself by casting my new Loomis GLX fly rod. A good fly rod is essential for dry-fly fishing, particularly on the Delaware. Your first cast should be your best cast to catch a wary trout.

It was mid-afternoon when we entered a favorite stretch of river, anchored above the tailout of a pool, and waited. As we stared intently at the water, Hendrickson's slowly began to appear on the surface, floating lazily in the steady current. Barry sat in front armed with a nine-foot four-weight Sage and peeled off line to ready his cast. After a few

John Morgan, a frequent visitor to the Upper Delaware, needs no lessons in casting. LEE HARTMAN

sporadic rises fish began cruising, sipping steadily on the struggling duns. Barry made a picture-perfect cast, placing the fly a foot above the nose of the fish. The trout ate it instantly! After a not-so-friendly struggle, the Equinunk resident landed a beefy brown trout. Two more trout came into our nets before the brief hatch ended.

Our day complete, we headed to the Long Eddy river access. Both of us have fished since we were kids, but the excitement of catching a fish never fades. The sun disappeared over the mountain as we chatted about the great start of the new season.

> *The only thing faster than the speed of thought is the speed of forgetfulness. Good thing we have other people to help us remember.*
> —*VERA NAZARIAN,* The Perpetual Calendar of Inspiration

Excited to fish again the following day, I discovered my GLX was missing from the car. Did I leave it at the access? Panic set in, and without

Barry Weinperl with a nice brown trout caught on a Hendrickson. LEE HARTMAN

hesitation I raced back to Long Eddy. It was not there. Delaware guide Adrian LaSorte was the only other boat on the river that day. Could Adrian possibly have picked it up? A phone call to him revealed he had not. I prayed an honest angler would find the Loomis and return it to me. The year went by without a phone call, and I lost any hope of getting it back.

The following season was a high-water year on the Delaware River. Garth Hallberg, a longtime friend and client, booked his usual midweek float trips during the month of May. The entire Upper Delaware River system had been blown out but was beginning to settle. Garth decided to buck the elements and fish.

The river high and clear looked like a deserted freeway. No boats, no anglers, and no bugs. The windless day was warm, bright, and without a cloud in the sky. Garth and I cruised the river edges until mid-afternoon when hunger set in. We stopped on the Pennsylvania side of the river for an hour to enjoy a shoreline lunch. Halfway through lunch I yelled to

There is approximately twenty-seven miles of designated trout water in the Wild and Scenic river section. LEE HARTMAN

Garth, "That looks like a rod floating!" Garth questioned my judgment. "How could that be, rods don't float." I watched it glimmering in the sun, still somewhat convinced it indeed was a fly rod.

We packed up our fold-out chairs and cooler into the boat and set out downriver. The rod now was gone from sight. Feeling hopeless of finding it, we headed to the New York side of the river to fish. After ten minutes of drifting, a shiny glimmer surfaced across the river. Was it the fly rod I saw previously?

A lone drift boat appeared upriver. It was Adrian LaSorte. I alerted him. "I believe a rod is floating ahead of you. Can you reach it?" Adrian mumbled something about me being crazy but continued drifting in the direction of the glittering object. He soon spotted the floating thing and scooped it up. "Hey dude! You got your GLX back," he yelled. "He's gotta be clowning with me," I thought. After I reached his boat, Adrian handed me the rod. He wasn't joking. The neoprene reel cover had kept the GLX rod afloat. My prayer was finally answered. I just nodded my head and smiled.

The 2006 Flood

The 2006 flood affected much of the mid-Atlantic region of the eastern United States. It was considered to be the worst flooding in the region since Hurricane David in 1979.

The river crept ever upward, soon lapping over the four-foot riverbank as two days of heavy rain continued to swell the Delaware River. Indian Springs Camp, which sits high on land and across from the railroad tracks, was out of harm's way—but my neighbors were not. A group of fishermen from Scranton, Pennsylvania, lease a sixteen-acre site located between the railroad tracks and the river. They use three trailers for sleeping quarters, and all are vulnerable to be swept downriver. Immediately I called camp watchdog Ned Holmes to warn him of the danger. Unfortunately, the Scranton native lived an hour away, which gave him no time to rescue the camp trailers.

The river was swelling unrelentingly and creeping over the bank so quickly. With little time before the area was flooded, I hooked up one of the trailers to my 1989 Blazer and drove the thirty-foot camper to Indian Springs, setting it on higher ground. I returned to retrieve a second trailer as the river continued to balloon, forcing Humphreys Brook, located a half mile away, to turn its flow into the campground. The water quickly gushed up from the railroad side while I latched down the second camper. Within minutes the river had surrounded the Blazer, just as I pulled the second camper out of harm's way. By the time Ned and his friends arrived, the river camp property was under three feet of water. The third camper survived, though was severely water damaged.

The following day, June 26, the sky broke loose again, slapping heavy rain against my recently purchased Pennsylvania home. The deluge breached the roof of an unfinished addition, and while tending to the leak there was a loud knock on the front door. It was the local emergency squad asking all residents to leave their homes, explaining Route 191 was partly underwater and still rising. "The road will be closing shortly. If you

A home suffers the aftermath of the storm near the mouth of Equinunk Creek.
LEE HARTMAN

don't leave now, you are on your own," he said convincingly. I wasted no time leaving.

One neighbor, who lived down the road from me in Stockport, did not regard the warning and stayed put in his million-dollar house next to the river. Five years prior to the June rainstorm, a New Jersey dentist had his dream home built next to the Stockport boat access frequently used by river guides. The former New Jersey resident was no friend of anglers. After his home was finished, Joe had lobbied Buckingham Township to close the historic Stockport river access, but his request was denied.

Elizabeth Davidson, a local architect, designed the beautiful dwelling in honor of the Delaware River. Her twenty years of experience living in the Upper Delaware region prompted her to voice concerns about building a home in the floodplain. She had suggested to Joe a six-foot aboveground foundation. He refused, insisting that the foundation be underground. With her reputation at stake, Liz resigned from the project, leaving the decision up to the builder.

On June 28 the floodwaters surrounded Joe's luxurious home, engulfing the building with water that reached the edge of the roof. With no way out and the highway flooded, he and his wife, shotgun in hand, crawled atop the roof to fire a few shots in the air, hoping to attract a rescuer. Bob Wills, a local river guide who lived nearby, became aware of the situation and launched his sixteen-foot drift boat from Route 191 into the raging floodwaters. He paddled the vessel to the edge of the roof and rowed the couple safely to shore. Overwhelmed by the trauma, the Stockport residents wanted no part of living next to the Delaware River and sold the property the following year.

Over the course of three days, the blockbuster rainstorm produced fifteen to seventeen inches of rain in the region, creating a wall of water in every stream in the Upper Delaware Valley and beyond. The town of Hancock was one of the hardest-hit areas and the town's surrounding tributaries took the brunt of the rainstorm. The rushing waters, now with a cargo of rocks and timber, scoured the stream banks, dragging along additional rocks and vegetation that took out bridges, roads, unsecured trailers, picnic tables, propane tanks, and small buildings until emptying into the Delaware. The floodwater was the fourth-highest recorded in the region with damages exceeding fifty million dollars in rural Wayne County, Pennsylvania, and one hundred million plus in Delaware County, New York.

The extraordinary flood was the third in three years. In the aftermath, the extreme devastation to property from the most recent flood triggered Hancock town supervisor Sam Rowe to undertake a massive course of action with regard to the streams and the river. The town elders vowed to do this with or without New York Department of Environmental Conservation (NYSDEC) permits. The NYSDEC soon buckled under the pressure and supplied the Town of Hancock with over four hundred permits. At a frantic pace, backhoes, bulldozers, and shovels dug out local New York tributaries to protect the town's buildings from future damage. The anglers who made yearly visits to the Delaware cringed as the spawning tributaries, the lifeblood of the river, were being damaged mercilessly.

Dredging Humphreys Brook in Lordville, New York. LEE HARTMAN

Friends of the Upper Delaware River (FUDR) filed a sixty-day letter of intent to sue the Town of Hancock, hoping it would lead to addressing the town about potential hazards of dredging and channelization. It was not to be. New York state senator John Bonacic rebelled, saying FUDR preferred "fish over people," a slogan that would haunt us.

FUDR was not at all about fish over people. After the previous two floods, the two-year-old organization had adopted a comprehensive flood-plain/tributary restoration initiative as part of a long-term flood mitigation/fisheries management plan for the Upper Delaware watershed. The organization engaged the services of LandStudies, Inc., an environmental engineering firm that specializes in floodplain restoration. The stream restoration plan sought to minimize flooding events by restoring these streams to their historic conditions by fully utilizing the region's natural floodplains.

While agricultural practices, sewage treatment facilities, and urban development often contribute to today's watershed problems, most flood-related difficulties in the Upper Delaware watershed actually stemmed from early settlements and industrial development dating as far back as the 1700s.

FUDR president Craig Findley reached out to Hancock town supervisor Sam Rowe after the June flood to offer any help we could provide. Sam thanked Craig, stated that everyone was helping as best they could, and told us that he did not know how to direct our group properly. Sam's answer was reasonable under the circumstances.

Sam Rowe invited me on a tour to see the work accomplished on many of the town's tributaries. Mr. Rowe was no average guy. The proud ex-Marine was a giant of a man who loved Hancock. He was proud of what he'd accomplished during the emergency for the town and its people. Three floods in three years had burdened the village residents and

Fish Creek, a tributary on the East Branch, after completion of restoration work.
LEE HARTMAN

their livelihood. It was too much for Sam to take, and he had done what he could to help protect Hancock and the surrounding communities.

Sam's tour was a blessing, as we both shared thoughts and Sam gained a better understanding of FUDR and what we are all about. Though channelizing a stream might have some immediate positive effects, expert studies demonstrate that in the long run they do more harm than good to property and the ecosystem. The results of channelization and dredging induce amplified stream velocity, bank erosion, and faster-rising water, which often create increased property damage.

A year after the 2006 flood event, FUDR's fallout with the village of Hancock was still being felt. Without the support of the local community, it was difficult for our organization to continue with any restoration plans for the flood-ravaged streams. Craig Findley, after serving four years as FUDR leader, resigned in 2008. Taking over his duties was Elmira, New York, native Dan Plummer, known to his peers as "Troutboy." He gained

Bouchioux Brook ravaged by the 2006 flood. LEE HARTMAN

the full support of board members and quickly focused on restoring FUDR's image with the local community by working with Sam Rowe to restore the damaged streams and properties.

The flood-damaged tributaries of Cadosia and Sands Creeks became the target of a fifty-five thousand dollar study funded by the FUDR and the National Fish and Wildlife Foundation, intended to restore flood-plains and habitat. "We cannot think of a better project designed to bring the Upper Delaware closer to its full potential than to restore these damaged tributaries that are spawning waters for the wild trout in the Delaware River," stated Troutboy. The study would provide a blueprint for stream restoration. "Millions of dollars were spent to do emergency flood repair work," said Sam Rowe. "More work on Sands and Cadosia Creeks is necessary to stabilize the floodplain and reduce bank erosion."

LandStudies, Inc. president Mark Guttshall explained that digging the stream deeper and building berms encourages bank erosion and catastrophic failures. A wider, connected floodplain will prevent banks from failing and trees from falling into the creek. A creek needs space to flood in a controlled manner without compromising houses or roads. FUDR later partnered with Trout Unlimited and in 2013 completed a large section of Sands Creek that restored a major floodplain.

Developing a New Release Plan

In 1954 the US Supreme Court issued a decree in *State of New Jersey v. New York and City of New York*, in which the court directed that the Delaware River Master perform multiple duties and functions including administering the provisions of the decree relating to yields, diversions, and releases; conserving waters of the river; compiling data on the water needs of the parties; checking and correlating streamflow measurements and records; observing, recording, and studying the effect of developments in the watershed on water supply and other uses; and making periodic reports to the court.

Water flows on the Delaware River are often extremely erratic. The River Master's performance of his or her duties can be difficult. Trying to satisfy a flow target one hundred miles away is a daily juggling act: how to combine natural and unnatural flows at Montague to make a flow of

Dr. Pete Bousum and Daniel Plummer expressing the need for proper releases to adequately protect the wild trout fishery. FUDR

1,750 cfs. The River Master must gauge seasonal changes, weather forecasts, and hydropower generator releases.

More than one billion gallons of water flow each day by gravity from the Delaware, Catskill, and Croton systems to meet the demands of more than nine million residents of New York City and surrounding communities. The city manages the system in a way that protects water supply reliability and balances multiple objectives including water quantity and quality as well as environmental and economic objectives.

The environmental consequences of any large dam are numerous and varied, and include direct impacts to the biological, chemical, and physical properties of a river and its streamside environment. Changes in temperature and the chemical composition, dissolved oxygen levels, and physical properties of a reservoir are often not suitable for the aquatic plants

226

and natural aquatic communities that have evolved within a given river system.

The alteration of a river's flow and sediment transport downstream of a dam often causes the greatest sustained environmental impact. Life in and around a river evolves and is conditioned by the timing and quantities of river flow. Disrupted and altered water flows can be so severe as to completely de-water river reaches and the life they contain. Yet even subtle changes in temperature caused by the quantity and timing of water flows have an impact on aquatic life, which can unravel the ecological web of a river system.

If you have fished under perfect conditions any of the rivers below each of the three NYC-owned dams, you could be missing the entire story. The trout fishery of the Upper Delaware, and the overall health of the river system, has yet to achieve its full potential due to erratic flows and poor water management. Reforming the Upper Delaware's flow management regime presents a unique challenge.

The East and West Branches, along with the Neversink River, all flow out of New York City water supply reservoirs. The flow management exercises have their roots in the early part of the twentieth century when New Jersey and Pennsylvania sued NYC in an effort to gain their fair share of water. The suit culminated in a consent decree issued by the US Supreme Court that divided up the water in the basin between NYC and downriver states. The decree did not include any minimum flows for ecological conservation or any other provision to preserve the health of the ecosystem.

With each new management agreement that has been reached since 1983, the cold-water fishery continued to remain irrelevant to those decision makers who decide the release programs. At the same time, increased demand for drinking water and unpredictable weather patterns have placed additional pressure on the system.

Regrettably, any flow regime change is dictated by a Supreme Court consent decree that can only be changed with the unanimous consent of the parties: New York, New Jersey, Pennsylvania, Delaware, and, in particular, New York City must be convinced that a more ecologically responsible flow regime will not threaten their water supply.

In 2004 Revision 7, with a 9,200 cfs/days thermal bank (equates to 92 days of 100 cfs/day of water), maintained summer water temperature of 72°F and no higher than 75°F at the Hankins gage located eighteen miles below Hancock. The increased flow, when called upon, kept average water temperatures a cool 68°F to 70°F at Lordville, nine miles above the Hankins gage.

The judgment by the NYSDEC to abandon Rev 7 in 2005, which curbed the flow out of Cannonsville to 225 cfs as measured at Hale Eddy, New York, proved costly to the Delaware ecosystem and threatened the health of the trout fishery. The Decree Parties announced that the bank-based release program under Rev 7 would be scrapped in 2007 for a more adaptive flexible release program based on reservoir storage levels.

The decision by the Decree Parties to initiate a storage-based release plan intrigued both Trout Unlimited (TU) and the Delaware River Foundation (DRF). FUDR regarded it as a positive step forward, though remained cautious on the application of the new plan.

The Flow Management Technical Advisory Committee, under the umbrella of the Delaware River Basin Commission (DRBC), created the Subcommittee on Ecological Flows (SEF), an implementation entity to mutually develop a new release strategy for support of ecological functions in the Upper Delaware River Basin. The objective of the subcommittee was to improve conservation flow requirements for maintaining a self-sustaining aquatics ecosystem in the tailwaters.

It was envisioned that a new release policy, without relying on a thermal bank, would be less labor intensive, reduce errors in predicting needed releases, and provide more stable base flows rather than the often rapidly rising and falling releases to meet temperature and flow targets.

The releases from Cannonsville played a dominant role in FUDR's thinking, because the water flows have a greater potential to maintain cold-water conditions on the main stem of the river. After a few FUDR board meetings, we agreed to visit New York congressman Maurice Hinchey (D-NY). The congressman appointed noted fisheries specialist Dr. Robert Bachman to the SEF. FUDR now became a cooperator to add input in gaining proper ecological flows in the Delaware system.

At the time the DRBC solicited The Nature Conservancy (TNC) to help develop sustainable water management solutions. TNC was employed to conserve biodiversity throughout the Delaware River Basin by investing in programs in each of the four basin states. It believed that only an agreement on a clear and comprehensive process would resolve the Delaware Basin flow management issues.

The SEF committee included representatives from TNC, NYSDEC, Pennsylvania Fish & Boat Commission, Delaware River Keeper, Academy of Natural Sciences in Philadelphia, New York City Department of Environmental Protection (NYCDEP), Pennsylvania Department of Conservation and Natural Resources (DCNR), US Geological Survey (USGS), TU, DRF, Columbia University, and FUDR.

Under the criteria and constraints of the Decree Parties, the committee came to an agreement to use the Delaware River Decision Support System (DRDSS)—a decision support framework for water management also known as the Bove' Study, developed by the USGS.

The Bove' Study proposed a series of four categorical protection levels for describing cold-water ecosystem management objectives for the Delaware tailwaters. The protection levels are for non-drought years and address both year-round habitat and summer water temperature, and are defined as follows:

Excellent—River sections with this designation will experience excellent year-round cold-water aquatic habitat and thermal protection and maintain opportunities for a year-round cold-water fishery. Summer water temperatures are routinely 68°F or less and would never or very rarely exceed a daily maximum of 75°F.

Good—River sections with this designation will provide cold-water aquatic habitat and thermal protection and maintain opportunities for a cold-water fishery. However, elevated water temperatures will occasionally be an issue in these sections, and the year-round abundance of cold-water species are not expected to be as prevalent as in sections with the Excellent protection level. Summer water temperatures will occasionally exceed a daily maximum of 75°F for short periods, and water temperatures greater than 68°F will occur more frequently than for sections with Excellent protection.

Moderate—River sections with this designation will experience adequate flow and some thermal protection for cold-water species and maintain seasonal opportunities for a cold-water fishery. Cold-water species will not be as prevalent as in waters with higher levels of protection. The thermal benefits from reservoir releases will diminish in these sections, and summer water temperatures will frequently exceed daily maximums of 75°F. However, stream flow will provide fish with sufficient access to cold-water refuges.

Minimal—River sections with this designation will experience adequate flow but only limited thermal protection. The thermal benefits from reservoir releases are greatly reduced in these sections, and the suitability of summer water temperatures in many years will not be optimal for cold-water species. The quality of the cold-water fishery will be generally seasonal and will vary from year to year. Flows should be adequate to enable trout to reach cold-water refugia and to protect dwarf wedge mussel populations in the vicinity of Callicoon.

The DRBC continued to apply a 75°F daily maximum water temperature as described in its management objectives. A thermal stress day applies when the maximum daily water temperature equals or exceeds 75°F with a limited minimum daily water temperature of 72°F for an entire twenty-four-hour period. Fish mortality becomes a worry if stress conditions persist for a period of several consecutive days with fish unable to move to cooler-water refugia. This threshold is intended to serve as an indicator of where maximum water temperatures may be a limiting factor for trout populations.

The Bove' Study noted that for optimal trout growth and survival, water temperatures need to remain below 68°F as detailed by many scientific studies and supported by the Cold Water Fishes designation under Pennsylvania Chapter 93 Water Quality Standards regulations and the New York State Division of Fish, Wildlife, and Marine Resources's "best thermal conditions" in its 1992 "Fishery Management Plan for the Upper Delaware Tailwaters."

The subcommittee's final consensus, based on the DRDSS flow reports, would employ the Tailwaters Habitat Protection and Discharge Management Program, which incorporated release tables based on reservoir storage levels—L-1 (highest level) through L-5 (lowest level). However, the initial release tables proposed by the Decree Parties was disappointing, and some members became concerned that an L-2 summer release level set at 260 cfs would not sustain the main-stem trout fishery during warmer months.

Dr. Bachman could not endorse a 260 cfs summer release, indicating that thermal temperatures during summer months would be too high for the main stem. Dr. Bachman stated, "This could threaten the survivability of trout 75 percent of the time."

Trout Unlimited and FUDR were equally concerned that the constraint the DRBC imposed in the interim Flexible Flow Management Plan (FFMP) was biased and inflexible in responding to low flows and high-water temperatures in the Upper Delaware. The DRBC and the City of New York felt otherwise, and on February 20, 2007, the Decree Parties adopted the initial FFMP for an interim five-year period to be reviewed and negotiated annually by the five Decree Party members.

The initial release tables in the new plan were tailored more to suit the cold-water habitat in the West Branch, upper East Branch, and Neversink River—each viewed as excellent trout streams, referencing the West Branch as one of the best wild brown trout streams on the eastern seaboard. In the signed resolution the signatory parties gave the brown trout its deserved acclaim, but curiously there was no mention of the rainbow trout, the most recognized game fish in the main stem of the Delaware.

In rivers, the water that you touch is the last of what has passed and the first of that which comes; so with present time.
—LEONARDO DA VINCI

The FFMP began on October 1, 2007. The initial release program performed somewhat as expected on the river branches during winter and

Cannonsville Storage Zone	Winter		Spring		Summer		Fall	
	Dec 1 Mar31	Apr 1 Apr 30	May 1 May31	Jun 1 Jun 15	Jun 16 Jun 30	Jul 1 Aug 31	Sep1 Sep 30	Oct 1 Nov 30
L1-a	1500	1500	225	275	1500	1500	1500	1500
L1-b	250	110	225	275	275	350	275	250
L1-c	110	110	225	275	275	275	140	110
L-2	80	80	215	260	260	260	115	80
L-3	70	70	100	175	175	175	95	70
L-4	55	55	75	130	130	130	55	60
L-5	50	50	50	120	120	120	50	50

The initial FFMP flow tables for Cannonsville Reservoir. LEE HARTMAN

early spring. By early June, thermal stress fears in the main stem became a reality. On four consecutive days the air temperature exceeded 90°F, which heated water to the lethal temperature of 81°F by June 10.

To alleviate the temperature crisis, FUDR quickly responded with phone calls and emails to NYSDEC asking for thermal relief water. The Decree Parties agreed to NYDEC's request and provided a two-day thermal release pulse from Cannonsville Reservoir that temporarily relieved the immediate crisis. The relief effort was a mere Band-Aid. River flows continued to be low during the remaining summer and no directed releases were called upon. By early August flows on the West Branch had become the lowest recorded for that time frame since the 1981 drought crisis.

NYSDEC continued its efforts among the Decree Parties to establish an emergency thermal protection release bank. Daily summer water temperatures measured at the Lordville gage equaled or exceeded 75°F for twenty days, with a trout-lethal temperature of 81°F. After five weeks of deliberation, a thermal protection bank was agreed upon by the Decree Parties. Unfortunately, it was so small the DEC had to constrain the summer releases, which made it nearly impossible to reach proper thermal conditions necessary for trout to survive.

A similar pattern occurred on the river at Callicoon during the months of July and September. The flow in each of those months dropped to the lowest level recorded during the previous thirty years—with one exception that occurred under Revision 7.

NYCDEP, in concert with the development of FFMP, was in the early stage of developing an Operation Support Tool (OST), calling it a state-of-the-art decision support system to aid operations and planning throughout the water supply system. OST, a forecast-driven simulation and analysis tool, would provide city operators and managers with likely predictions of future system events, such as forecasting meteorological episodes, to help determine the minimum flow necessary to satisfy the court-mandated target at Montague.

When the well's dry, we know the worth of water.
—*BENJAMIN FRANKLIN*

On September 4, 2008, the city predicted a major rain event that triggered a rapid reduction of water releases from Cannonsville Reservoir three days in advance of the rainstorm.

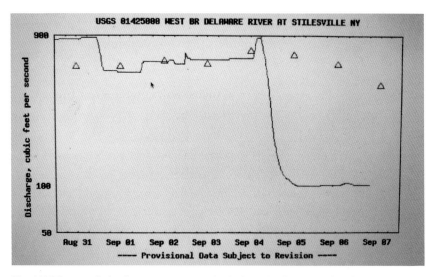

The USGS recorded release rates one mile below the Cannonsville Dam.
KEN BOVE'

The flow at the Lordville gage on September 4 measured 905 cfs. The following day river flows suddenly dropped to 333 cfs during the twenty-four-hour period, displaying a boneyard of rocks and exposing river bottom life halfway across the river. A day later the flows fifteen miles downriver plunged to 519 cfs at Callicoon, approaching its minimum record level of 438 cfs and threatening the dwarf wedge mussel colony, listed as an endangered species. The flexible flow plan proved that it was not flexible at all and was no better than any past revision.

At the end of the season, the Decree Parties promised a new flexible flow strategy to manage the resource that would balance the vital drinking water needs of the city, the flow considerations of downriver residents, and the sensitive environmental resources of the river.

The DRBC decided to withdraw its proposal to amend the water code that would legitimize the interim FFMP. Trout Unlimited and FUDR welcomed the decision and, along with many other groups, agreed this was a correct and responsible action.

In 2009 the FFMP/OST's slightly improved flows benefited the East Branch and Neversink; however, no flow changes were made on the West Branch. There were growing concerns again that the interim agreement had fragile benefits for the renowned wild trout fishery within the upper main stem and scenic corridor. With fewer mandated releases during summer months, the river continued to be vulnerable to high water temperatures and yo-yo releases that raised fears within the environmental community.

The limiting factor in any cold-water ecosystem is temperature. The bottom releases from the NYC Delaware Basin reservoirs once established a wild trout fishery as far down as Callicoon, New York. You can't measure improvement by fish surveys, creel studies, or number of anglers, nor even by the number of restaurants, gas stations, or fly shops—but flows, temperatures, and releases at Lordville. Any reputable biologist should know that the upper limit of a cold-water ecosystem is 68°F. The difficult part is to get the decision makers to understand that trout live precariously during extreme flow and temperature fluctuations.

The bottom line is that low summer flows and high temperatures determine the standing stock of wild trout in any stream or river. The

River level September 4, 2008, at Lordville, New York. LEE HARTMAN

River level September 5, 2008, at Lordville, New York. LEE HARTMAN

reservoir managers must look at what flows are achievable to maintain 68°F. That is what protecting the cold-water ecosystem means, and not anything else. As Lewis Carroll said in *Alice's Adventures in Wonderland*, "If you don't know where you are going, any road will get you there." We are going all right, but we still have not agreed on where we want to go.

In 2010 the NYSDEC fisheries division and the Pennsylvania Fish & Boat Commission were equally concerned about the tailwater trout fishery on the Upper Delaware. Together they published a white paper describing recommended river flows for the Upper Delaware River system from a cold-water ecosystem perspective. The two state fisheries agencies worked with the Decree Party representatives and associated work groups to revise the FFMP reservoir storage rule curve. The Decree Parties agreed to increase summer releases out of Cannonsville during June 1 to August 31. The one-year interim agreement was adopted by the Decree Parties and went into effect for June 1, 2011 through May 31, 2012.

The revised Flexible Flow Management Plan improved the flows on the West Branch and upper main stem. However, New Jersey continued to challenge NYC's water allocations each year and refused to sign the 2016 interim FFMP agreement.

After a year of negotiating, a new agreement was reached on October 21, 2017, by the Decree Parties, and New Jersey signed the 2017 FFMP. The two-part, ten-year agreement (through May 31, 2028), reviewed on the fifth year (2023), now guides the current Delaware River management operations.

There are two parts of the agreement that quickly became major concerns for the environmental groups. The agreement called for maintaining the water temperature at Lordville, New York, at 75°F, no higher than 77°F, with a 2,500 cfs thermal bank to protect the main-stem fishery.

The 2017 FFMP agreement was a giant step backward for the cold-water habitat in the Upper Delaware. The new plan exceeds the normal thermal stress level for trout by 9°F and is one degree away from the trout-kill temperature of 78°F. A 2,500 cfs/days thermal bank of water under long-hot summer periods is not nearly enough to cool to proper trout-friendly temperatures in the Upper Delaware River. It will be like trying to use a garden hose to put out a house fire.

- 12 -

Rainbows Under a Pot of Gold

High water quality and the presence of clean water releases with a free-flowing character all give the Delaware River some of the most important fisheries habitat in the Northeast. The Delaware enjoys a diverse and well-balanced biological ecosystem. The uppermost segment of the river is also unique among large rivers in the East due to its relatively cold temperatures. This stretch supports an abundant population of wild rainbow trout offering some of the finest trout fishing, which attracts anglers from every part of the country. In the river's southern reaches, below Callicoon,

The scenic river corridor is a water trail through a timeless valley that is immersed in nature. The beauty is in the journey. LEE HARTMAN

Rainbow trout are notoriously strong, often leaping freely downriver after it is hooked on a fly. LEE HARTMAN

you can discover many species of warm-water sport fish including small-mouth bass, sunfish, eel, striped bass, shad, and walleye.

Many people ask what my fondest memory as a guide on the Delaware River is. It's a reasonable question to ask but a very difficult one to answer. After spending thirty years guiding on this treasured river, I have numerous stories to select from to suit whomever I'm talking to—like telling a big fish story (there were many) or seeing a bald eagle dive from a treetop and swoop up a fish next to your dry fly, or telling about the huge black bear lying on its back in the river shallows to cool off from the summer sun.

These stories are all great recollections—and often shared with others—but there is one incident that triggers my warmest memory, but one I seldom reveal. There happens to be a large rock that sits under three feet of water, which can be seen while floating into the confluence with the East and West Branches of the river. Each time I pass by this boulder, it evokes the memory of where I caught my first rainbow trout forty-five years ago.

Although not bragging-size, the sixteen-inch trout grabbed my fly next to that rock and suddenly bolted fifty feet downriver, tail-dancing across the water into the setting sun, before I secured the feisty, colorful fish into the net. The remembrance of catching that rainbow and its antics to escape the hook was a life-changing event that kept me coming back to the Delaware, where I live today.

That fishing experience on the Upper Delaware in 1973 placed me at the headwaters between Pennsylvania's Appalachian plateau and New York's Catskill Mountains. Since the completion of the Cannonsville Reservoir in 1968, large volumes of frigid water have been released, enough to numb your feet and fill the river with a ghostly mist on a hot summer day.

The New York State Department of Conservation (NYSDEC) recognized the value of the tailwater with its wild trout and reclassified the Upper Delaware River between Hancock and Callicoon as a cold-water fishery. The century-old rainbow trout dominated the twenty-seven-mile stretch, which soon turned into one of the finest "wild trout" fishing spots in the northeastern United States.

My daughter Nicole with her husband, Pete Merges, canoeing on a misty morning. LEE HARTMAN

In a country where nature has been so lavish and where we have been so spendthrift of indigenous beauty, to set aside a few rivers in their natural state should be considered an obligation.
—SENATOR FRANK CHURCH FROM IDAHO, ARGUING FOR PASSAGE OF
THE 1968 WILD AND SCENIC RIVERS ACT

When John Hutzky was appointed as the first National Park Service (NPS) superintendent of the Upper Delaware Scenic and Recreational River in November 1979, he was tasked with the formation of the Upper Delaware River Management Plan (RMP). The river plan entered into uncharted waters.

Since the signing of the National Wild and Scenic Rivers Act on October 2, 1968, the process to create a river management plan for the Upper Delaware has been most unusual. Normally, on a designated scenic river the NPS would buy the land required for the national park. In this case the NPS was ordered by Congress to work with state and local governments, other agencies, and community groups to develop a plan

America's bird, the bald eagle, can be seen throughout the scenic river valley.
LEE HARTMAN

240

in which federal jurisdiction would be limited to the river surface and a small amount of property, while the majority of land remained privately owned.

Many residents along the river were extremely skeptical about the intentions of government officials regarding acquisition of land. Some of it had been purchased by eminent domain from unwilling sellers during the planned Tocks Island Dam project in the middle Delaware River. In earlier decades, New York City had condemned thousands of acres of land to create the Neversink, Cannonsville, and Pepacton Reservoirs, which ended with many homesteads forever covered by water. With that historical backdrop, the challenge for the NPS was to convince residents of the Upper Delaware Valley that the primary mission was to protect the natural resources of the area, and not take land by condemnation.

In 1980 the creation of the Upper Delaware River RMP began. NPS personnel from the Denver office—working with local officials from five counties and with input from a group of local county planning professionals called the Upper Delaware Clearinghouse—drafted two river management plans, both of which were soundly rejected by residents. The general consensus was that the Denver planners did not understand the importance of home rule. Major concerns that residents had included overregulation, the use of eminent domain, loss of local control, and issues such as the right to fish, hunt, and use the river corridor in ways that families had for generations.

After a third attempt to draft a plan, the Denver-based planners withdrew from the process. Local citizens and politicians were brought in, and a group of seven Pennsylvania townships and eight New York towns along the river formed the Conference of Upper Delaware Townships (COUP) in 1981. COUP became involved in an important way. Several community groups pushed for de-authorization of the plan with the hope that the NPS would leave the valley. A California rights activist came to the area promoting the film *For the Good of All*. The film told the story of the US Army Corps of Engineers and the NPS regarding the Cuyahoga Valley National Recreation Area in Ohio in the late 1970s and early 1980s. According to the rights activist, the number of homes purchased by the federal government to create the area was well over three hundred.

He said, "The small community was destroyed and schools closed—their tax base eroded by unnecessary land acquisition." The film touched off a squabble that gave support to those calling for de-authorization.

Soon after came vandalism aimed at the NPS. In February, five vehicles in the NPS motor pool were painted with black swastikas. By July, five towns and townships had endorsed de-authorization, while other towns came in support of the Upper Delaware legislation. COUP hired a consulting firm to assist them in rewriting the plan.

On June 4, 1986, more than three hundred people attended the first public hearing on the proposal, held in the Damascus school. A large majority of people opposed the plan. As the meeting was called to order, an organized disruption began with cowbells and other noisemakers. Chants of "No park, no plan, no way" broke out and continued for ninety long minutes, which prevented anyone from speaking. Eventually, the representatives of COUP and the NPS left the podium.

The following meetings on June 6 and 7 were orderly, and testimony from seventy-four individuals was taken, with 256 written comments received. Later that month, COUP sent a letter inviting fifteen eligible towns to participate in a new plan revision committee. Nine of the fifteen towns and townships chose to participate, and their representatives held several hearings through October 23.

During the summer, tensions ran high. The *River Reporter* newspaper had been supporting the NPS and the adoption of the river management plan, which drew the ire of those who favored de-authorization. In August 1986 the home of the publisher and editor of the paper burned to the ground. While no one was ever charged with setting the fire, many residents remained convinced that the fire was connected to the NPS controversy.

The plan committee made some four hundred changes over the next few months to strike a balance among the entities. In November 1986 the plan was adopted. The Upper Delaware Council was officially incorporated on February 18, 1987, and became the oversight body to implement the RMP. The voting membership included representatives of eight New York towns: Hancock, Fremont, Delaware, Cochecton, Tusten, Highland, Lumberland, and Deer Park; four Pennsylvania townships: Lackawaxen,

Damascus, Shohola, and Westfall; and the two states. The Delaware River Basin Commission and the National Park Service are non-voting members. Three Wayne County townships—Buckingham, Manchester, and Berlin—are eligible for membership but have not yet chosen to join.

Congress, using the Wild and Scenic Rivers Act, designated the Upper Delaware River as a unit of the National Park System and a component of the National Wild and Scenic Rivers System. Two reaches of the Delaware River were included in the system. The uppermost section extends 73.4 miles from the confluence of the East and West Branches at Hancock downstream to a railroad bridge in the vicinity of Mill Rift, Pennsylvania. The second section covers about 40 miles from the junction south of Port Jervis, New York, downstream to the Delaware Water Gap.

The scenic designation put a spotlight on the river, attracting anglers, boaters, and sightseers. The Hancock region soon was surrounded by river outfitters, campgrounds, and lodging establishments catering to their customers. The National Park Service currently permits sixty-six fishing guides and twelve canoe liveries to operate within the Upper Delaware

John Morgan with a nice rainbow caught in the Wild and Scenic corridor of the Delaware River. LEE HARTMAN

Scenic and Recreational River. By 2018 the cold-water fishing and boating industry was adding to the regional economy an estimated $305 million annually, including an additional $105 million in the real estate value of second homes.

The Wild and Scenic Rivers Act affirms that the Upper Delaware shall be preserved in free-flowing condition, and that the "immediate environments shall be protected for the benefit and enjoyment of present and future generations." The act also states that land managers will work to "preserve other selected rivers or sections thereof in their free-flowing condition to protect the water quality of such rivers and to fulfill other vital national conservation purposes."

Ed Van Put, noted Catskill angler, author, principal fish and wildlife technician (forty years) with NYSDEC's Bureau of Fisheries, and friend of the Upper Delaware River wrote:

> *Tributaries are the life-blood of the river. The river's wonderful fisheries cannot exist without these cold-water streams and their healthy trout habitats. Based on my experience with other large rivers, I doubt that rainbows spawn directly in the Delaware. That does not mean that spawning does not take place, but I doubt that it is successful. I have walked many tributaries during spawning season in Region 3, and my observations convince me that spawning recruitment comes from them. Streams such as Hankins Creek, Basket Creek, Hoolihan Creek, and Pea Brook all have spring runs of rainbow trout, and I suppose all tributaries to the river do. If you look at topo maps of tributaries leading into the Delaware from either Pennsylvania or New York, you will see that there are few, so each is extremely important for providing trout spawning habitat. The value of streams like Cadosia Creek and Sands Creek cannot be overestimated.*

A small but important point is the additional value of tributaries as refugia for trout when main-stem water temperatures get too warm and adult trout seek cooler water for survival. Vegetative cover along these tributaries is essential to keep water temperature cold. The tributaries are

President Jimmy Carter hooking up with a nice fish on the Upper Delaware River in 1984. ED VAN PUT

trout nursery areas, in some ways equally as important as the Delaware main stem in creating these fisheries.

The Lenape would have never witnessed the brown and rainbow trout that exist in the river today. Their livelihoods in the undammed river relied mostly on shad, sturgeon, and eel, all natural to the Delaware. The rainbow trout, native to the northwest Pacific region, have nevertheless flourished in the scenic corridor and become an important component of the river. People are now the caretakers of these precious, painted fish, descendants of those northwestern trout that made their home in the treasured river.

It is our responsibility—as good citizens and good fisherman—to do our part, and that means to do whatever it takes to make state, local, and city agencies recognize the value and plight of the wild rainbow trout. Only we can guarantee that our children's children will enjoy these fish a century from now.

Connecticut angler Stan Beirut holding a brown trout nearly as long as his arm.
LEE HARTMAN

Brown trout were introduced from Europe in the nineteenth century and are present in the river, though they maintain greater numbers in the upper reaches. It has been estimated that 50 percent of the rainbow population is born in the streams located within the Wild and Scenic section of the Delaware River between Lordville and Callicoon. The East Branch also has significant spawning streams vital to their survival.

When Seth Green first introduced his hatchery-farmed fingerlings to smaller tributaries in the late 1800s, he had no idea brown and rainbow trout would find their way into the Delaware and persevere. Since the days of the disappearing brook trout, these fish have learned how to survive, and they continue to persist in limited ways despite the most unlikely conditions.

The Delaware River rainbow are not ordinary nor are they stocked. The non-native rainbow rarely reproduces in northeastern streams—the exception being the Upper Delaware River tributaries. Vital to their existence are the many streams that enter the river. The small feeder streams in the scenic corridor, many of which were not specifically acknowledged, are biologically important to the value of the fishery. These tributaries became natural rainbow trout factories and were administratively recognized by the State of New York and the Commonwealth of Pennsylvania as proven spawning and nursery waters for the hearty rainbow in the spring season.

Based on fish counts, rainbow trout numbers have been slowly declining in recent years. Moving the thermal target from Hankins to Lordville is a contributing factor. Among other influences are stream blockages caused by numerous flood events, failed flow management practices, and, more recently, increasing the temperature target at Lordville while lowering the thermal "bank." These factors can further debilitate the trout in the main stem.

The number of New York streams that enter the river were determined by NYSDEC as classified C(t) (trout spawning) areas between Hancock and Callicoon, none of which are stocked streams.

The Delaware River tributaries in the scenic corridor are nature's hatchery for rainbow trout. LEE HARTMAN

On the Pennsylvania side, all tributaries entering the Upper Delaware are designated as an exceptional-value, high-quality, cold-water fishery by the Commonwealth of Pennsylvania under the Clean Stream Law. This designation, designed to improve water quality and habitat, permits no degradation of exceptional value streams. It also permits no degradation of high-quality, cold-water fishery streams, unless overriding social and economic justification/benefits exist. The streams that enter the Delaware in the scenic corridor known to have spawning trout are:

New York Tributaries
- Humphries Brook
- Abe Lord Creek
- Pea Brook
- Hoolihan Creek
- Basket Creek
- Hankins Creek
- Callicoon Creek

Pennsylvania Tributaries
- Stockport Creek
- Equinunk Creek*
- Factory Creek
- Little Equinunk Creek
- Cooley Creek
- Hollister Creek

*Stocked with brown and brook trout only

In the warm-water fishery, generally considered below Callicoon, both brown and rainbow trout can be caught in the vicinity of stream-bed springs and cold tributary stream mouths. The smallmouth bass and walleye pike were first introduced in the Delaware during the late 1800s. The bass are cool water fish and primarily located between Hankins, New York, and down to Port Jervis, New York. Because of environmental limitations smallmouth bass is, however, fished for over a longer period of time each year than any other species of fish in the Delaware River.

During the past thirty-five years, reductions in conservation releases from New York City's reservoirs have adversely affected the quality of the trout fishery in the scenic corridor. The city's Municipal Water Efficiency Program, which was begun in 1979 by the New York City Deartment of Environmental Protection, has since reduced NYC's water consumption by 65 percent—a substantial savings of Delaware River water. In addition the Croton Reservoir system has been resurrected to supply NYC additional water each year, which also increases water storage in the Delaware Basin reservoirs. And yet, with each new flow agreement, the cold-water wild trout fishery continues to suffer the fate of not gaining a fair share of saved water for protecting the fishery.

The walleye pike is another cool-water fish, predominantly found throughout the upper reaches of the river, that can be fished throughout much of the year. Because of its secretive behavior, the walleye is generally not an easy catch, particularly on warm, sunny days. Walleye are night feeders. Dark, cloudy weather and late-night fishing are favorite periods for dedicated walleye anglers.

The American shad, once removed in great numbers by netting and pollution, are an important sport fish in the Upper Delaware system. Today the Delaware is the only natural shad river in the Northeast (from Maine to West Virginia) free of man-made barriers and industrial pollution to allow passage of these migratory fish. Up to five hundred thousand migrate to the upper reaches. The most important spawning grounds and nurseries are in the river between Callicoon and Hancock and into the East Branch as far as Downsville, New York. Following hatching the young shad are found during the summer months in nursery areas throughout the river corridor; in fall they migrate to sea.

The scenic portion of the river classified as trout water is not void of other problems during warm-water events. Ed Van Put noted, "When these fish are in stress due to high water temperature they will gather at the mouths of cold-water tributaries, and over an extended period of time the fish can become subject to illegal fishing (i.e. snagging, netting, predation etc.). At times under the undesirable condition, stressed trout develop sores on their body from argulus, a parasitic fish louse that attaches itself on a host fish."

Fish lice generally are not lethal unless fish are severely stressed during prolonged high-water temperatures. It's not known if, or how many, trout will die from these parasites. Van Put also has seen argulus on shad as they become stressed from spawning and their long journey.

From the mighty striped bass to the shy mudminnow, a wide variety of fish inhabit the clean waters of the Delaware River—including native and non-native species. Of the sixty-one total fish species within the National Park System, forty-four are native to the region, fourteen are native to North America but probably did not naturally occur in this region, and three are introduced alien species not native to North America.

Ten of these species have been listed as rare, threatened, or endangered by the states of New Jersey and/or Pennsylvania. Two species, the ironcolor shiner and the bridle shiner, may also inhabit national park waters. However, the last report of the ironcolor shiner in park waters was in 1978, and only one known population remains in Pennsylvania.

Native fish in the park include fallfish, striped bass, brook trout, eastern mudminnow, American shad, yellow perch, and pumpkinseed.

The following species were introduced to the eastern region before the creation of the park on the Delaware River and now inhabit park waters: rainbow trout, smallmouth bass, largemouth bass, bluegill, green sunfish, black crappie, channel catfish, walleye pike, muskellunge, gizzard shad, alewife, and fathead minnow.

Four native anadromous species can also be found within the national park reaches. Anadromous species begin their lives in fresh water but later migrate to the ocean, where they spend the middle part of their lives, then migrate back to fresh water to spawn. The four anadromous species in the park section are striped bass, American lamprey, American shad, and the alewife. Juvenile sea lamprey may remain in freshwater streams for fourteen years before migrating to the ocean, whereas juveniles of the other anadromous species migrate to the ocean in the first year of life.

One catadromous species, the American eel, occurs in the Delaware River within the park. Catadromous species begin their lives in the ocean but migrate to fresh water, where they spend the middle part of their lives, then migrate back to the ocean to spawn. Female American eels migrate from the Atlantic Ocean into the Delaware River when they are about one year old, and typically remain for about ten years. Unlike the females, it seems that male eels typically do not migrate into fresh water but remain in the brackish waters of estuaries. Thus, it is likely that all, or almost all, American eels inside national park waters are females.

The alien species are the common carp, native to Asia and Europe; goldfish, native to Asia; and brown trout, native to Europe.

Endangered Species Considerations

The Endangered Species Act of 1973 requires federal agencies to protect federally listed or threatened or endangered species and habitat critical to their survival. The objective of the threatened and endangered species section is to identify and protect rare, threatened, and endangered species within the river corridor.

Two federally endangered species are known to occur in the Upper Delaware tailwaters—the dwarf wedge mussel and the bridle shiner. The cold-water aquatic community in the Upper Delaware River and its tributaries was not expected to cause harm to these species and may provide limited benefit as described in the Bove' Study. To further protect these orders, additional information on the habitat requirements and limiting factors in the main-stem Delaware tailwater is necessary to fully assess the impact of reservoir releases on them.

Jeffery C. Cole of Frostburg State University Department of Biology, in a cooperative agreement with the US Department of Interior, was assigned the task to predict flow and temperature regimes at three dwarf wedge mussel (Alasmidonta heterodon) locations in the Delaware river. Cole's report in 2008 suggested that a flow requirement of approximately 930 cfs at the US Geological Survey gage at Callicoon is needed to fully protect dwarf wedge mussels and other mussel species. Similarly, the impact of such a target on drought events and whether it would be needed on a year-round basis or only during the summer needs further investigation. Seasonal and life-stage requirements for dwarf wedge mussels continue to remain poorly defined.

Lead, Follow, or
Get Out of the Way!

"Upper Delaware river watchers should stop crying about how the New York City reservoirs are managed and look to the existing federal law that protects this river. The city's draining of Cannonsville Reservoir, curtailment of downstream releases, and the apparent acquiescence of Delaware River Basin Commission officials to those actions run in the face of federal law.

"The Wild and Scenic Rivers Act of 1968 (Public Law 90-542) was drafted to include language to protect the Upper Delaware from contradictory water management by the states or federal government. Sections of the law, cited successfully some years ago, discouraged NYC diversion plans, which then presented a threat to the nationally protected river.

"The 1968 law listed the Upper Delaware as a 'study' river, and as such, no agency of the federal government would 'license or abet any unit of government or commercial enterprise who proposed anything that would impact upon the original designated rivers' or 'study rivers,' period. This prohibition includes the New York State Department of Conservation, the City of New York, and everyone else.

"The muscle of the law has already been invoked. In the 1980s, New York proposed to sell off any hydropower from its release valves to the West and East branches, respectively, as well as the collecting tunnel that carried these waters from lower elevations of the reservoirs to the Rondout collecting reservoir. Water going through tunnels for hydropower was not going to come down the river.

"In my position then as National Park Service superintendent, I drafted a lengthy response to the Federal Energy Regulatory Commission (FERC) and all other parties. Granting the license would have circumvented the Wild and Scenic Rivers Act and the authority of Congress. FERC stood up and took notice; so did the city. They had second thoughts and the plan died.

"This wasn't the only instance where the federal designation protected residents from competing water-management plans. The NPS earlier successfully intervened at Shohola Township's request when a developer wanted to dam Shohola Creek for hydroelectric power. The same provisions of the Wild and Scenic Rivers Act applied.

"Upper Delaware Council executive director Bill Douglas and I made frequent trips to let them know that the Upper Delaware was not only a player, it was the five hundred-pound gorilla. But the DEC and DRBC were well represented, and at this time, we stepped back and let them lead. Was it a mistake?

"Stop wringing your hands and pointing fingers, and get off your duffs. Fight this or there won't be any Upper Delaware worth fighting for. If you don't demand action from the agencies, ask for congressional oversight before everything goes to hell in a bucket. Ask your congressmen and congresswomen whether running the tailwater dry is what Congress had in mind in 1968 and 1978.

"Running the river dry in winter is extremely dangerous. I didn't spend sixteen years of my life working on behalf of the valley to see another winter flood like the drought year of 1981. Because of that flood, everyone was ready to condemn the NPS for not issuing a warning. We listed and entered into an agreement with the US Army Corps of Engineers Cold Weather Research Station in Hanover, New Hampshire, to monitor winter ice conditions. Is that agreement still in effect? Many rescue personnel, including several NPS rangers, put their lives on the line that fateful night and the next day to help rescue people.

"Now it's the ecosystem's turn. Let the NPS in Washington, DC, or Philadelphia, and the Secretary of the Interior—or at least his stand-in—know what's going on. You didn't hesitate to contact Congress when you thought your homes and livelihoods were threatened. Well, they're threatened again. If you don't use the law, this is all but just sound and fury signifying nothing."

—John Hutzky, NPS superintendent,
Upper Delaware River (1979–1995)

National Trout Unlimited, with its Delaware River Committee representatives from Pennsylvania, New York, and New Jersey, has taken the lead and continues to play a major role to improve water releases from the NYC Delaware River Basin reservoirs to help sustain the river flows in order to maintain and restore this unique wild trout fishery.

Since the inception of Friends of the Upper Delaware River in 2004, the organization has evolved to become a major influence in the local region and remains committed to its fundamental mission of maximizing water releases to ensure the ecological balance necessary to protect the cold-water habitat.

Trying to harness more water for the recognized tailwater fisheries under the constraints of the court decree and continually weakened flow plans that are designed to minimize releases is a task that can only be done with a strong declaration from the communities and those who rely on the economic benefits gained from the river.

Under the leadership of the Friends of the Upper Delaware River (FUDR), chairman Dan Plummer and executive director Jeff Skelding together played a key role in the formation of the Upper Delaware River Tailwaters Coalition. The organization—which is composed of the towns of Hancock, Hamden, Masonville, Sanford, and Tomkins, the village of Hancock, Broome County, Upper Delaware River Business Coalition, Equinunk Watershed Alliance, Trout Unlimited, and Friends of the Upper Delaware River—added a new voice, which helped gain the attention of the US Congress; state legislatures in New York, Pennsylvania, and New Jersey; and local governments throughout the Upper Delaware River watershed.

In October 2016 President Barack Obama signed a landmark piece of legislation that created the first federally authorized program established to protect and restore the entire Delaware River watershed from the Catskills to the Delaware Bay.

Many other iconic water bodies in the United States, like the Chesapeake Bay and the Great Lakes, have longstanding federal authorizations that create funding streams for local waterway projects designed to protect and restore water quality, address pollution threats, improve aquatic habitat, and revitalize local economies.

A surveyor prepares for the stream restoration project on Sands Creek, located in the town of Hancock, New York. LEE HARTMAN

The new federal authorization for the Delaware River created the Delaware River Basin Restoration Program (DRBRP). In 2018, the fiftieth anniversary of the Wild and Scenic Rivers Act, the US Congress approved a five-million-dollar appropriation to support a restoration grant program. Nonprofit organizations and municipal governments are eligible to receive these funds to undertake local projects that protect and restore the Delaware River watershed. FUDR's Sands Creek Restoration Project, completed in 2016, is an example of the type of projects this new program will fund.

In December 2018, FUDR and the Upper Delaware River Tailwaters Coalition received a $250,000 DRBRP award for three projects in the Upper Delaware watershed that will protect trout spawning beds, remove fish migration blockages, and improve water quality in the vital river tributaries.

In 2019 the US Congress approved a $6 million appropriation for the DRBRP in the second year of the federal program. FUDR and the UDRTC seized upon the opportunity and secured $750,000 in grant awards for on-the-ground stream restoration projects for the Upper Delaware River watershed. Combined with $500,000 in grants awarded to Trout Unlimited, the Upper Delaware River received $1.2 million in federal grants to protect water quality, enhance recreational opportunities, enhance aquatic habitat, and mitigate the dangerous impacts of local flooding. These projects include activities such as culvert replacements to remove stream blockages and allow for fish passage; reconnecting waterways to their floodplains, which slows the water down after rainfall and reduces sedimentation and flooding; and building trails and other river-based recreational opportunities to provide public access to the river and increase awareness about the ecological and economic importance of the resource to local people and communities.

There are many modern-day heroes that continue to fight hard to expand the funding for the DRBRP to ensure that a reliable long-term and sustainable source of funding will be available every year to preserve the specially protected waters from Hancock to the Delaware Bay.

INDEX

Academy of Natural Sciences, 229
acid factories, 69–72, 193
acid mine drainage, 8, 16
Ackley, H. A., 75–76
Ainsworth, Stephen, 76
Albert, Richard C., 103–4, 122
alien species, 250, 251
Alosa Sapidissima. See shad
American Sportfishing
    Association, 170
anadromous species, 38, 87,
    112, 250
anthracite coal, 3, 4–7, 7–11. *See
    also* coal
Appalachian Mountains, 24
aqueducts, 148, 152, 210–12
ark of 1814, 3–7
Army Corps of Engineers, US, 98,
    102, 105, 127, 253

Bachman, Robert A., 202–8, 211,
    228, 231
Baird, Spencer, 78, 82, 86
Barnes-Williams Environmental
    Study report, 123–24
Barnhart, Gerry, 208–10
bass, 175, 249, 250
Beaver Kill River, 87, 168,
    169, 188
Behnke, Robert, 79, 80, 87
Billingsley, Craig, 182

Blackford, Eugene J., 83–84
blind casting, 162–63
bottom releases, 171
Bousum, Pete, 226
Bove' Study, 229–31, 251
Brant, Joseph, 135, 138–39
brook trout, 27, 65–89
brown trout, 42, 85–88, 161, 164,
    169, 171, 213, 246, 248
Bureau of Marine Fisheries,
    NJ, 124

Cabot, John, 91, 92
Cadosia Creek, 225, 244
Callicoon Creek, 45, 177, 248
Cannon, Benjamin, 139, 147
Cannonsville, NY, 139–40, 146–48
Cannonsville Dam, 171, 174–83,
    186, 195
Cannonsville Reservoir, 132–33,
    145, 146–48, 182, 188,
    210, 241
  cold water releases from, 239
  floods in 1996, 165
  flow out of, 228
  mandated releases, 191, 194–95,
    196
  releases and spills, 199–200, 208
  water crisis, 2001-2002, 183–87
catadromous fish, 38, 87, 112,
    250–51

Catskill Rivers Coalition, 179, 186
Catskills, 44–49, 131, 134–39, 142
Caucci, Al, 160, 198
channelization, 224
Chase, Phil, 179, 185–87, 198
Chehocton, 38, 130
Clean Water Act of 1972, 104, 122
clear-cut forests, 71
coal, 1–22, 115–16. *See also*
    anthracite coal
Cochecton, 38, 46, 50, 242
cold-water ecosystem, 234, 236
cold-water fisheries, 188, 190, 196,
    231, 239, 244, 249
cold-water releases, 133, 171, 188,
    191, 195, 196, 229–30
cold-water tributaries, 166
Cole, Jeffery C., 251
Columbia University, 229
Compact. *See* Delaware River
    Basin Compact
Conference of Upper Delaware
    Townships (COUP), 241–42
Connie (hurricane), 97
conservation, environmental,
    72–73. *See also* Trout
    Unlimited
Costolnick, Jim (Coz), 198
COUP (Conference of Upper
    Delaware Townships),
    241–42
Court Decree (1954 US Supreme
    Court), 143, 145, 174, 186,
    198, 225, 227, 254. *See also*
    Supreme Court, US

Cowley, St. Leger, 135–38
Croton Reservoir, 141–42, 249
Crozier, Marty, 125–26

Damming the Delaware (Albert),
    103–4
dams, 98–107, 140, 193
    Cannonsville (*See* Cannonsville
        Dam)
    Downsville, 174
    in early 20th century, 115–16
    environmental consequences of,
        226–27
    and hydroelectric power, 195–96
    to supply NYC drinking water,
        133, 143–44
    Tocks Island (*See* Tocks Island
        Dam Project)
De La Warr, Lord, 91
Decker, Sam, 162–63
Decree Parties, 187, 198, 228, 229,
    231, 232–33, 234, 236
Delano, PA, 9–10
Delaware Aqueduct, 210–12
Delaware River
    battle for water rights, 140–44
    brown trout in, 246, 248
    cold-water releases, 171, 191,
        195
    dams on, 98–107, 140, 175, 193
        (*See also* dams)
    East Branch (*See* East Branch
        (Delaware River))
    economic impact of trout fishing
        on, 170

elevated water temperatures, 168
fish die-off, 69, 182, 185, 188, 189
fisheries habitat, 237
floods/flooding, 165–67, 219–25
guide services on, 44, 215–17
management program, 236
and NYC water consumption, 185–87
overview, xviii–xix
pollution, 8, 9–10, 120–21, 121–22
rainbow trout, 74–82, 161, 237, 246, 248
release volumes, 191–92
and shad, 117–18, 121, 123–24, 124–25, 249
sturgeon, 125–28
temperature/flow relationship, 175–82
tributaries, 6, 20, 143, 205, 246–48
trout in, 44, 129–48, 160
trout movement study, 166–70
upper (*See* Upper Delaware River)
and US Supreme Court, 143–44, 145–46
warm-water fisheries, 237–38, 248–49
waste-treatment plants, 122
water crisis, 2001-2002, 183–87
water flows, 225–26
water level, 208
watersheds, 14, 18, 254–56

West Branch (*See* West Branch (Delaware River))
as Wild and Scenic River, 161, 246
Delaware River Basin, 142–44, 174, 187
Delaware River Basin Commission (DRBC), 99, 106, 121–22, 178–83, 228, 229, 230, 234, 243
Delaware River Basin Compact, 99, 146
Delaware River Basin Fish and Wildlife Management Cooperative, 124
Delaware River Basin Restoration Program (DRBRP), 255, 256
Delaware River Club, 198
Delaware River Decision Support System (DRDSS), 229
Delaware River Foundation (DRF), 195, 199, 228, 229
Delaware River Keeper, 229
Delaware River Master, 183, 225–26
Delaware River Treaty, 142–44
Delaware Riverkeeper Network, 127–28
Delaware Valley Conservation Association, 101–2
Delaware Water Gap, 90, 97, 99
Delaware Water Gap National Recreation Area, 105, 107

Department of Conservation
and Natural Resources,
Pennsylvania, 229
Department of Environmental
Protection, New York City
(NYCDEP), 143, 211, 229,
233–34
Diane (hurricane), 97–98
Dickinson, Jesse, 139
Douglas, William, 200, 253
Downsville Dam/Reservoir,
144, 174
DRBC. *See* Delaware River Basin
Commission (DRBC)
DRBRP. *See* Delaware River
Basin Restoration Program
(DRBRP)
dredging, 224
DRF. *See* Delaware River
Foundation (DRF)
Drinker, Henry, 31, 33–34, 35, 37
drinking water, 13, 104,
140–41, 234
droughts, 178–83, 183–87,
201, 253
Duff, James H., 16–17
Dutch settlers, 93–94
dwarf wedge mussel, 234, 251

East Branch (Delaware River), 47,
131, 133, 143, 168, 209
cold water habitat, 231
damage from poor water management, 189
rainbow trout in, 161, 246

reservoirs on, 174
shad in, 249
tributaries, 166, 223
water flows, 227
East Branch Valley, 144
ecosystem management, 229–30
eels, freshwater, 38–41, 251
endangered species, 127, 234,
250, 251
Environmental Conservation Law
(Article 15, Title 8), 175
Equinunk, PA, 55, 69–70, 129, 151
Equinunk Creek, 27–28, 37, 47,
220, 248
Erie Railroad, 37–38, 45, 57, 58,
59, 61, 66, 140, 150
ERQ (excessive release
quantity), 183

Federal Energy Regulatory
Commission (FERC),
195–96, 252
Federal Water Pollution Control
Act, 121
feeder streams, 246–48
FERC. *See* Federal Energy
Regulatory Commission
(FERC)
FFMP. *See* Flexible Flow
Management Plan (FFMP)
Findley, Craig, 196–98, 223–25
Fish and Wildlife Service, US,
105, 118
Fish Commission, New York,
81–82

Fish Commission, US, 78, 79–80, 85

Fish Creek, 223

fish culture, 88

fish hatcheries. *See* hatcheries, fish

Fish & Wildlife Service, US, 78

fish/fishing, 114

die-offs, 69, 182, 185, 188, 189, 230

flow management issues in Upper Delaware, 204–8

and thermal stress (*See* thermal stress)

warm-water sport fish, 237–38

fishing camp. *See* Indian Springs Fly Fishing Camp

Flexible Flow Management Plan (FFMP), 231–32, 234, 236

Flood Control Act of 1962, 99

floodplain restoration, 222, 225

floods/flooding, 98, 165–67, 208, 219–25, 253

flow, water, 200

on Delaware River, 225–26

environmental impact of alterations in, 227

management in Upper Delaware River, 204–8

relationship with water temperature, 175–77, 188

Flow Management Technical Advisory Committee, 228

Fontinalis Fly Fishermen, 179

For the Good of All (film), 241–42

freestone rivers, 65, 168

French and Indian War, 49, 90, 97, 154, 155

French Woods Sports & Art Center, 162

Friends of the Upper Delaware River (FUDR), 198–208, 222, 223–25, 228, 229, 232, 234, 254

Frisbie Island, 47, 129, 149

FUDR. *See* Friends of the Upper Delaware River (FUDR)

Fuller, Roger, 147–48

Gale, John (Bunny), 133

Garlick, Theodius, 75–76

Ginter [Ginder], Philip, 1–3

Green, Seth, 76–78, 80, 81, 86, 87, 88–89, 246

green drake hatch, 109, 213, 214

Gregory boys, 55–57

Grey, Zane, 60–64

guide services, 215–17

Hallberg, Garth, 217–18

Hancock, NY, 38, 130, 221–25, 243

Hankins gage, 208, 209, 228

Hardenberg Patent, 44, 134

Hardy, Charles, 120–21

Harvey, George, 25, 26, 29

hatcheries, fish, 75, 77, 78, 79–80, 82, 85, 86, 88–89

hemlock forests, 49, 68, 69, 70

Hendrickson hatch, 215–17

Hinchey, Maurice, 175, 228

Hollister Creek, 27, 46, 248
Holt! T'other Way! (Wood), 49, 50, 53
home rule, 241
Homer, "Doc," 157–58
Hudson, Henry, 91, 92
Humphreys, Joe, 23, 25–29, 42
hurricanes, 97–98
Hutzky, John, 240, 252–53
hydroelectric power, 140, 186, 191–92, 195–96, 208

impoundments. *See* reservoirs
Indian Springs Fly Fishing Camp, 109, 156–61, 219
industrialization, 119
interstate water projects, 142–44
Iroquois, 44, 47, 95, 97, 134–35

Jones, Ruth, 101

Kostmeyer, Peter, 106–7

Lackawaxen, PA, 57, 61, 62–64
Lackawaxen River, 44, 60, 63, 64, 191–92, 195, 200–201, 201–2, 205
Lake Wallenpaupack, 191, 195–96, 200, 208, 210
LandStudies, Inc., 222, 225
Langan, Dave, 166–67
LaSorte, Adrian, 217, 218–19
leaks, aqueducts, 210–12
Lehigh Coal Mining Company, 3, 142

Lehigh River, 3, 4, 18, 19, 20–22, 115
Lenape Indians, 13, 18, 30, 44, 46, 92–93, 94–97, 155, 245
Lewis, John Fred, 120, 122, 123
logging industry, 70
Long Eddy, NY, 56–57, 166, 192–93, 216
Lord, John, 149–51
Lordville, NY, 38, 149–70, 235, 236

Marrazzano, William, 178
Mather, Fred, 81, 86, 87
Mid-Atlantic Fishery Management Council, 124
mines/mining, 3, 6–7
Minisink, NY, 47, 90, 100, 135
Minsi Indians, 44–45, 47
Minuit, Peter, 92–93
Mohawk Indians, 134–35, 136
Mohawk River, 131
"Molly Maguires," 7
Montague flow, 196, 200, 201, 208
Morgan, John, 216, 243
mortality, fish. *See* fish/fishing
Municipal Water Efficiency Program (NYC), 249
Munsee Indians, 30, 90, 94, 96–97, 153–56
Murphy, Greg, 125–26
Myers, Dan, 70

National Environmental Policy Act, 104, 105

National Marine Fisheries
Service, 127
National Park Service,
240–42, 243
National Wild and Scenic River,
18, 106, 107
National Wild and Scenic Rivers
Act, 105
National Wildlife Foundation, 105
Neversink Reservoir, 144–46, 148,
176, 182, 186, 189, 210, 241
Neversink River, 143, 227, 231
New Jersey v. New York. See
Supreme Court, US
New York Board of Water
Supply, 143
New York City
aqueducts, 148, 210–12
and Cannonsville Reservoir, 196
effect of reservoirs on trout
fisheries, 249
ERQ, 183
**1954 Supreme Court Decree,
186**
rebels against controlled releases
by NYSDEC, 177
reservoir release program, 175
reservoirs, 177, 227, 241, 252,
254
search for drinking water,
140–44
Supreme Court water allocation
decision, 145–46
water conservation, 182–83
water consumption, 179, 185–

87, 211, 226, 241, 249
water impoundments, 133, 171
New York State Department of
Environmental Conservation.
See NYSDEC
NYCDEP. *See* Department of
Environmental Protection,
New York City
NYSDEC (New York
State Department
of Environmental
Conservation), 166–67, 221,
229, 232–33, 236, 239
controlled releases, 175, 177
trout study, 169
NYSTU (New York State Trout
Unlimited). *See* Trout
Unlimited

Operation Support Tool, 233–34

Papagonk, 139
Paraziewicz, Piotr, 187–90
Parks, Josiah (Bos'n), 32, 47–49,
50–51
Parks, Melvin Emmet, 69–70
PATU (Pennsylvania Council of
Trout Unlimited). *See* Trout
Unlimited
Penn, Thomas, 95–97
Penn, William, 13, 94–95, 112
Pennamite Wars, 47, 48
Pennsylvania, early history, 93–95
Pennsylvania Fish & Boat
Commission, 229, 236

Pennsylvania Fish
    Commission, 105
Pennsylvania Power and Light
    (PPL), 191–92, 195–96,
    199–208
Pennsylvania Scenic Rivers, 20
Pepacton Reservoir, 144–46, 148,
    174, 176, 182, 186, 210, 241
Philadelphia, PA, 3, 114,
    119–20, 121
Pinchot, Gifford, 72–73
Piotr Study, 187–90, 198, 200
Plummer, Dan "Troutboy,"
    224–25, 226, 254
Pohpakton River, 131
politics, water, 191
pollution, water, 8, 69, 71, 104, 141
    Delaware River, 9–10, 120–21,
    121–22
    Schuylkill River, 15, 16–18,
    120–21
power plants, 186. *See also*
    Pennsylvania Power and
    Light (PPL)
PPL. *See* Pennsylvania Power and
    Light (PPL)
Preston, Samuel, 30–37
public lands, 73
pulsed releases, 206–7

Quick, Tom, 149, 153–56
Quillen, "Boney," 59–60

Rachuck, Mike, 20–22

radiotelemetry program, 166,
    167–68
rafting, timber. *See* timber rafting
rainbow trout, 27, 80, 231, 238
    decline of, 247
    in Delaware River, 74–82, 161,
    237, 246, 248
    and in eastern rivers, 81
    importing from California,
    83–85
    spawning, 169, 244, 247
    in Upper Delaware, 171, 213,
    239, 245
releases, reservoir, 175, 177,
    183, 199–200, 206–7, 228,
    237, 254
reservoirs. *See also* specific reservoir
    in Delaware River Basin, 174
    New York City, 177, 241, 252, 254
    water releases (*See* releases)
restocking programs, 117–18
Revision 7, 190, 196, 199, 208–10,
    228, 233
Roebling Bridge, 152
Rondout Reservoir, 148, 178,
    186, 210
Roosevelt, R. B., 77, 82
Roosevelt, Theodore, 72, 100
Roundout Creek, 143
Rowe, Sam, 221, 223–25
Runge, Bob, 162–63, 164

Safe Harbor, PA, 37, 47, 49
salmon, 108, 112
Sands Creek, 225, 244

Sands Creek Restoration
    Project, 255
Save the Delaware River
    Coalition, 105
sawmills, 53, 54–55, 69
Sawyer, Isaac, 135–38
Schoharie Indians, 135–38
Schuylkill River, 6, 13–18
    dams and canals, 115
    designated National Wild and
        Scenic River, 18
    pollution, 15, 16–18, 120–21
    shad in, 115
sewage, 19, 120–21, 141
shad, 108–28
    catch reports in 1980s, 122
    early history in America, 112–18
    effect of industrialization on,
        119
    feeding habits, 113–14
    harvesting, 116–17, 117–18
    population decline, 114–15, 117,
        118–25
    protection of, 125
    restocking program in 1870s,
        117–18
    return to Delaware River, 121,
        123–24, 124–25
    spawning, 108, 112–14, 249
    in Upper Delaware, 249
Shad, Edward, 179–82
Shehawken Creek, 28
Sheppard Study, 175–77
Shukaitis, Nancy, 100–105
Skelding, Jeff, 254

Skinner, Daniel, 42, 44, 46–47,
    49–51
Smith, Richard, 109–12
spawning
    eels, 38, 41
    rainbow trout, 244, 247
    shad, 108, 112–14, 249
    trout, 167, 169
Stipulation of Discontinuance,
    177, 186
Stockport, PA, 23–41, 220
Stone, Livingstone, 78–79, 82
stress, thermal. See thermal stress
sturgeon, 125–28
Subcommittee on Ecological
    Flows (SEF), 228, 229
Supreme Court, US, 143–44, 145.
    See also Court Decree (1954
    US Supreme Court)
Swinging Bridge Reservoir, 208,
    209–10

tailwaters, 239
Tailwaters Habitat Protection
    and Discharge Management
    Program, 231
tanneries, leather, 67, 69–72
temperature, water, 168, 175–77,
    188, 205–6, 228, 230–31, 234,
    236, 237, 244–45, 249–50. See
    also thermal stress
Thayendenegea, Chief. See Brant,
    Joseph
The Nature Conservancy, 229
Theodore Gordon Flyfishers, 179

thermal stress, 168, 175, 176, 177, 189, 209–10, 230, 232, 236, 250

Thompson, Frank, 106–7

threatened species, 250, 251

timber rafting, 42, 46, 49–60, 140, 151, 193

Tockpollock Creek, 30, 32, 35

Tocks Island Dam Project, 98–107, 140, 241

tributaries
 cold-water, 166
 Delaware River, 143, 205, 246–48
 East Branch, 223
 Lehigh River, 20
 as refugia for trout, 244–45
 Schuylkill River, 6
 Upper Delaware River, 244

Tri-State Delaware River Commission, 142–44

trout. *See also* specific types
 in Cannonsville Reservoir, 132–33, 175
 and cold-water releases, 171, 195
 deaths in Delaware River, 182
 in Delaware feeder streams, 27
 in Delaware River, 44, 129–48, 160
 effect of NYC Municipal Water Efficiency Program on, 249
 flow/temperature fluctuations, 234, 236
 movement study in Delaware River, 166–70

and pulsed releases, 206–7
 radiotelemetry program, 167–68
 spawning, 167, 169
 sport fishing for, 72, 80
 and thermal stress, 175, 176, 189, 209–10
 in Upper Delaware River, 27, 80–82, 169–70, 197, 236
 use of tributaries as refugia, 244–45
 and water temperature, 231
 in West Branch, 187–89, 197

Trout Unlimited, 9, 44, 199, 202, 225, 228, 229, 234, 256
 National, 25, 26, 167, 185, 190, 254
 New York State, 166, 167, 179, 182
 Pennsylvania, 26, 176, 179, 182, 201
 study on economic impact of fishing on Delaware River, 170

Turner, Ray, 40–41

Uniform Fishing Laws, 118

Upper Delaware Clearinghouse, 241

Upper Delaware Council, 242–43

Upper Delaware River. *See also* Delaware River
 changes in aquatic life with introduction of cold water, 171
 cold-water fisheries, 196, 239
 endangered species, 251
 flood mitigation program, 222

flow management, 204–8
management plan, 240–43
part of National Wild and Scenic Rivers System, 243
rainbow trout in, 239, 245
restoring health of, 189
shad in, 249
tributaries, 244
trout in, 27, 80–82, 87, 169–70, 197, 213, 236
trout movement study, 169–70
water temperature/flow relationship, 175–77, 237
watershed, 256
Upper Delaware River Basin, 228
Upper Delaware River Tailwaters Coalition, 254, 255, 256
Upper Delaware Scenic and Recreational River, 124, 243–44
Upper Delaware Valley, 45–46
urban growth, 119
US Geological Survey (USGS), 229

Van Put, Ed, 132–33, 244, 249–50
van Rossum, Maya, 127
von Behr, Lucius, 86, 87

Walking Purchase, 95–97
Walpak, NJ, 102–3
warm-water fisheries, 248–49
waste-treatment plants, 19, 120, 121, 122

water, clean, 104, 140–41, 237
water management, 187, 211
water rights, 140–44
watersheds, 14, 18, 166, 254–56
Weinperl, Barry, 215–17
weirs, 39–41, 180
West, Thomas, 91
West Branch (Delaware River), 47, 55–57, 131, 139, 143, 168, 209
cold water habitat, 231
damage from poor water management, 187–89
rainbow trout in, 161
temperature/flow relationship, 176, 179–82
trout fishing on, 193, 197
water flows, 227, 232
West Branch Angler Resort, 194, 195, 197
Wheeler, James and Ebenezer, 52–53
Wild and Scenic Rivers Act, 18, 161, 240, 243, 244, 252–53, 255
Wilson, Brian, 43–44
Wood, Bob, 69–70
Wood, Leslie, 49, 50, 53
wood chemical industry, 70
Worrell, James, 117

Youngblood, Ray, 176, 182

About the Author

Leo (Lee) Hartman, born in Hazleton, Pennsylvania, now lives along the Upper Delaware River in Equinunk, Pennsylvania. He is a forty-five-year veteran on the Delaware system and former owner of Indian Springs Fly Fishing Camp in Lordville, New York. Lee Hartman continues to guide on the river and host anglers to great fly-fishing destinations throughout the world. A staunch conservationist, Lee cofounded Friends of the Upper Delaware River (FUDR) and is currently co-chairman of the Delaware  River Committee for the Pennsylvania Council of Trout Unlimited. Lee accepted a Community Service Award from the Upper Delaware Council in 2014 and also received US Congressional recognition for outstanding and invaluable service to the community.